Faith Healers and the Bible

FAITH HEALERS AND THE BIBLE

What Scripture Really Says

Stephen J. Pullum

An Imprint of ABC-CLIO, LLC

Santa Barbara, California • Denver, Colorado

Library of Congress Cataloging-in-Publication Data

Pullum, Stephen Jackson, 1957–
    Faith healers and the Bible : what scripture really says / Stephen J. Pullum.
        pages cm
    Includes bibliographical references and index.
    ISBN 978-1-4408-3213-0 (print : alk. paper) — ISBN 978-1-4408-3214-7 (e-book)
    1. Healing in the Bible.   2. Spiritual healing—Biblical teaching.   3. Healers. I. Title.
    BS680.H4P85 2015
    234'.131—dc23   2014033998

ISBN: 978-1-4408-3213-0
EISBN: 978-1-4408-3214-7

19 18 17 16 15   1 2 3 4 5

This book is also available on the World Wide Web as an eBook.
Visit www.abc-clio.com for details.

Praeger
An Imprint of ABC-CLIO, LLC

ABC-CLIO, LLC
130 Cremona Drive, P.O. Box 1911
Santa Barbara, California 93116-1911

This book is printed on acid-free paper ∞
Manufactured in the United States of America

Contents

Introduction

Faith healers, as they are referred to in popular parlance, are a group of individuals within Christianity, broadly speaking, who believe that while they themselves have no special powers, God has called them to be his instrument through whom the sick or ailing can receive a divine, miraculous cure, provided these individuals have enough faith in God. This so-called healing usually, though not always, comes after the faith healer has laid his or her hands on those who are sick. Faith healers are a part of what has sometimes been called "The Faith Movement." According to Ankerberg and Weldon, individuals within this movement—whether faith healers or individuals who trust in faith healers—believe "that the human mind and tongue contain a supernatural ability or power." By positively expressing their faith in divine laws, they believe they can invoke a "'divine force' that will heal, produce wealth, bring success, and in other ways influence the environment." In other words, "God automatically responds and accomplishes what we command when we positively confess our needs and desires in faith."[1]

In 1999, I published *"Foul Demons, Come Out!": The Rhetoric of Twentieth-Century, American Faith Healing.*[2] This book was an introduction to seven very prominent and successful faith healers of the twentieth century, some of whom lived into the twenty-first century, a few of whom are still preaching and practicing today. In this book, I explained from a rhetorical perspective (i.e., using principles of communication) why faith healers were so successful. And while this book fulfilled a need, it was not as critical toward faith healers as it could have been or should have been. There is so much more about them that I believe needs to be addressed than what I initially discussed in my previous work. For example, are the things that faith healers preach supportable from a biblical perspective?

Every year since the late nineties, I have taught a course at the University of North Carolina, Wilmington, titled The Rhetoric of Faith Healing (Com 458). This course has been and continues to be very popular among students at UNCW. The very first day of the semester, I always explain three things to my students. First, I make it clear to them that I am a person of faith. I disclose, however, that while I believe in God—as many people in academia do,[3] contrary to popular belief—I do not believe in contemporary miracles, as ironic as that might sound to some. Later in the book I will explain why, but for now, let me suggest that it is not a contradiction, as it might appear on its face, to believe in God but not believe in contemporary miracles. Indeed, it is very possible for one to be even deeply religious yet not believe in contemporary miracles.

Early in the course, I also explain to my students that the concept of a supernatural being back of the universe—what many of us simply refer to as God—cannot be proven empirically. In other words, we cannot roll the heavens back and say, "See, here God is" or "See, here he isn't." The concept of God is a metaphysical question. (The word *metaphysics* is a combination of the Greek *meta*, meaning "after" or "beyond," and *phusikos*, meaning "physics" or "nature."[4]) We cannot prove the existence of God using sense data or experience. However, this is not to say that there are not cogent arguments for the existence of God. There are many, which are beyond the scope of both this book and the class that I teach. I mention all of this here simply to say that I do not come at the topic of faith healing as an agnostic or as an enemy of those who profess belief in a divine being back of the universe.

My attempt in the current book is to meet faith healers and those who embrace their doctrine on their home turf, to show that much of what they teach cannot be supported by the Bible, even though they would like their audiences to believe so. In fact, most of what they teach actually runs contrary to the Bible. It would be too easy for faith healers to dismiss me as just another unbelieving academician—someone who is antagonistic toward the Christian faith and really knows nothing about the Bible. This they cannot do.

Another point that I make on the first day of class is that the course I teach is actually a confluence of many disciplines. While I approach the topic of faith healing primarily from a rhetorical (i.e., communication) perspective, as readers will note in the first chapter we cannot talk about faith healing without discussing other factors such as religion, psychology, sociology, history, and to some extent medicine. Students expect me to be able to answer any and all of the questions they pose, regardless of what type of question it is. However, the majority of the questions that individuals present to me have historically been of a biblical nature. It has been my experience that most students really want to know what the Bible has to say about faith and healing and concomitant subjects. To inquiring minds, it is irrelevant into which of the above categories their question falls. They just want it answered. I like to think that, over the years, I have become more informed on issues related to faith healing, by having to address the objections and questions that students have thrown at me. This is not to say that I have all the answers. However, I believe I know more today than I did seventeen years ago when I first started teaching the course, because I had to learn how to address tough questions. My students have made sure of that. This book has grown out of much of what I have discussed with students, both in and out of the classroom, about faith healing—its rhetoric, its theology, and its psychology, among other things. So I have written this book primarily with my students in mind. That's not to say that others will not profit from reading it, but first and foremost, I publish for my students.

This book deals with so many more issues than my earlier work did. Although in my previous book I raised numerous objections to twentieth-century faith healing, other relevant topics went unaddressed. My aim is to deal with these issues in the current book. For example, after showing in chapter 1, which was previously published in a multivolume set,[5] the rhetorical pattern that faith healers use to convince their listeners that they can receive a divine, miraculous cure, in chapter 2 I offer the reader some guidelines for reading and understanding the scriptures while illustrating from the preaching of faith healers where they have run afoul of these guidelines. I believe that many theological teachings that emerge in the preaching of faith healers and other contemporary religious leaders have grown out of a failure to interpret biblical texts correctly. Thus, in chapter 2, I will offer some tips for correct interpretation.

In chapter 3, a version of which I also published previously in a multivolume edition,[6] I go into greater detail regarding how the miraculous differs from the providential. I have often said that the word *miracle* may be the single most misunderstood word in the English language. I believe that not only faith healers but people of faith in general often make the mistake of thinking that God always has to act miraculously when he responds to prayer. When God acts, could he not act providentially without acting miraculously? I believe that he not only can but does. My experience also suggests that individuals are quick to call something a miracle if they cannot explain it, even though they themselves may not be of any particular religious persuasion. Should they? Moreover, does God really ever respond miraculously? These are the types of questions I hope to explore in the following pages.

In addition to what constitutes the miraculous, in chapter 4 (a version of which was also previously published[7]) I address the topic of demon possession, a theme that is not only inherent in the preaching of faith healers but also popular among other people of faith today. The reality is that one really does not have to be a faith healer to believe in demon possession, as I will show later on. This belief can be found among Protestants and Catholics alike, who are anything but faith healers.

Another topic I believe needs to be addressed is the call of God. In chapter 1 I point out how faith healers have traditionally relied upon claims of being called by God, among other rhetorical strategies, to establish their legitimacy. In chapter 5, I analyze whether we should believe them or anyone else who says they have been called by God to do certain things. Does the Bible actually teach that God has called some people to be ministers of healing? For that matter, does the Bible teach that God has called individuals into any type of occupation, whether faith healing or anything else? Simply put, if there is a call of God, what does this calling look and sound like from a biblical perspective?

In chapter 6, I address the well-known biblical expression, "All things are possible," which appears in Matthew 19:26, Mark 9:23, Mark 10:27, and Luke 18:27 (ASV). Faith healers loosely throw this phrase around as proof that one can receive a divine miraculous cure, provided that an individual has enough faith. After all, what person of the Christian faith is going to argue with the Bible? In fact, the phrase "All things are possible" is so popular among faith healers to prove that divine, miraculous cures are not only possible but probable that the historian David Harrell used it as the title of his book on the history of healing revivals within this country in the twentieth century (*All Things Are Possible: The Healing & Charismatic Revivals in Modern America*).[8] But does "all things" really mean everything? I hope to show that there is more to this phrase than initially meets the eye.

I believe that one of the biggest reasons faith healers and other individuals of the Faith Movement have taught what they have through the years is because they have failed to understand the work of the Holy Spirit. Who is the Holy Spirit? What is the baptism of the Holy Spirit? What does it mean to say that the Holy Spirit dwells in Christians today? If, as Romans 8:14 teaches, "For as many as are led by the Spirit of God, these are the sons of God," how does this happen, and what does the Holy Spirit cause individuals to do, if anything? The Holy Spirit, then, is the subject of chapter 7.

The gospel of health and wealth is another topic that needs to be addressed. Although this theme is not shared by all faith healers, it crops up enough times in their preaching—and in the preaching of other contemporary evangelists—to warrant a biblical examination, which I offer in chapter 8. Finally, in chapter 9, I attempt to answer the question "So what?" by providing seven reasons why we ought to care what faith healers preach.

I realize that there are some who would criticize me for writing a book like this. "Why don't you leave faith healers and those who follow them alone?" some might ask. "After all, they're honest and sincere men and women of God who are merely trying to do his will to the best of their understanding." Others, as I often have heard my students do, would quote Jesus's words in Matthew 7:1, "Do not judge so that you will not be judged. For in the way you judge, you will be judged; and by your standard of measure, it will be measured to you" (NASV). On the surface, these might sound like compelling reasons not to engage in the type of study I have undertaken. The problem with what I call "argument from sincerity" is that—besides the fact that what faith healers teach simply cannot be supported from the scriptures, which makes their doctrines counterfeit—I believe that the potential to do harm far outweighs any good that might come from their work.

For instance, what if individuals with diabetes or some other disease were to throw away their insulin or other medicines because they believe they have been healed, when in reality they have not? The physical consequences would be grave at best, if not altogether lethal. Readers who think this example is far-fetched, that no one would ever do this, should reconsider. In his book *Christianity in Crisis*, Hanegraff cites the story of Larry and Lucky Parker, who allowed their son Wesley to slip into a diabetic coma because they believed that he was healed, simply because they had affirmed their faith. After they took him off of his medicine, they continued to "positively confess" their son's healing as the healer had exhorted them to do. Tragically, Wesley died. "Even after Wesley's demise," writes Hanegraff, "the Parkers, undaunted in their 'faith,' conducted a resurrection service rather than a funeral." For a full year afterward, they believed that their son would resurrect from the dead just as Jesus did.[9]

Ankerberg and Weldon cite the case of the "Faith Assembly" Movement of Hobart Freeman, where "well over 100 unnecessary deaths (including Freeman's)" occurred. Then there were the "End Timers" of

North Central Florida, who "allowed several dozen children and adults to die prematurely."[10] A similar case occurred in February of 2014, when, Jamie Coots, the snake-handling pastor of the Full Gospel Tabernacle in Jesus Name in Middlesboro, Kentucky, refused medical treatment after receiving his ninth bite from a large rattlesnake, because he believed that faith in God alone would cure him. Eventually, he died.[11]

In his book *Healing: A Doctor in Search of a Miracle*, medical doctor William Nolen personally interviewed twenty-three individuals who had supposedly received a divine, miraculous cure while attending a revival led by the well-known faith healer Katherine Kuhlman in the 1970s. Nolen discloses how he had "mixed emotions about the follow-up study." He acknowledged that Kuhlman "was a sincere, devout, dedicated woman who believed fervently that she was doing the Lord's will." In no way was Nolen out to "hurt her." "On the other hand," though, he points out how he "wasn't sure that whatever good Miss Kuhlman was doing wasn't outweighed, far outweighed, by the pain she was causing."[12] So he decided to proceed with his study. Nolen did not find a single cure—let alone a miraculous one. Furthermore, he found that many of the people who believed they had been healed at Kuhlman's revivals had actually died within a few weeks of their "healing." Suffice it to say, there are people of great faith who might very well withhold medicines either from themselves or from their children because they believe they are either already healed or will be healed shortly if they just confess their faith.

In regard to the notion that we should not judge others, more often than not individuals fail to realize what Jesus taught in John 7:24: "Judge not according to appearance, but judge righteous judgment" (ASV). Here is an explicit command that, on its surface, looks contrary to what he said in Matthew 7:1–5. But was Jesus contradicting himself?

Actually, what Jesus was condemning in Matthew 7:1 was not judgment per se but hypocritical judgment; that is, using a different standard to judge oneself than to judge someone else. In this type of judgment one is quick to point out the flaws of others (e.g., that there is a "mote . . . in thy brother's eye") when one has a "beam" (i.e., plank) in his or her own eye, as we see in Matt. 7:3–4 (ASV). Jesus is admonishing an individual to take care of one's own problems first. Then he or she can see clearly to help others. To criticize someone else when we ourselves have the same problem is to engage in self-condemnation. We should never use one standard to judge ourselves but a higher standard to judge others around us.

In John 7:24, Jesus is not only suggesting that it is okay to judge others but actually requiring it. Such judgment, however, must be administered fairly and according to principles of truth (i.e., "judge with righteous judgment," NASV). The fact is, it is impossible to go through life without judging others. This principle is at the very core of Fritz Heider's Attribution Theory, which says that humans cannot help but judge others.[13]

Among other things, according to Heider, we make implicit—if not explicit—judgments all the time about where to go, what to do, and with whom we should do these things. The minute we say, "I don't like what you're doing" or "I don't want to get involved in this person's life," we have made a judgment. Without the ability to judge others, biblical statements such as "Evil companionships corrupt good morals" (I Cor. 15:33, ASV) would have no practical benefit. Although it may be true that good behavior is corrupted by bad company, in order to benefit from this truth, practically speaking, one has to judge whether a potential companion is good or bad and to what extent one should keep company with that person. Further, when Jesus said in Matt. 7:6 to "Give not that which is holy unto the dogs, neither cast your pearls before the swine," one must first make a judgment to determine who the dogs and swine are.

So, what appears in the following pages is based on many years of thinking and teaching about what faith healers and other people of faith have espoused. I can recall, as a boy, sitting in front of my family's black and white television in the 1960s, watching the young faith healer Oral Roberts and trying to figure out what was actually unfolding before my eyes. In my teenage years, growing up in an area where faith healing was popular, I continued to study what the Bible had to say about these issues. What I was reading in the Bible did not square with what I saw and heard around me in some religious circles. In the early eighties, when I first caught a glimpse on cable of the well-known contemporary faith healer Ernest Angley of Akron, Ohio, my fascination with this subject was still strong. The fact is, throughout the years, this allure really has never left me. Thus, in this book, I would like to provide an alternative view of such a popular and controversial movement, albeit from a Christian perspective, to help others make sense of what is being taught.

By nature, I am not a contentious individual. It is not my intent in this book to be rude and disparaging. I try to follow the Apostle Paul's advice in Rom. 12:18: "If it be possible, as much as in you lieth, be at peace with all men." However, there are times when error needs to be exposed, and doing so does not endear one to those who are being criticized. In pointing out the shortcomings of faith healers and others in the faith movement, my hope is that I might have a positive impact on both my students and anyone else who may have been seriously contemplating these issues from a religious perspective. If I can persuade one person to see where the truth lies, my efforts will not have been in vain.

Communication scholar Otis Walter points out how public speaking, which includes preaching, "now and then becomes a powerful force affecting individual men and whole civilizations." Historically, suggests Walter, "wherever . . . religious . . . revolutions have arisen, speaking has played an important role—sometimes desirable and sometimes disastrous." And while many ideas are disseminated through the written word, suggests Walter, "the spoken word, active and vibrant, has an impact that written passages rarely, if ever, can match." It is because this discourse is such a "powerful force" upon us, that "man needs profound and searching insight into the speeches he hears—into their truth or falsity, their wisdom or stupidity, their profundity or emptiness, into their subtle greatness or disguised and hidden meanness."[14] Walter's ideas are clearly relevant to the discourse of faith healers and televangelists. In fact, if preaching of any type is not relevant to what Walter is talking about, then no type of public communication is.

When listening to or reading the discourse of faith healers, there are a number of legitimate questions that audiences should be asking. In fact, we should be asking these questions about all types of rhetoric, even of the book you are reading. Is it ethical? Is it practical? Is it harmful? Should it be followed or rejected? To what extent is it socially beneficial or intellectually sound? Is it reasonable?[15] In the case of what many people of faith are espousing, specifically we should be asking, "Is it scriptural? Is it theologically sound?" Communication scholar Barnett Baskerville supports these questions when he suggests, "Today's critic often side-steps inquiry into the basic soundness of the speaker's position, offering the excuse that truth is relative, that everyone is entitled to his own opinion."[16] James Andrews, retired professor of rhetoric and public address at Indiana University, points out that "Ideas and evidence in the speech must withstand the careful scrutiny of reasonable men and women."[17] Andrews is talking about any type of public address, whether political or religious in nature. I believe that the "ideas and evidence" in the preaching of faith healers is sorely lacking. Ernest Wrage, who, before his death, was a long-time professor of rhetoric at Northwestern University, once argued that, "In the long view the ideal critic is concerned with ventilating and improving our public talk."[18] That is what I am trying to do in this book. By pointing out the shortcomings in the preaching and teaching of faith healers, my hope is to equip us, from a theological and a rhetorical perspective, with a better understanding of the issues with which we are confronted.

Finally, allow me to say a word about how I use the Bible. Throughout this book, I cite a number of scriptures. Sometimes the citation is in the text. Sometimes the citation is in an endnote. Whether in the text or in an endnote, I have tried to show the reader where from the Bible faith healers have taken their ideas or where I have drawn mine. At times I give either a full quotation or a partial quotation from the Bible within the text itself. On other occasions, however, I merely paraphrase the idea of a verse. Whether I provide full or partial quotations, or whether I merely paraphrase the idea contained within a verse, depends on how necessary I believe it is to do so at the time. In general, I have tried to avoid long-winded quotations, which tend to bore most people. Whether I have been successful in this endeavor will be up to the reader to determine.

Throughout this book, I have relied on three biblical translations. First and foremost, I have employed the American Standard Version (ASV) because I am most familiar with it. I have been using this version in my personal studies for close to forty years. However, to avoid archaic pronouns such as "ye," "thee," and "thou," I have occasionally opted for the New American Standard Version (NASV). In a few cases, I have used the King James Version (KJV) because the particular wording of a passage fits the discussion better than the other two versions. All of these translations are legitimate, credible, and acceptable for almost everyone in the Faith Movement if not within Protestant Christianity in general. All biblical references hereafter will come from the ASV unless otherwise noted.

Let us turn now to an introduction of prominent historical and contemporary faith healers, to see not only what they have taught through the years but why they have been so persuasive. This will serve as a foundation for what will follow. We will then be in a better position to analyze from a biblical perspective some of the various themes that emerge in their preaching.

1

❖

"Hallelujah! Thank You, Jesus!": Selling the Miraculous in the Preaching of Faith Healers

They are as much a part of the American culture as Harley-Davidson motorcycles, baseball, and Barbie dolls. They have given rise to movies such as *Leap of Faith*, starring Steve Martin, and pop songs such as Neil Diamond's *Brother Love's Traveling Salvation Show*. Robin Williams, Sacha Baron Cohen, and other comedians have frequently used them as subjects of religious parodies.[1] Bart Simpson even played the role of one in an episode of *The Simpsons*.[2] Faith healers, as they are popularly called (a label they generally despise), are a cadre of male and female Christian evangelists who criss-crossed this country throughout the twentieth century and into the twenty-first century, preaching spiritual and physical deliverance from sin, sickness, and disease, provided individuals had the necessary faith in God to heal them.

Historically many well-known faith healers in the United States came from other countries. One of the earliest faith healers in America, for example, was Alexander Dowie, who arrived from Scotland via Australia in 1888 before settling in Chicago. Smith Wigglesworth, who preached in America in the 1920s and '30s, was English. Aimee Semple McPherson, who was enormously popular before her death in 1944, was born in Canada. She eventually obtained U.S. citizenship when she married her second husband, Harold McPherson, in 1912.[3]

The end of World War II brought with it an explosion of American-born independent healing revivalists. For example, Oral Roberts (born near Bebee, Oklahoma), Asa Alonzo Allen (born in Sulphur Rock, Arkansas), and Jack Coe, Sr. (born in Oklahoma City), to name a few, took center stage. William Branham, another post-War faith healer—born in Burkesville, Kentucky, and eventually establishing his headquarters just over the Ohio River in Jeffersonville, Indiana—was one of the most popular traveling evangelists of his day. Perhaps more of the world would have known him were it not for his premature death in 1965 as the result of a car wreck near Amarillo, Texas.[4]

Ernest Angley, a prominent, albeit elderly, contemporary faith healer—who was born in Mooresville, North Carolina, in 1922 and who began his successful career in the 1940s—is currently headquartered in Akron, Ohio. Although born Palestinian in Tel Aviv, Israel, on December 3, 1952, Benny Hinn, one of the most well-known faith healers in the United States today, is headquartered in Grape Vine, Texas, near Dallas.[5] Gloria Copeland, wife of well-known televangelist Kenneth Copeland, is another prominent healing evangelist in her own right, whose base of operation since 1967 has been Fort Worth, Texas. These are only a handful of the many faith healers who have preached, and continue to preach, in this country.

Throughout their careers, these men and women, among many others like them, have been enormously influential, amassing large followings and raking in millions of dollars. Throughout each decade, thousands upon thousands have turned to them, seeking miracles of one type or another. Why? Perhaps an even more interesting question is, how? In other words, how have faith healers been able to sustain such large followings throughout their lifetimes? What was it about their preaching that endeared them to so many people, that caused multitudes to flock to them? These, I believe, are worthwhile questions, especially given the fact that faith healers have been so successful economically, socially, and religiously.

Using a sales metaphor, in this chapter I will address three separate but related questions in an attempt to account for such a popular phenomenon: (1) Exactly what were these faith healers "selling"? (2) To whom were they "selling"? Or more to the point, who was "buying"? (3) How was it that they were "selling" it? Simply put, what rhetorical strategies did they either consciously or unconsciously employ, as a group of preachers, to persuade individuals to accept their message? In examining this last question, I will attempt to demonstrate that there exists a body of faith healing discourse, a genre of faith healing rhetoric, crucial to this enterprise. Although there may be subtle differences in each of the above individuals' preaching and method of operation, in general one will find that they made similar types of promises, preached to comparable types of audiences, and relied primarily on the same types of proofs.

APPROACH

In attempting to answer the above questions, I analyzed books of printed sermons, magazine articles, and other primary literature produced by faith healers Branham, Roberts, Allen, Coe, Angley, Copeland, and Hinn. Additionally, I examined countless hours of audio and video tapes of these men and women. Chronologically, these artifacts ranged from shortly after World War II to the present day. In a number of instances, I was personally able to attend the actual healing services conducted by some of these individuals, most notably those of contemporaries Ernest Angley, Gloria Copeland, and Benny Hinn.

In critiquing the discourse of faith healing, I proceeded inductively, looking at a number of specific instances before drawing conclusions. Rhetorical theorist Sonja Foss, for example, advises that when taking this approach, an individual should follow four steps: First, one determines whether "similar situations, removed from each other in time and place, seem to generate similar rhetorical responses." Second, one collects several samples of rhetoric that may be indicative of the genre. Preferably, these artifacts should come from various periods of history. Third, one seeks to discover shared "substantive or stylistic features" in the samples. In doing so, one need not follow any prescribed methodology. Instead, one merely allows the rhetorical artifacts to speak or "'suggest' . . . important similarities and differences." Finally, one should "formulate the organizing principle that captures the essence of the strategies" that the rhetorical artifacts share. Foss notes that "labeling the organizing principle actually may occur simultaneously with the delineation of substantive and stylistic strategies since the elements identified may come to the critic's attention grouped around an obvious core or principle."[6]

For our purposes, there are at least two important reasons for doing a generic analysis: First it "provides a history of communication rules."[7] As will become evident, I am not advocating that we emulate the communication rules and patterns of faith healers, any more than I would advocate that we emulate the rhetoric of Adolf Hitler. Nonetheless, recording the rhetorical history of faith healers, in and of itself, is a worthwhile goal. Second, and perhaps more importantly, generic criticism "serves as an index to social and cultural reality."[8] That is, it helps us to understand how groups and subgroups view the world around them. As in the case of faith healers, sometimes this reality is intriguing. At other times it can be frightening, with an entire set of consequences often overlooked by both the faith healers themselves and an unsuspecting public. In saying this, I am not suggesting that faith healers are or have been inherently evil people. To the contrary, most of the faith healers in this study were morally upright individuals who were (and still are) sincere about what they perceived as a good work. Ostensibly, they truly believed in what they practiced. In spite of their sincerity, however, their realities left much to be desired, as I hope to demonstrate not only in this chapter but throughout this book. Let us turn first to an examination of their discourse.

WHAT HAVE FAITH HEALERS SOLD?

A close look at what faith healers have taught throughout the years reveals the preaching of three types of deliverance, assuming one had the necessary faith in God: (1) deliverance from sin; (2) deliverance from bodily afflictions, diseases, and addictions; and (3) deliverance from financial worries, which I will address in detail in chapter 8.

The fact that faith healers preached deliverance from sin raises no eyebrows. Within Christianity, the idea that humans are in sin, that Jesus died on the cross to reconcile them to God, and that all they need to do is accept him in order to avoid eternal punishment and enjoy the bliss of heaven is really no different from what is taught in most Protestant, conservative, Evangelical churches. While there may be differences in how the sin was obtained or what an individual must do to be forgiven, generally what faith healers taught regarding deliverance from sin would be accepted by many religious people in the broader culture of American Christendom, Catholic and Protestant alike. Indeed, this common teaching may account for part of faith healers' appeal, especially among people who know little, if anything, about Christian theology.

In addition to preaching deliverance from sin, faith healers have taught that one could receive bodily healings as a result of the atonement of Jesus on the cross. Or, to use the words of the contemporary faith healer Ernest Angley, "Come right on. Whatever it is, God will heal."[9] Post–WW II faith healer A.A. Allen stated this idea as well as any: "At Calvary something happened that will be beneficial not only for your soul but also for your body . . . Jesus not only died for the sins of the world but before he ever died . . . they placed the stripes on his back and the scripture says, 'whereby ye were healed.'"[10] The scriptural allusion is to Isaiah 53:5, which states, "But he was wounded for our transgressions, he was bruised for our iniquities; the chastisement of our peace was upon him; and with his stripes we are healed" (ASV). Faith healers have traditionally misinterpreted this passage to mean that one can be healed physically and financially (as well as spiritually) because of Jesus's death on the cross.

Faith healers have believed that many—not all, but many—physical afflictions and addictions to bad habits, such as cigarette smoking and drug addiction, are caused by demons possessing people. Perhaps Oral Roberts illustrated this best when he suggested that "deaf and dumb demons do take the hearing and speech of some people." Roberts contended that there are numerous types of demons, such as epileptic demons, lying demons, and sex demons.[11] Jack Coe once quipped, "I think if there's anything that's of the devil, it's a cancer."[12]

Roberts often told stories about casting demons out of people. Whenever this occurred, one would likely hear him yell something like, "Thou foul tormenting demons, I adjure thee in the name of Jesus Christ of Nazareth, come out of this woman! Loose her and let her go free!"[13] When laying his hands upon those in his healing lines, A. A. Allen would often yell, "Thou devil of deafness, I rebuke you!"[14] On one occasion, I witnessed Benn Hinn attempt to convince a woman, and more than twenty thousand other people in attendance, that he cast out a cancer demon from the bottom of her foot and that it wiggled off the stage.[15] I also watched Ernest Angley lay hands on individuals in his prayer lines and scream in their face, "Loose her, thou foul, tormenting spirit! . . . Yeaaaaaha, come out!"[16]

Before going any further, we need to address a question that occasionally arises. What is wrong with faith healers praying for the sick? After all, is not this taught in almost all Christian churches today because it can be found in the Bible? It is true that just as faith healers have believed that one could be healed through prayer, so today do many churches throughout America. The difference, however, between what faith healers have traditionally taught and practiced and what many other Protestants believe—and this is a big difference—is the expectation that God would heal miraculously exactly as miraculous healings were recorded in the Bible. What is being sold is not so much prayer for the sick but belief that the one prayed for would be healed wholly and miraculously of whatever ailed him or her. Unlike other Christian groups, faith healers fail to make a distinction between the providential, wherein it is believed that God acts behind the scenes to heal through the laws of nature, and the miraculous.

One is left to conclude that faith healers really don't understand what a miracle is in the first place. Both the eighteenth-century Scottish philosopher David Hume and the twentieth-century theologian C. S. Lewis at least agree on this point. Each suggests that a miracle is a violation or interruption of the laws of nature. To borrow Lewis's words, miracles "interrupt the orderly march of events, the steady development of nature according to her own interest, genius or character."[17] To illustrate this principle, Lewis suggests that if a virgin were to conceive without a man, the conception would be miraculous because it initially violates the laws of nature regarding procreation. Once the conception occurs, however, the birth itself would not be miraculous. Lewis argues, "If God creates a miraculous spermatozoon in the body of a virgin, it does not proceed to break any laws. The laws at once take it over. Nature is ready. Pregnancy follows, according to all the normal laws, and nine months later a child is born."[18]

In the New Testament—the very book that faith healers themselves appeal to, in part, as proof that what is happening in their revivals is miraculous and, hence, God-ordained—one can read that dead people were made alive (Matt. 9:18–25, Luke 7:11–17, John 11:17–46; ASV). What is ironic about these examples is that these individuals had no faith whatsoever. How could they when they were dead? Also in the New Testament, one reads about withered hands instantaneously made whole (Matt. 12:9–14). The deaf and mute were made to hear and speak immediately (Mark 7:31–37). These are just a few of the more than thirty examples of miraculous cures that one can find in the New Testament. All of these healings involved a violation or interruption of the laws of nature. And what is more, these miracles were visually verifiable, something many of the so-called miracles performed throughout the twentieth and twenty-first centuries have not been.

Faith healers in our day most often call out ailments such as back aches, diabetes, sinus problems, heart conditions, nerves, addictions, and so on.[19] The problem is, one cannot see these types of cures. They simply are not empirically verifiable like those recorded in the scriptures. Moreover, because they are not empirically verifiable, they are non-falsifiable, which is advantageous to faith healers. One must simply take the word of the individual with the affliction as to whether he or she was really healed. This is also problematic, because often the individual thinks he or she is healed when in reality no healing has occurred at all. Certainly nothing miraculous occurred.

Medical doctor William Nolen looked at dozens of cases of so-called miraculous healings, which supposedly occurred during the ministry of popular faith healer Kathryn Kuhlman during the 1970s, and concluded that he could not find a single case of the miraculous. While some individuals who claimed a cure gradually became better over time, only to relapse, others showed no improvement at all. In fact some whom Nolan interviewed who claimed to have been healed at a Kathryn Kuhlman crusade died shortly after his interview with them.[20]

In addition to the above, contemporary audiences of faith healers who witness "miraculous healings" really do not know to what extent the person who claimed a healing was sick or ailing in the first place. Perhaps the individual him/herself does not even know. Audiences simply have to take the word of the person on stage if they want to know how sick or ailing a person really is. While we cannot nor should not accuse an individual of lying about his or her disease, one has to wonder to what extent an individual is dramatizing his or her physical problems. After all, there is a certain expectation for these people who are standing under the spotlight in front of thousands of onlookers to perform in the heat of the moment, not to disappoint both the faith healer and the audience. In short, we are talking about religious theatre where the healer, the subject seeking healing, and the audience all know their roles. All of them know what is expected of them—what to say, when to respond, and how to respond.

In his article *Ritual Expectation in Pentecostal Healing*, William Clements rightfully argues that "Religious ritual and dramatic performance exhibit a number of parallels." He points out that "Participants in both kinds of performance have definite anticipations of what the outcome will be." If "expectations" on the part of all parties involved are not met, the "ritual" (i.e., drama) "would be profoundly disturbing."[21] Clements concludes that, "In ritual as in drama as in most of life's experiences, we get pretty much what we expect we are going to get."[22] Of course, the more dramatic the "theatre" in a faith healing revival, the louder the applause one will receive. Everyone goes away happy, as if something miraculous has indeed occurred. Everyone has played his or her role perfectly.

On rare occasions, audiences do not even know what the ailment to be healed is. The minister merely lays hands on the individual, and he or she walks off the stage, leaving the audience wondering what just happened.[23] Nonetheless, audiences clap in approval because they know what is expected of them, regardless of what they have just witnessed.

As I have argued elsewhere, it matters little whether one believes the New Testament accounts of miraculous healings.[24] The fact is, faith healers themselves do. Further, they believe that these types of miracles are still occurring today just as they were recorded in the Bible. However, by the standard that faith healers set for themselves—namely, that of the Bible—they fail to show the authentication indicated in the Bible.

Jack Coe, who was typical of most faith healers in his own day and now, illustrates the point well. A young man with "old deaf ears" once came into Coe's healing line, with a friend who served as interpreter. Coe laid his hands on him, and the man was supposedly healed of deafness. To demonstrate to the thousands in attendance, Coe whispered three words in the man's ear—"baby," "boy," and "mama." When asked to repeat these words, the young man could not. Instead, he often muddled "mama" when Coe wanted him to say "boy" or "baby." In resignation, Coe turned to the young man's interpreter and said, "Somebody's gonna have to teach him."[25] I have witnessed similar incidents with Benn Hinn[26] and Ernest Angley.[27] Obviously, no healing took place, let alone anything miraculous. If the man had been healed of any inability to speak in the first place, which is often characteristic of deaf-mutes, why did Coe not emphasize the wonderful fact that this man was even talking at all? Instead, Coe disappointedly said that someone was going to have to teach him. Moreover, why didn't Coe just obviate the need for a teacher altogether and miraculously cure the man of his inability to speak? If the man could be healed of deafness, why could he not also be cured of his inability to talk?

The main point to be understood throughout this discussion is that faith healers have believed that a divine, miraculous healing could and would occur upon their praying for an individual, just as recorded in the Bible, provided that individuals had the prerequisite faith. For faith healers, prayer for the sick involved more than just a healing—something that can be found in almost any Protestant denomination. Instead, prayer on the part of faith healers was intended to provide a miraculous cure, and here is the proverbial rub. This, in part, was what was being sold to the public, and many were buying.

TO WHOM HAVE FAITH HEALERS SOLD?

If one were to ask the faith healers in our study, "To whom are you preaching?" no doubt they would have responded, "To anyone who is listening." Ostensibly this may be true, but the reality is that faith healers were and are acutely aware of their predominant audiences. They know that not just anyone accepts their message. Rather, it is the physically afflicted, or their relatives, who in many cases have exhausted all hopes of being cured by medical doctors, who seek them out. For these people they are in business. Most audiences are composed of Pentecostals or Charismatics, those who already believe that the nine spiritual gifts mentioned in I Corinthians 12 are normal occurrences for Christians today.

William Branham, for example, once relayed the story about "a fine [non-Pentecostal] brother" who had just finished preaching to about eighteen hundred "nice, well-dressed [non-Pentecostal] people, intelligent-looking people" before Branham took the stage of the same auditorium. Contrasting that audience to his own, Branham sullenly continued, "I thought, 'My, that's very nice.' But here come [sic] my group in. Mine come [sic] in on crutches, wheelchairs, [and] straitjackets."[28]

Oral Roberts believed his audiences were the "incurably ill,"[29] who "in most cases have exhausted the resources of medical science, and now their only hope is faith in God."[30] Roberts frequently made these types of statements. He also believed his partners were primarily "hard core Pentecostals"[31] who had "fallen on hard times"[32] economically. Roberts once described them as "the simple, uneducated, uninhibited, with few sidelines to whom God means all, and who worship with their hands, feet, and voices."[33]

A. A. Allen was also acutely aware of who his followers were. Among them were the "sick" and "suffering."[34] Stating the obvious, Allen once remarked how "hundreds of people are rolled under this tent, on this ramp, on stretchers, in dying condition."[35] Regarding his followers' educational level, Allen disclosed that his revival "isn't breaking out among the intellectuals. The Bible says much learning hath made thee mad. So we're making no special effort to reach intellectuals."[36] Journalist William Hedgepeth once described those in attendance at an Allen revival as "skeletal men in bib overalls, chubby matrons, scrawny teenies and septuagenarians." Additionally, there were "blind ladies," "lunatics," and people with "faded eyes," "varicose veins," and "hook hands." He further described these individuals as having "bottomless frustrations" and "unlabeled loneliness."[37]

Jack Coe realized to whom he was primarily speaking when he once asked an audience, "How many believe he's [Jesus] here to smite that old cancer, to heal that old tumor, to open them [sic] blinded eyes, to cause them [sic] old lame legs to leap for joy?"[38] Jack Coe Jr. reveals that "as a young man" he remembered "hundreds of people coming to my father's tent revivals on stretchers and in wheelchairs."[39]

Those in attendance at more contemporary healing revivals mirror those who flocked to the tents of post-War faith healers. These audiences include those with withered or malformed limbs, those reliant on oxygen tanks, and those dependent on crutches, stretchers or wheelchairs. Further, while there appears to be at the revivals of Benny Hinn, Gloria Copeland, and Ernest Angley a number of financially well-off people who dress in fine clothing and sport what looks like expensive jewelry, the predominant picture is one of people in flannel shirts, tee shirts with various logos, sweatshirts, blue jeans, and casual footwear such as tennis shoes and boots. In short, these individuals appear to be ordinary people.

Moreover, judging by the number of people who close their eyes, look upward, stretch their hands toward heaven, and respond to the preaching with "Amen," "Hallelujah," "Thank you, Jesus," "Praise the Lord" or some similar expression, these individuals are already highly religious and know the routine.[40] Clearly these people are "true believers" in the first place.[41]

In his essay "Charisma and Media Evangelists: An Explication and Model of Communication Influence," communication professor Todd Lewis points out that the situational crises in which audiences find themselves serve as perceptual filters: "If audience members believe that their immediate context is hopeless, stress-producing, or threatening, their scope of perception narrows until they locate a leader/communicator who can remedy their exigence."[42] Similarly, medical doctor William Nolen suggests that once doctors admit that they can no longer help people, these individuals "go looking for salvation elsewhere."[43] Certainly the crises that audiences of faith healers find themselves in have contributed to their eagerness to "buy" the wares that faith healers are "selling."

HOW HAVE FAITH HEALERS SOLD THEIR MESSAGE OF HEALING?

Having looked at what faith healers have traditionally preached and who their primary audiences have been, the next logical question is, how have they been able to persuade their followers to accept their message despite evidence to the contrary? Simply put, what rhetorical strategies have they consciously or unconsciously employed in selling the idea of miraculous cures to their constituencies?

GOD HEALED ME

In examining the discourse of faith healers, one of the first things that audiences hear them preach, as proof of miraculous cures, is that they themselves have been personally healed by God. Oral Roberts frequently reminded those in his healing lines that God healed him of both tuberculosis and stuttering.[44] In fact, on one occasion Roberts told the once-popular talk show host Merv Griffin that "the greatest miracle I ever saw was my own personal miracle when God healed me of tuberculosis and loosed my stammering tongue."[45] Ernest Angley reminded audiences that God had healed him of a bone disease in one of his legs "that almost destroyed me as a child." After many nights of prayer, "King Jesus came and made me whole, made me well. I knew he could heal. I didn't doubt his healing power."[46] Although not specific about the nature of her illness,

Gloria Copeland reminded her audience that God had healed her and that, because of this, "nobody believes in healing more than I do."[47] Jack Coe told of how he had been so sick that he weighed only one hundred thirty-four pounds and the doctors had given up on him. They "folded their hands and shook their heads." Then "Dr. Jesus came into my room" and healed him. Coe, a big man in the first place, humorously suggested that now he weighed "two hundred thirty-five pounds and none of your business how much more."[48] A. A. Allen told of how God had healed his damaged vocal cords. After a friend prayed for him and the demons left his body, "My 'ruined' vocal cords were as good as new."[49] William Branham claimed to have been healed from "stomach trouble."[50] Benny Hinn tells of being healed of both stuttering[51] and a bleeding heart valve.[52] Now, he assures his audiences, he's so "anointed" that God "has even kept my teeth from cavities."[53]

Lewis refers to these types of claims as "conquered physical imperfections." He suggests that audiences are "drawn to . . . leaders whose defects have been surmounted and those who exist despite possible difficulties."[54] When faith healers tell such stories about personal healings, they embody the beliefs, values, and hopes of the group. Audiences reason that if God could heal the preacher, surely he can heal them. To borrow the term of rhetorical theorist Ernest Bormann, the faith healer him/herself became the "ultimate legitimizer" of what he or she was preaching.[55]

GOD CALLED ME

Faith healers have always been quick to remind their audiences that they were called by God. And what is more, these callings—according to faith healers—often came through miraculous visions or audible voices. William Branham, for instance, often told of how at the age of seven an angel warned him not to "drink or smoke or defile your body in any way, there'll be a work for you to do when you get older."[56] Branham also frequently disclosed how on May 7, 1946, at the age of 37, he was visited by an angel and commanded to "go to all the world and pray for the sick people." The angel continued, "If you get the people to believe you, and be sincere when you pray, nothing shall stand before your prayers, not even cancer."[57]

Oral Roberts often reminded his audiences of how, while he was lying flat on his back in his study in 1947, the Lord spoke to him: "Son, from this hour you will heal the sick and cast out devils by my power."[58] Roberts assured his audiences that since this visitation from God, he had "prayed for thousands upon thousands of these cases and in many instances the

Lord has set them free and made them whole."[59] Like Branham and Roberts, A .A. Allen told how God appeared to him while he locked himself in a closet to pray. "Then, like a whirlwind, I heard His voice. God's voice. Speaking to me."[60]

Ernest Angley claimed that God called him one night at the age of seven, when he was lying in bed. Like a scene from *The Wizard of Oz*, Angley describes how "the bed began to spin around and around until I was out in space under the stars."[61] Showing him millions of stars in the heavens, the Lord told Angley that he would eventually lead unlimited souls to Christ. Angley also recalled how one night in 1945, the same night he was healed of a stomach ulcer, Christ appeared to him in a blinding light and told him "that He would give me his power of healing others and that I was to carry the ministry of healing to the multitudes."[62] Benny Hinn recalled the day in April of 1974 when he was called to preach: "I saw someone standing in front of me. He was totally in flames, moving uncontrollably; his feet were not touching the ground. . . . At that moment, the Lord spoke to me in an audible voice. He said, 'Preach the gospel.'"[63]

The fact is, faith healers have frequently reported that God, or angels, appeared to them with a message. Most of them claimed to have had numerous supernatural encounters, and they were quick to remind their audiences of such. It is as if these experiences were their stamp of approval. God had validated, in other words, what they were teaching and practicing, and audiences loved it. Lewis suggests that it is natural for audiences who are "driven by the frustrations and stress of their situational crises" to seek out "a leader with a 'messianic destiny.'"[64] Certainly, the faith healers in this study claimed to have had such a destiny.

GIVE GOD THE CREDIT

Unlike what many people believe about faith healers, those in this study were really not arrogant individuals. Ostensibly, most appeared to be humble servants of God, which accounts in part for their relative popularity. Historically, faith healers never claimed to have the power to heal people. Instead, they always gave any credit or honor associated with what they were doing to God. Furthermore, they went to great lengths to make sure that their audiences understood this. Their followers loved them for their humility, giving them appropriate respect and credibility.

In attempting to explain what he was about, Jack Coe once stated, "I am not a healer. I never claimed to be a healer. I believe there's only one healer, and his name's Jesus." Coe went on to explain, "We do not claim to heal any of these people, but it's the prayer of faith that I pray for them."[65] Making sure that the audience did not think more highly of himself than they ought to, Coe once quipped, "I didn't come to you with a degree from any big college."[66] William Branham was incredibly humble. He taught, "I do not claim to do one thing myself. I have no power within myself to do anything."[67] He believed "there's no great people and big people in the kingdom of God. We're all one."[68]

Time and time again, A. A. Allen reminded his followers, "I'm not a healer, but I'm a believer."[69] "I'm not a healer. I couldn't heal anybody."[70] "We are not a healer, but the healer is here."[71] On one occasion, Allen humorously remarked, "I do not play at being God. . . . I am not a healer. A. A. Allen couldn't cure a fly with a headache."[72]

Before calling people into his healing lines, Oral Roberts would remind those in attendance, "I'd like to tell you friends as we start praying for the sick tonight. I'd like you to understand how God works through me. I am not the healer. I cannot heal. Only God can do that. But I am an instrument in his hands, which he is using to bring healing to many, many people."[73] Among more contemporary faith healers, one can hear similar disclaimers. Gloria Copeland, for instance, teaches that "you come to receive healing from the Lord Jesus Christ . . . healing that will flow out of my hands into you, but it's not my anointing. It's the anointing of the Holy Spirit."[74]

Ernest Angley is equally disavowing when he publicly prays, "Thou knowest, oh God, that I never take any of the honor. I never claim any of the glory. I am just a weakness to your greatness."[75] Once Angley disclosed to Cleveland television personality Fred Griffith that "everything" he did "is centered around Jesus, not around Ernest Angley."[76] Benny Hinn reminds would-be critics, "I don't heal anybody. The Lord is the healer."[77]

These types of claims help faith healers increase their ethos with their "partners," a term that some use to refer to their constituencies. Audiences love speakers who appear to be genuinely humble. Conversely, they despise the arrogant. Not claiming to have any personal power is advantageous to faith healers for two reasons: (1) not only does it help them increase their credibility with their audiences, but (2) it can also be used as an excuse when healings do not occur. Rather than shoulder the blame themselves, all faith healers have to say is that they never really claimed to have power to heal in the first place. The problem, therefore, must lie with the individual seeking the healing. Obviously, he or she did not have the necessary faith in God. Nonetheless, giving glory to God is one way that faith healers have "sold" what they do to a compliant constituency.

THE BIBLE SAYS SO

Had there been no Bible, or had the Bible not contained stories of miraculous cures, there probably would never have been Christian faith healers as we know them. For despite the fact that healers of one type or another (witchdoctors, shamans, etc.) have ministered in almost every community almost everywhere in the world since prehistory, Christian faith healers themselves take their marching orders from the miracle stories in the New Testament. They often remind their audiences that they practice what they do because they believe they can find evidence for it in the scripture. This strategy appears to work.

Throughout his sermons, for example, Jack Coe made numerous references to healings in the Bible. Coe pointed out that healing begins in Genesis 17 and runs "like a scarlet thread" throughout it. He reminded his audiences that "the Bible said that all who came to Jesus was [*sic*] healed." So sure of his right and ability to heal people because of what he believed the scriptures taught, he challenged, "I dare any fair-minded person to take this blessed old book that I hold in my hand and make a fair-minded, open investigation of the word of God in divine healing." Coe believed that he had "enough Bible to back it up."[78] Like other faith healers, Coe often quoted Hebrews 13:8 ("Jesus Christ the same yesterday, today, and forever") as a proof text that healing occurs today just as it was recorded in Jesus's day.[79] In fact, this passage has probably been quoted more than any other verse in the entire Bible to prove that miraculous healings should still be expected.

Similar to Coe, A. A. Allen also practiced what he did because he believed he could find a basis for it in the New Testament. Once, seemingly out of frustration, Allen earnestly pleaded with his listeners, "Listen to me. I am giving you biblical, scriptural proof."[80] Like Coe and other faith healers, Allen relied on Hebrews 13:8,[81] I Peter 2:24,[82] Matthew 8:17,[83] and Mark 16:17[84] among others. Allen even had a portion of Mark 16:17 plastered on a long banner, which hung behind the pulpit in his tent to remind those in attendance: "These signs shall follow them that believe." So confident was Allen in using the Bible to "prove" miraculous healing that he often began statements with "my Bible says"[85] and then commanded the audience to "say amen if you believe everything in God's word."[86]

Oral Roberts also relied heavily on the Bible as proof of miraculous cures. Hebrews 13:8 was one of his favorite passages.[87] Once Roberts labeled Matthew 8:5–13 as "the greatest healing chapter in the Bible."[88] There was never a time when Roberts did not attempt to ground what he was practicing in the scriptures.

Nowadays, Gloria Copeland often assures her audiences that "It says so in the Bible" or "I'll prove it to you from the word" when referring to miraculous healing. "God doesn't use cancer to teach the church," she says; "He uses the Holy Spirit and the word." "Scripture teaches," explains Copeland. Copeland once preached, "The same word that we [she and her husband Kenneth] listened to twenty-five years ago, we still listen to because it's the same word with the same power."[89]

Many other examples could be cited, but these are sufficient to show that references to the Bible have been a central rhetorical staple in the preaching of faith healers. Furthermore, such strategy works for the predominantly Pentecostal and Charismatic audiences who believe the Bible to be the inspired word of God. It matters not to them that some of these passages have nothing to do with miraculous cures. Many times, they are not even aware of this. The fact is, faith healers use these verses repeatedly, and their listeners accepted them as proof. Certain verses (e.g., Heb. 13:8; Isa. 53:5; 1 Pet. 2:24; Mark 16:17) have become part of the faith-healing culture. When audiences hear the same verses over and over again, it becomes difficult for them not to believe that these passages teach what the preacher says they teach. In this way, use of the Bible has become a major inducement for audiences to believe.

I'VE SEEN IT WITH MY OWN EYES

In an attempt to persuade those in attendance to believe in miraculous cures, faith healers cite example after example of individuals they have personally witnessed who, they claim, have been cured. Gloria Copeland tells of how, during various years of her ministry, people with "all kind [*sic*] of terminal diseases, serious things, just absolutely serious things . . . were healed."[90]

Jack Coe seemed to thrive on this type of proof. In February 1956, Coe was arraigned in a Miami, Florida, courtroom on charges of practicing medicine without a license. Eventually the charges were dropped, but the sassy Coe seized the opportunity to let the authorities of Miami know how little he appreciated being questioned about his authority to preach and practice healings. In one sermon preached during his Miami revival shortly after his arrest, Coe offered example after example of individuals he had seen healed. In bold fashion, he told of how "last Saturday night" a man had been healed of blindness, and Sunday afternoon his wife testified that "God has given him back his eyesight." He reported that a woman was "here last night who had never heard or spoke [*sic*]" before but who was healed. After citing the healing of Naaman in the Bible (2 Kings 5) and his own personal healing, Coe cited the example of a Mr. Chumley, a Baptist preacher from Plainview, Texas, who had been healed. Now Mr. Chumley is "out preaching divine healing," Coe assured his audiences. In graphic detail, Coe boasted of the healing of Christine Carmichael of Tulsa, Oklahoma, who was dying of a brain tumor: "Pus and blood ran from her brain." He told of how after he laid hands on her she "spit up" her tumor and coughed it from her mouth. "I tell you, that's the best cancer operation you'll ever undergo."[91] Coe often used these types of graphic examples to persuade audiences to accept divine healing.

William Branham boasted to his audiences how he had seen "better than three hundred cases of cross-eyeds [sic] healed in less than six months' time." He told of people who were healed of paralysis, withered hands, demon possession, and crippling diseases. He assured his audiences that he had seen miraculous cures "hundreds of times" during his ministry.[92]

Likewise, Oral Roberts assured his audiences that thousands of people had been cured after he laid hands upon them and prayed for them.[93] A. A. Allen often cited examples of people who had been healed under his tent.[94] Among the many examples that Ernest Angley has given, he once told his audience that one woman "flew in from Russia to get her miracle" before having to return.[95]

No matter who the faith healer, examples have commonly been employed in an attempt to prove to onlookers that God can and does heal people miraculously. Like the other rhetorical strategies, use of examples appears to contribute to the speaker's ability to persuade.

IF IT HAPPENED TO ME, IT CAN HAPPEN TO YOU

In addition to citing concrete cases of people being healed, faith healers often allow these individuals to stand in front of audiences to recount their own stories. Often they return with envelopes containing x-rays or medical papers as proof that tumors or other ailments are now gone. Once, for instance, Oral Roberts called Fred Odel from Oakland, California, to the stage to testify of how he was clear of lung cancer after being healed in a previous Oral Roberts crusade. When asked by Roberts what was in the envelope he was carrying, Odel confidently responded, "That's my proof." Odel had returned with an x-ray and a doctor's letter, verifying his cure. If only for a few minutes, Odel reveled in the spotlight, and the audience loved it. Roberts, too, appeared to relish the occasion. In fact, Roberts liked these moments so well that he often allowed individuals to return at a later date to testify to audiences about their healing. Like the other faith healers, he realized the inherent value of such testimonies.[96]

Not only have faith healers allowed individuals to stand in their services to testify about their healings, but they have often published these testimonies in their monthly magazines. Among the numerous others, for example, A. A. Allen once published a testimonial entitled, "I Took My Cancer to Church in a Jar."[97] Other claims involved being healed of hemophilia, growing an arm longer, passing an open safety pen from the stomach up the esophagus and through the mouth, being set free from demons, or having one's lungs cured of cancer.[98] One individual even testified that God had miraculously filled one of her teeth with gold.[99] Suffice it to say that testimonials, whether spoken or printed, were often employed in an attempt to sell the idea of miraculous cures to audience. Just as advertisers rely on various individuals to endorse their products, so too, have faith healers relied on testimonials to "sell" the miraculous. It appears to work. But how?

As I have argued elsewhere, testimony is effective for several reasons.[100] First it is entertaining. Audiences simply like to hear peoples' stories. They find them interesting. The more sensational the story, the more entertaining the testimony. Second, if audiences perceive that an individual is credible and has received a healing, they begin to think that a healing could happen to them, too. While the nature of the ailment may not be identical, the fact that both are human and both have suffered a sickness or affliction provides sufficient common ground. Finally, the tendency to identify with another individual is particularly strong when the ailments are identical, especially if an individual has exhausted all other hopes of being cured. The testimony of one individual offers hope for another.

JUST SEE FOR YOURSELF

Empirical demonstrations have been central to the healing lines of faith healers. After persons have claimed to have received a healing, faith healers have often commanded them to bend over and touch their toes, swirl their backs in circles to demonstrate a cure, or run across the stage to show that not only could they walk but they could now run after being confined for years to a wheelchair. The deaf and mute have often been asked to parrot some simplistic expression that the preacher would call out, such as "baby," "boy," or "mama." Others have been asked to repeat "Thank you, Jesus," "Hallelujah," or "Praise the Lord." These expressions have varied little from one faith healer to another. The healers often move several feet away from the individual to demonstrate to audiences just how well the person could now hear.[101]

On one occasion, in an attempt to demonstrate just how well off a man with a bad back had become, A. A. Allen jumped into the man's arms and commanded him to carry him across the stage.[102] On another occasion, after raising a man off a stretcher, Allen had him eat a ham salad sandwich and drink a carton of milk to demonstrate to the audience that he had been healed of stomach cancer.[103]

In his attempts to be empirical, Jack Coe was often rough with those who sought healings. It was not uncommon for him to place his hands on their neck and force them to bend their back forward or ram his knee into their back and force them to bend backward to demonstrate that they were healed. Also, Coe frequently grabbed a person with a locked arm or shoulder and physically moved it up and down for the individual to demonstrate to the audience that he or she was now healed. "Up! Down! Up! Down! Up! Down! Up! Down!" Coe would sometimes command an individual in rapid, repetitive fashion after freeing his or her arm. Coe also attempted to show how cancers would fall off of people's faces into his hands.[104]

Once after supposedly healing a woman with a goiter on her neck, Oral Roberts pulled at the woman's throat and told the audience that the goiter was leaving because her skin was "loose and flabby" and "as smooth as it can be."[105] Roberts often affirmed to his television audiences that what they had seen was real: "Now after you've seen with your own eyes and felt with your own heart what God's done for the people in the healing line tonight, I want to offer prayer for you personally, there in your room, for the Lord to heal you."[106]

Aware that many people were skeptical about what they were seeing, A. A. Allen once assured his television audience, "The camera picks them [miraculous healings] up just as they happen. Actually, it's a part of the service."[107] One could cite many other examples, but suffice it to say that from William Branham through Gloria Copeland and Benny Hinn, faith healers have relied heavily on individuals to demonstrate in some physical way to those in attendance that they were healed. Apparently this strategy worked, judging by the immense applause and numerous outbursts of "Praise the Lord" or other expressions of exultation that one could hear at these healing revivals.

There is a problem, however, with these "empirical" demonstrations. Often onlookers have no idea of how severe a problem an individual has, if any at all. As I have argued previously, audiences are at the mercy of the individual's testimony. They are asked to assume that the individual is truly afflicted and merely take their word for it. When a person throws away his or her crutches or stands up out of a wheelchair, audiences just assume the individual could not walk at all before. Who really knows, though, to what extent these individuals lack the ability to walk? Who really knows to what extent a person has arthritis, cancer, or any other ailment for that matter?

YOU DON'T NEED THOSE CRUTCHES ANY MORE

In addition to having people who supposedly were healed demonstrate their cures in an empirical way, some faith healers such as Jack Coe and Benny Hinn have appealed to their audiences' visual senses with references to abandoned medical apparatuses (e.g., crutches, canes, wheelchairs, oxygen tanks). These have served as nonverbal symbols of inducement. Jack Coe intentionally displayed hundreds of crutches, strung on ropes around the inside of his tent, to show audiences that individuals had come into the healing line on crutches but no longer needed them after being healed. In fact, at the beginning of Coe's television programs, aired in the 1950s, the camera would pan the inside of the tent and a narrator would ask "what is the meaning" of these crutches and braces. He would then invite people to stay tuned so that they would find out for themselves.[108] Once when trying to persuade an audience to believe in what he was practicing, Jack Coe brashly pointed to the medical apparatuses hanging around the tent and told the audience, "I want you to see all of those crutches and all of those braces, and all of those wheelchairs that came off of the people's spines here in the city of Miami."[109] No doubt Coe was using them as symbols to induce audiences to believe in miraculous cures.

Similarly Benny Hinn employs "abandoned" medical devices to convince his followers. After calling out scores of healing in the audience, Hinn's ushers begin to line the stage as quickly as is humanly possible with discarded wheelchairs, walkers, oxygen tanks, and crutches. No doubt these are placed there for a reason. Hinn wants everyone in attendance to see them. Empty wheelchairs, of course, imply that people are cured. They are symbols of healings, and Hinn understands this, which is why he has his ushers to place them on stage for everyone to see in the first place. Once Hinn remarked, seeing so many wheelchairs on the stage, "We have a traffic jam on the platform."[110] The audience, already worked into a frenzy, erupted in more praise and applause.

There is a limit, though, to the types of discarded medical aids one will see. Typically, they have been limited to crutches, braces, wheelchairs, oxygen tanks, and the like. It is interesting to note that one will never see prostheses such as artificial arms, legs, hands, teeth, eyes, or ears, because the fact is, these are never miraculously regenerated.

LET ME ENTERTAIN YOU

In his model of communication influence of media evangelists, Lewis points out that one factor that makes a speaker so charismatic and hence persuasive is the speaker's delivery. Elements such as "vocal force," "rapid delivery," and "nonverbal qualities" (i.e., physical attractiveness, gestures, facial expressions, clothing, touch, and crowding) contribute to the selling of the miraculous. Audiences respond favorably to varied volume, pitch, and stress of certain words. Moreover, rapid delivery, interspersed with short pauses and repetition of key phrases (e.g., "Hallelujah! Thank you, Jesus!"), "forestall[s] the possibility of immediate critical analysis" and "short-circuits the reflective process."[111]

All of the faith healers of this study employed one or more of these elements, whether consciously or unconsciously, in appealing to their followers. Physically, A. A. Allen was a dynamic preacher, often athletically jumping around in the pulpit. While preaching, he frequently jumped up and down, making a chopping motion with his right hand, all the while yelling at the top of his lungs. During his healing lines, more often than not he would grab an individual's head with both of his hands or firmly place his index fingers in their ears, working them in a circular motion as he cast out some type of demon. Not since the days of Billy Sunday had America seen a more animated, acrobatic speaker in the pulpit.

After being introduced like a game show host by his associate pastor Bob DeWeese, Oral Roberts would bound through a back door onto the stage with a smile on his face. No one had more spring in his step than Roberts. Moreover, he was tall (about 6'2"), dark, and handsome. He was always impeccably dressed, as were all of the other faith healers in this study. While preaching, Roberts would place one hand in his coat pocket, pick up the five-foot-long chrome microphone stand with the other, and pace across the platform. He preached so adamantly that his black hair would frequently fall limp across his forehead. While healing people, he would sit in a folding chair, take off his coat, and lay his hands firmly on the forehead of an individual standing a few feet below him on another platform.

With a body like Santa Claus, Jack Coe was a large man, well over two hundred thirty-five pounds and "none of your business how much more." He had a large stomach, which was noticeable, in part, because he often took off his suit coat in an attempt to stay as cool as he could in the summer heat. Due to his size, Coe did not jump around in the pulpit as did Allen. Instead he used his voice and facial expressions to emphasize his points. Coe also frequently repeated himself for emphasis. Once, when defending his right to practice healing, he read from the Bible about Jesus's ministry. With a sassy smirk on his face, Coe yelled that Jesus went about all Galilee preaching "and healing aaaaaaall manner of sickness and aaaaaaall manner of diseases with-out-a-license. I said with-out-a-license."[112] Coe's nonverbal mannerisms and vocal inflection dared anyone to take issue with what he preached.

Benny Hinn is one of the most animated faith healers one will ever watch. His performances are nothing short of theatrical. In fact, Hinn once disclosed that when he is on stage, he is under "pressure to produce": "People don't come just to hear you preach; they want to see something."[113] If people "want to see something" certainly Hinn does not disappoint them. Holding a cordless microphone in one hand, Hinn roams widely across the platform while preaching or calling out healings. He frequently takes off his coat and swings it around and around in lasso fashion while running across the stage to "slay someone in the Spirit," which I will say more about in the next chapter.

Slaying people in the Spirit is one of Hinn's specialties. Like Ernest Angley, after Hinn places a hand on their forehead, individuals fall backward into the waiting arms of an usher, trained to catch people. Often the ushers themselves fall out under the power of the Spirit. Even Hinn will fall backward as if overcome by the Holy Spirit. Once I witnessed Hinn's ushers catch him just in time before he crashed into the drum set. Audiences burst with side-splitting laughter when they see such histrionics. Although critic Ole Anthony describes Hinn's behavior as "goofy,"[114] audiences find him highly entertaining. It is doubtful that they would have a better time at a stand-up comedian's concert.

Less dramatic in her stage presence than any of the above faith healers, Gloria Copeland is still a dynamic speaker, physically restrained but bold in speech nonetheless. Often she directs her comments forcefully and adamantly toward the devil himself. One woman in Copeland's audience explained to me that she likes the healer so much because "She's so powerful—dynamic." When asked what she liked about Copeland, another woman replied, "Her strong faith. Her healing is real—very real!" In addition to her dynamism, Copeland is physically attractive. Standing approximately five feet five inches tall, with a smooth complexion and blonde hair, Copeland is always well dressed and visually appealing.[115]

Both Ernest Angley and William Branham were also forceful speakers. Although their power came more from their voices than from their physical presence, they still were entertaining to watch, especially when laying hands on individuals to be healed. There can be no doubt that part of the success of faith healers was due largely to the way they conducted themselves on stage, which was generally very entertaining.

CONCLUSION

In summary, the faith healers we have discussed in this chapter have typically attempted to sell the miraculous to uncritical, highly religious, not-well-educated audiences who were afflicted with various physical and emotional problems. Supposedly, these ailments were often the results of demons inhabiting people. Faith healers have traditionally used a number of strategies, often consciously, to persuade those listening that miraculous healings are normative for the here and now. These have included (1) testimonies of the healers themselves being miraculously cured, (2) claims of being miraculously called by God, (3) disavowing personal power and giving God the credit, (4) references to various passages throughout the Bible, (5) use of examples seen by the faith healers, (6) public testimonies of individuals who claimed to have been healed in prior revivals, (7) empirical, physical demonstrations, (8) use of nonverbal artifacts, and (9) commanding stage presences of the faith healers.

These strategies are powerful factors in persuading audiences that they can receive a miraculous cure, particularly when used in combination with each other. It is hard for unsuspecting religious followers to deny the claims that faith healers make, when constantly bombarded with these rhetorical practices—especially if an individual has already exhausted all that medical science has to offer. Given that humans will always suffer physical and mental afflictions, one should not look for faith healers to go out of "business" any time soon. In fact, it is doubtful that such will ever be the case. For now, at least, all over this country people continue to flock to large auditoriums, seeking relief, just as they fled in hordes into the tents of post-WWII faith healers, and as they came flocking to Jesus in the biblical narratives. Like the faith healers who evoke them, the expressions "Hallelujah! Thank you, Jesus!" will not likely fall silent any time soon.

The haunting fact, of course, that leaves us all wondering, is that despite the foibles of some of the faith healers, and despite what many outside observers would say is little more than high drama and sensationalism rather than proof of claims, individuals continue to cling to the belief that miracles, demon possession, visions, and the like continue to happen just as we can read about in the Bible. In the remaining chapters we will be looking more closely at some of the beliefs that are articulated not only by faith healers but by people of faith in general, to determine to what extent these beliefs really are biblically based.

2

―――――・✦・―――――

"Do You Understand What You Are Reading?"[1]: Making Sense of the Bible

Having introduced in the previous chapter some of the things that faith healers have traditionally taught, and how they have been able to convince certain audiences to accept their messages, we turn now to a discussion of how we can make sense of the Bible when we read it, particularly when it comes to the things that faith healers espouse. The principles that I will introduce in this chapter, which I will also reference from time to time in the remaining chapters of this book, when understood, can help us to evaluate what we hear when listening to the preaching of faith healers.

According to a 2011 Gallup poll, 3 out of 10 Americans say they believe the Bible is the "the actual word of God." While this number is down from the 1970s and '80s, it is similar to what Gallup reported a few decades ago. According to the same poll, "A 49% plurality of Americans say the Bible is the inspired word of God but that it should not be taken literally." Another 17% report that they believe the Bible is little more than a book of legends and fables. However, among churchgoers, not surprisingly, 54% "of those who attend religious services on a weekly basis" believe that the Bible is the actual word of God and should be taken literally. This number is "more than twice the percentage of those who attend church less often."[2]

Those who are more inclined to believe that the Bible is literally true are Protestants (as opposed to Catholics or Mormons). In fact, two-thirds of all Protestants who attend church on a weekly basis believe that the Bible is the actual word of God and should be interpreted literally. In summarizing the above data, author Jeffrey Jones writes, "In general, the dominant view of Americans is that the Bible is the word of God, be it inspired or actual, as opposed to a collection of stories recorded by man. That is consistent with the findings that the United States is <u>a predominantly Christian nation</u> and that Americans <u>overwhelmingly believe in God</u>" (underlined in original).[3]

It is one thing to believe that the Bible is the inspired word of God and that, in many cases, it should be taken literally, but it is quite a different matter to read it and study it. According to the 2007 Religious Landscape Survey conducted by the Pew Research Center, only 27% of adults between the ages of 18 and 29 say they read the Bible on a weekly basis. This number is not much better among older adults. Only 36% of those thirty years or older report reading the Bible at least once a week.[4] A more recent study conducted by the Barna Group for the American Bible Society suggests that while 80% of all Americans believe the Bible is sacred, only 1 in 5 actually reads it "on a regular basis." In fact, 57% of those surveyed say they read their Bibles only "four times a year or less."[5]

The National Study of Youth and Religion (NSYR) project, based at the University of North Carolina at Chapel Hill, reports that among U.S. Protestant teenagers, only 32% say they read the Bible alone at least once a week. This means that the "majority of U.S. Protestant teenagers say that they read the Bible either less frequently or not at all." Among all U.S. teenagers, only 26% report that they read the sacred texts of their religious affiliations once or more a week.[6] Christian Smith, Director of the NSYR, argues that it would be a mistake to say that U.S. adults are reading the Bible any more often than teenagers. He suggests, "It could be that most Protestant adults are not very good role models for their teenagers when it comes to basic, personal religious practices like reading the Bible."[7] Suffice it to say that, although many Americans believe the Bible is the inspired word of God, not many of them are actually reading it, let alone studying it. In other words, not much reading is being done by not many people.

And herein is the problem. If Americans in general, and Protestants in particular, are neither studying the Bible nor reading it—in spite of the fact that they believe it is sacred—then from whom are they receiving their religious instruction, if they are receiving any at all, especially on topics that faith healers preach about—miracles, demons, the call of God, the Holy Spirit, the gospel of health and wealth, or any other biblical topic for that matter? Perhaps they are acquiring whatever religious knowledge and beliefs they have from misguided family and friends, from movies or other media, or from some misinformed religious authority figure, including faith healers or other disreputable televangelists. It is quite possible, if not probable, that this is the case. Thus, to say that it is important to study the scriptures for oneself is an understatement. Equally important, when one studies, an individual needs to understand some basic rules of interpretation so that he or she does not draw wrong conclusions or is not steered down the wrong path, which leads me to the purpose of this chapter. What I would like to do is discuss some elementary, yet indispensable, principles by which we can comprehend the scriptures that deal with the themes that one can hear among faith healers. While I will be the first to admit that there is much about biblical analysis that I do not know, there are a few simple ideas that, if followed, can help any reader come to a proper understanding of the scriptures. After all, the Bible was meant to be read and understood by everyone alike (Eph. 3:2–19, 1 John 2:1). If, after reading this chapter, the reader would like to learn more about how to extrapolate meaning from biblical texts, there are several excellent books available.[8] My hope in this chapter, in part, is to help an individual comprehend what he or she might possibly read from the Bible as well as to empower him or her with the confidence to conclude that what faith healers have traditionally taught has been foreign to the scriptures—in spite of their claims to the contrary—because they have violated one or more principles of Biblical interpretation mentioned below.

Before going further, two related words are important for the reader to understand: *hermeneutics* and *exegesis*. These words are often found in the same context and are occasionally used interchangeably, even though they are technically not the same. Greek in origin, *hermeneutics* is derived from *Hermes*, messenger of the Greek gods, whose job "was to explain divine decisions to humans."[9] According to the *American Heritage Dictionary of the English Language*, hermeneutics is from the Greek *tekhne* ("art") and *hermeneutikos* ("of interpretation"), meaning the art of interpretation.[10] The *Oxford English Dictionary* (OED), defines *hermeneutics* as "the interpretation of scriptural texts; such interpretation as a subject of study or analysis, esp. with regard to theory or methodology." The OED also states that "such study often addresses the issue of how spiritual truths may be either revealed or obscured by the language of translated texts; it is commonly distinguished from *exegesis* or practical exposition."[11]

Exegesis, on the other hand, is from the Greek *exegeisthai* ("to show the way," "expound").[12] The OED states that *exegesis* means "to interpret, to guide, lead," as in to guide or lead out of. It is the "Explanation, exposition (of a sentence, word, etc.); esp. the interpretation of Scripture or a Scriptural passage."[13] When one exegetes a passage of scripture, he or she shows the way or guides others by drawing the meaning out of the text.[14] In his work *Toward An Exegetical Theology*, Kaiser concludes, "while hermeneutics will seek to describe the general and special principles and rules which are useful in approaching the biblical text, exegesis will seek to identify the single truth-intention of individual phrases, clauses, and sentences as they make up the thought of paragraphs, sections, and, ultimately, entire books." Hermeneutics, then, is the "*theory* that guides exegesis" while "exegesis may be understood . . . to be the practice of and the set of *procedures* for discovering the author's intended meaning."[15] Likewise, in his book *Exegetical Fallacies*, Carson points out that "exegesis is concerned with actually interpreting the text, whereas hermeneutics is concerned with the nature of the interpretative process. Exegesis concludes by saying, 'This passage means such and such'; hermeneutics ends by saying, 'This interpretative process is constituted by the following techniques and pre-understandings.'"[16] Faith healers, as I will show in more detail in subsequent chapters, have had a difficult time in these two areas of study.

INTERPRETING VERSES WITHIN THEIR CONTEXT

One of the first lessons that an individual should keep in mind when studying the scriptures is to interpret them within their proper context. *Context* is derived from the Latin *con* (meaning "together") and *textus* (meaning "woven"). Kaisar writes, "Hence when we speak of the context, we are talking about the connection of thought that runs through a passage, those links that weave it into one piece."[17] The job of the exegete, according to Kaisar, is "to find this thread of thought which runs like a life stream through the smaller and larger parts of every passage."[18] Biblical scholar John Broadus warns us that often a context can range from a few verses to a few chapters and may not necessarily begin or end with a chapter where a text is found.[19] Robinson, in his book *Biblical Preaching*, points out that "An expositor pulls up his chair to where the biblical authors sat. He attempts to work his way back into the world of the Scriptures to understand the message. . . . As much as possible the expositor seeks a firsthand acquaintance with the biblical writers and their ideas in context."[20] Schmidt reminds us in his booklet *How To Study the Bible* that the "basic questions to ask about any Scripture are: Who, What, When, Where, How and Why."[21] In critiquing "reader-response criticism," which suggests that one should not take into account either the author or historical or literary context of a verse but to let a verse speak to an individual any way that individual sees fit, thus making the reader "(and the reader alone) . . . responsible for the production of 'meaning,'" Fee argues that such a philosophy of biblical interpretation "stands in unrelieved tension with the biblical revelation—that it was the one true God who chose to reveal himself to creation and to Israel and the church, and to enshrine this revelation in the texts cherished as the Christian Bible." This later belief, "necessarily commits the interpreter to historical and literary inquiry. Readers must seek to understand how God revealed himself to people then and there, so that they can grasp how God speaks the Word that is once and for all."[22] In other words, one must take into account who said what to whom, for what purpose(s), with what effect. One must interpret a verse in light of its context. Let me illustrate the principle of context with a relatively non-controversial issue.

In Romans 14:10, the apostle Paul writes, "But you, why do you judge your brother? Or you again, why do you regard your brother with contempt? For we will all stand before the judgment-seat of God" (NASV). If a person were to pluck this verse out of its context, he or she might wrongly interpret it to mean that we should never judge anyone—that God frowns on all judgment. After all, that is what it looks like it is teaching on its face. In fact, as I pointed out in the introduction to this book, this is the type of thing I hear my students say on a regular basis: "The Bible says that we shouldn't judge."

However, a closer look at the verse in its context tells a different story. Although the apostle Paul may have appeared to imply that we should not judge, he is really suggesting that we should not judge others (i.e., condemn) solely on matters of opinion, as opposed to matters of law. How do we know this? In this context Paul is specifically referring to eating meats which have probably been sacrificed to idols. (See 1 Cor. 8 for a parallel chapter.) In Romans 14:3, he tells his readers, "The one who eats is not to regard with contempt ["despise" KJV] the one who does not eat, and the one who does not eat is not to judge the one who eats, for God has accepted him" (NASV). Paul's point is that it is neither sinful to eat nor sinful to abstain from eating, depending on what one's conscience will allow (vss. 14–15). Just because a person's conscience will not let him or her eat meat, this does not give an individual the right to condemn someone else who does. Likewise, those who eat meat should not condemn those whose conscience will not allow them to do the same. Thus, Paul suggests in verse 13, "Let us not therefore judge one another anymore." Paul is not talking about all judgment, though. Rather he is discussing in this context only matters of opinion, specifically in regard to eating meat.

An individual might easily draw the wrong conclusion about a verse—as many people have about what Jesus said about judging others in Matthew 7:1—if he or she were to isolate these verses from their context.

Missing the context is where faith healers have often run afoul of the truth. They believe, for instance, as I will discuss in much greater detail in chapter 7, that all Christians ought to receive the baptism of the Holy Spirit, with evidence of speaking in tongues like what Luke records happened on the day of Pentecost in Acts 2. Citing verses such as Matthew 3:1–12, John 14:26, and Acts 1–2, for instance, faith healers leave the impression that they know what they are talking about and that what they are talking about is grounded in the Bible, which makes their arguments rhetorically successful. In other words, although boasting that what they teach is biblically based is persuasive, in reality it is merely a facade. In truth, they have failed to understand what is going on in these contexts.

In Matthew 3, John the Baptist was talking to two groups of people: (1) the Pharisees and Sadducees and (2) the apostles. John did not have everyone in mind, even in his immediate audience, when he said, "I indeed baptize you in water unto repentance; but he that cometh after me is mightier than I, whose shoes I am not worthy to bear: he shall baptize you in the Holy Spirit and in fire."

In John 14:26, when he promised to send "the Comforter, even the Holy Spirit," who would "teach you all things and bring to your remembrance all that I said to you," Christ was talking only to his disciples, not to anyone else, and certainly not to people today. Thus, when the baptism of the Holy Spirit came in Acts 2, it fell only on the apostles, as Christ had promised them in Luke 24:49 and Acts 1:4. Failure to understand who the speaker was and to whom he was speaking in these contexts has caused faith healers and other Charismatics to utterly miss the point. They believe that Christians today ought to receive the same thing that the apostles received, but there is not one shred of evidence to support their claim.

Likewise, when Oral Roberts and others argue from the Bible that verses like Galatians 6:7 ("for whatsoever a man soweth, that shall he also reap") prove the doctrine of seed faith, a topic I discuss in greater detail in chapter 8, they have also failed to take into account the context. In the context of Galatians 6, the apostle Paul was talking metaphorically about sowing deeds, not money. In fact, Paul concluded, "let us work that which is good toward all men, and especially toward them that are of the household of faith" (Gal. 6:10). When Paul reminded the Galatians that they would reap what they sowed, the reaping that he had in mind was eternal life, not something in the present life. This is clear when Paul said, "but he that soweth unto the spirit shall of the Spirit reap eternal life" (Gal. 6:8). When one fails to take into consideration the context, misinterpretation is usually the result.

One should never make a verse say what he or she wants it to say, which is what faith healers often do. This is called *eisegesis*. In *eisegesis* (as opposed to *exegesis*), one imports his or her own ideas into a verse to make the verse say what he or she would like it to mean, thus giving others the impression that what is being taught is biblically grounded. This is equivalent to driving a square peg into a round hole. Ultimately one might force the peg into the hole, but there is going to be collateral damage in the process. What a person would like a verse to say may not always fit the context.

There is a truism among Biblical scholars that any text taken out of its context is merely a pretext for a prooftext.[23] A pretext (i.e., an ostensible excuse to believe something) is a good way to describe what faith healers often offer when they attempt to prove from the Bible many of the things that they teach. Kaiser warns that "We must not make a pretense of exegeting a text just because the wording is to our liking. That, in essence, would be a deliberate misleading of the congregation, for they would assume we are pointing to that text as authoritative for the matter under consideration."[24]

Nowhere is the idea of making a verse fit what one would like it to mean more evident than when faith healers attempt to justify the practice of being "slain in the Spirit," which I introduced in chapter 1. The expression "slain in the Spirit" is found nowhere in the scriptures; moreover, neither is the concept, even though faith healers would argue otherwise. According to Hanegraaff in his book *Counterfeit Revival*, there are several "scriptural pretexts,"[25] used to support the idea. However, according to Hanegraaff, all of these verses have been taken out of context and made to mean something that they do not mean. Let us look at a few of them.

According to Hanegraaff, Genesis 17:3 is a verse that is sometimes used to justify being "slain in the Spirit." This verse says that "Abram fell on his face and God talked with him" (NASB). Does this verse really teach that Abram was "slain in the Spirit"? Hanegraff suggests that unlike what is seen in the services of faith healers today, "the Almighty did not cause Abraham to fall through a blow that stupefied and knocked him senseless; rather Abraham fell of his own accord in response to the majesty of the Almighty." Hanegraff goes on to argue that "it is important to note that God is more concerned with the attitude of our hearts than He is with the position of our bodies. While God most certainly has the power to overwhelm us with His presence, a basic principle communicated in Scripture is that God has created us as volitional beings" who can either submit or rebel.[26] Voluntary submission is really what Abraham was doing.

A second verse that is sometimes used to justify being "slain in the Spirit" is Acts 10:9–10, where Peter "fell into a trance" while praying. Hanegraaff suggests that "biblical trance states like that experienced by Peter are sovereignly initiated, not self-induced or induced through human agency," like what happens in the services of faith healers. In contrast, Hanegraaff continues, "unbiblical trance states can be self-induced, induced through socio-psychological manipulation, or initiated by the touch of a shaman/sorcerer." Hanegraaff points out that Peter's trance "cannot be used as a precedent for people today" because "as an Apostle [he] was foundational to the church (Eph. 2:20)." God put Peter in a trance to explain to him that he wanted him to preach the gospel to Cornelius, the first Gentile convert to Christianity. The context clearly indicates this. Trances were never intended to be normative for Christians over two thousand years later.

Then there was the apostle Paul who, as he traveled on the road to Damascus as Saul of Tarsus to persecute Christians, "fell upon the earth" after seeing a light shine from heaven (Acts 9:4). This verse is also used to prove that Christians today can be "slain in the Spirit." First, it should be noted that Paul's experience was unique. The context suggests that it was given to qualify him to be an apostle. For example, God's words to Ananias, the man whom God called to teach and baptize Paul, were that he was "a chosen vessel unto me" (Acts 9:15). Paul remained blind for three days thereafter. Hanegraaff cleverly states, "one wonders how many . . . devotees would line up to experience the slain in the spirit phenomenon if they truly believed that there were a chance that they, like Paul, would end up blinded for three days." According to Hanegraaff, "parallels between what happened to the apostle Paul" and what happens to people today who claim to have been "slain in the Spirit" "are conspicuous by their absences."[27]

In Revelation 1:17, John records, "And when I saw him, I fell at his feet as one dead. And he laid his right hand upon me, saying, Fear not." This verse, too, is sometimes used to prove that individuals can be "slain in the Spirit." The fact is John was not necessarily knocked unconscious by the Holy Spirit; what purpose would that have served? The context suggests that he did what he did out of godly fear and respect. In his book *The Avenging of the Apostles and Prophets*, Ogden points out, "John was so awed by what he saw he fell down as dead. He had just seen a manifestation of the glory of the Lord and the perplexities of the occasion were more than the human mind could fathom. In this respect, he was no different than Ezekiel or Daniel who under similar circumstances likewise fell under the pressures of the occasion (cf. Ezek. 1:28; 3:23; 43:3; Dan. 8:17; 10: 7–10).[28] In his commentary on Revelation, MacArthur suggests that John was "overwhelmed with terror at the manifestation of Christ's glory," which caused him to fall prostrate as if he were a dead man.[29] Robert Mounce, in his commentary on Revelation, suggests that John was "experiencing a supernatural phenomenon of such magnitude that to stand as an equal would be tantamount to blasphemy."[30] John did what he did of his own volition out of respect to Christ, not because he was somehow overwhelmed by the Holy Spirit, which he could not withstand.

Hanegraaff suggests that John 18:6 is occasionally cited as a proof text that people today can be "slain in the Spirit." This verse discusses what happened to "the band of soldiers" who sought Jesus the night that Judas betrayed him. It reads, "When therefore he [Jesus] said unto them [the soldiers], I am he, they went backward, and fell to the ground." While the scriptures really do not say why the soldiers hit the ground—and thus to surmise would be pure speculation at best—it would be presumptuous to read into this verse the power of the Holy Spirit. The soldiers were not converts to Christianity. There is no reason to think they would be recipients of the Holy Spirit or would know that the Holy Spirit even existed, for that matter. The only people today who claim to be "slain in the Spirit" are people of faith in the first place. Even the *Dictionary of Pentecostal and Charismatic Movements* states, "There is no mention of the Spirit here, and John portrays no relationship between Spirit, power, and Jesus. The text remains enigmatic, especially since John offers neither explanation for, nor effect of, their fall. Obviously they were not converted, because they proceeded to arrest Jesus."[31]

Matthew 17:6 and Matthew 28:1–4 are other passages that are sometimes used to prove the notion of being "slain in the Spirit." Matthew 17:6 records how the disciples of Christ "fell on their face, and were sore afraid" when they heard the voice of God from heaven. Matthew 28:4 reveals that "for fear of him [an angel] the watchers [Roman guards] did quake, and became as dead men." *The Dictionary of Pentecostal and Charismatic Movements* has this to say about these two verses: "Both the Matthean texts refer to instances of fear. One is clearly a normal response of awestruck worship . . . while the other is probably simply a figurative way of saying the guards were 'petrified.' Even if the guards were 'slain,' their experience is entirely secondary to the story and did not have any redemptive value as far as the text is concerned."[32] Something similar to what happened to the disciples of Christ and the Roman guards in the above contexts probably occurred to the apostle John in Revelation 1:17.

Second Corinthians 12:2 is also occasionally used to justify the practice of being "slain in the Spirit." Here the apostle Paul talks about knowing a man in Christ who was "caught up even to the third heaven." He may or may not have been talking about himself. Nonetheless, this verse is not remotely related to what is seen today in the services of faith healers. Regarding this verse, *The Dictionary of Pentecostal and Charismatic Movements* suggests that "While this is appealed to as evidence that Paul experienced being slain in the Spirit, there is simply not enough data to justify the conclusion that the 'third heaven' and the state of being 'slain in the Spirit' are identical." Faith healers will have to look elsewhere for proof of this phenomenon.

A final passage used to prove the idea of being "slain in the Spirit" discussed by Hanegraaff is Ephesians 5:18. Here the apostle Paul instructed the Ephesians, "And be not drunk with wine, wherein is riot, but be filled with the Spirit." Hanegraaff correctly argues, "Paul . . . is not saying that drunkenness is desirable and has a spiritual counterpart. Rather, in context he is presenting a consistent series of contrasts between cultic and Christian behavior . . . [H]e makes it clear that as Christians we must be 'alert and sober' rather than being in an altered state of consciousness or slain in the spirit."[33]

The preceding passages are really only a few of the verses that faith healers sometimes employ to leave the impression that what they are teaching regarding being "slain in the Spirit" is biblically based. Yet these verses are being forced to say something that in reality they do not mean. Faith healers are practicing *eisegesis*. They are reading into these verses what they would like them to say. The conclusion to the matter of being "slain in the Spirit" is best articulated by *The Dictionary of Pentecostal and Charismatic Movements*: "The evidence for the phenomenon of being 'slain in the Spirit' is thus inconclusive. From an experiential standpoint it is unquestionable that through the centuries Christians have experienced a psychological phenomenon in which people fall down; moreover, they have attributed the experience to God. It is equally unquestionable that there is no biblical evidence for the experience as normative in Christian life."[34] We are forced to the conclusion, then, that being "slain in the Spirit" is little more than a dramatic, humanly induced physical experience in search of scriptural backing.

Before proceeding to the next section, let me suggest that one of the biggest blunders faith healers and Charismatics alike have made interpreting an idea within its context has to do with the length of time miracles in general were to remain with the infant church. As I will discuss in greater detail in chapter 3, in the middle of a long context about miraculous gifts, which runs for at least three, if not four, chapters, 1 Corinthians 13:8 tells us that "Love never faileth; but whether there be prophecies, they shall be done away; whether there be tongues, they shall cease; whether there be knowledge, it shall be done away." Prophecies, tongues, and miraculous knowledge are merely synecdoche, parts standing for the whole. In other words, Paul is using these three spiritual gifts to refer to all nine of the spiritual gifts that he mentioned in 1 Corinthians 12. Nonetheless, all were to be done away when "that which is perfect is come" (1Cor. 13:10). But the question is, does the context shed any light on what the "perfect" was to be?

As I will discuss in more detail later on, faith healers and Charismatics have interpreted the "perfect" to be Christ. Simply put, they believe that miracles were to stay with the church until the *parousia* (i.e., the second coming of Christ—see verses such as 1 Cor. 15:23, 1 Thess. 4:15, 1 Thess. 5:23, and 2 Thess. 2:1.), Christ himself being perfect or sinless. And since the second coming of Christ has yet to occur, miracles must still be with us.

However, the context suggests otherwise. The word "perfect" (from *teleios*, meaning "complete," "fully grown," or "mature"[35]) does not mean "sinless." Therefore it must be referring to something other than Christ, who was someone who was sinless (1 Pet. 2:22). Even if one does not know what the Greek is, the context helps us understand what the "perfect" might be. Miraculous spiritual gifts are described as that which is "in part," "childish," or analogous to seeing "in a mirror darkly." They are juxtaposed to that which is "perfect," mature, or analogous to seeing "face to face"—that is, seeing clearly. And even though the context never explicitly says that the "perfect," mature, or clear thing to be seen is the written revelation of God, it allows for it to be—what James once referred to as the "perfect [*teleios*] law of liberty" (James 1:25). While there are other interpretations of what "the perfect" in 1 Corinthians 13:8 is (other than the completed revelation of scripture[36]), at the very least, the context is talking about neither Christ himself nor heaven. Here is why. Within the broader context of spiritual gifts, which begins in 1 Corinthians 12, Paul told the Corinthians that while they were to "desire earnestly the greater gifts," he would eventually show them "a more excellent way" (1 Cor. 12:31, KJV), suggesting that spiritual gifts (i.e., miracles) were to be temporary. There would be a better way for the Corinthians—and, by extension, the entire Christian church—to edify each other and know the will of God while on this earth than through spiritual gifts, which was their purpose in the first place (1 Cor. 14). It is highly unlikely that the apostle Paul wanted them to wait until the second coming of Christ before this could occur. Moreover, it is highly unlikely that Paul wanted the church to wait until their "entrance into heavenly glory" or "the believer's entrance into the Lord's presence"[37] for tongues to cease. By that time, it would have been too late. So a better way for the church to be edified and know God's will than through spiritual gifts (i.e., immature, childish things) would be through something more mature—probably the completed revelation of scriptures.

Furthermore, the context of 1 Corinthians 13 suggests that faith, hope, and love would abide even after "that which is perfect" had come. If the "perfect" were referring to Christ during the *parousia*, or Christians' glorious entry into the presence of the Lord (i.e., heaven itself), there would be no need for faith. It would be turned into sight. There would be no need for hope. Hope would become a reality. Yet, Paul says that faith and hope would abide even after "that which is perfect" had come. So, it is highly unlikely that 1 Corinthians 13:10 is referring to Christ or heaven as "that which is perfect." It most probably refers to the completed revelation of the scriptures, through which the New Testament church was to receive its edification (2 Tim. 3:16-17).

INTERPRETING VERSES ACCORDING TO THE LARGER PICTURE OF BIBLICAL TRUTH

Just as it is important to understand the context before determining what a passage of scripture is teaching, it is equally important to understand the larger picture of truth that the Bible reveals about a subject. Occasionally we may not know what a verse means. Indeed, we may never know exactly what a verse means. However, often we can be sure of what it does not mean, because to make it mean one thing may cause it to fly in the face of some other clearly established truth. The Bible should never contradict itself in principle. Unfortunately faith healers do not seem to understand this rule. Or, if they do, they are ignoring it. In his article "The Battle of Armageddon," Tyler argues, "Obscure passages should be studied, understood and accepted in the light of [other] plain understandable texts. The plain, comprehensible passages must never be sacrificed, altered or compromised for some fanciful interpretation of an obscure Scripture."[38] In other words, a difficult passage should not be made to mean one thing if, in doing so, it contradicts clearer, more easily understood verses on the same subject. Likewise, Puckett, in his article "How the Spirit Indwells," advises that a concept be studied "in the light of the totality of divine revelation." He suggests, "a fundamental rule of interpretation is that no interpretation or construction can be placed upon a passage of scripture that does violence to, or runs counter to what is taught somewhere else."[39] Even though he was talking specifically about Postmodernists and other individuals who do not believe "that there is an omniscient God who actually stands behind all of the Bible," what Carson says in his book *Exegetical Fallacies* about the way these people interpret the Bible could also be said about faith healers: "they feel free to read parts of it in ways that are deliberately set over against other parts of the Bible." This is what happens, according to Carson, when one tries to interpret the scriptures while ignoring "the Bible's story-line,"[40] what Fee in his book *New Testament Exegesis* refers to as "the metanarrative of the whole of Scripture."[41] In other words, when one fails to take into consideration the Bible's larger picture of truth—its overall theme—one is likely to misinterpret not only a piece of scripture but an entire context. Broadus reminds us that if a passage "may have two senses, owing to the ambiguity of some word or construction, [or] to the doubt whether some expression is figurative, etc., then one must choose one which accords with what the Bible in general plainly teaches rather than one which would make the Bible contradict itself."[42]

This is where faith healers run into trouble with the topic of the baptism of the Holy Spirit. When the apostle Paul affirmed in Ephesians 4:5 that there is "one baptism" (not two) to which we must be amenable, he did not have Holy Spirit baptism in mind. Rather he was most likely discussing water baptism, the same baptism that he had in mind a chapter later when he asserted that the church is sanctified and cleansed "by the washing of water with the word" (Eph. 5:26). To imply that all verses that talk about the Holy Spirit in Christians mean that they have received (or should look to receive) Holy Spirit baptism would cause Paul to contradict the broader truth of what the New Testament teaches about water baptism and what Paul explicitly says in Ephesians 4:5 (i.e., that there is only one baptism). Moreover, it would run counter to the fact that there were only two cases of Holy Spirit baptism granted in the New Testament—and those occurred only in the first-century. The broader truth about Holy Spirit baptism, which I will take up later in this book, is that it was given to a limited number of people for limited purposes, which no longer exist.

Likewise, to argue that demons still possess people today the same way that we read about in the synoptic gospels and Acts, as faith healers so confidently affirm, would cause the New Testament to contradict itself. Here is why. If as the apostle Paul suggests, miracles would be done away when "that which is perfect is come," and "that which is perfect" (i.e., the completed written revelation to mankind) has already arrived (indeed, it has been with us for close to twenty centuries), then miracles have ceased, period. To say, therefore, that demons can be exorcised would imply that miracles are still occurring, which would be a contradiction of a greater principle of biblical truth. Moreover, if miracles have ceased yet demons continue to inhabit people as faith healers and others would have us to believe, then victims of demon possession would be utterly helpless to do anything about their condition. What is a poor individual possessed by demons supposed to do?

To argue that miraculous healings occur today just as one reads about in the synoptic gospels because Hebrews 13:8 tells us that "Jesus Christ is the same yesterday and today, yea and forever," is to ignore the larger biblical truth that miracles have ceased. Instead, Hebrews 13:8 is referring to the loving, compassionate, forgiving character of Jesus, among other personal attributes. It is not suggesting that he is still operating in the same manner today that he used to as told in the synoptic gospels. In fact, he cannot be because he is not on earth to do as he once did, if we are to take faith healers' interpretation to its logical conclusion. Regarding this verse, Pratt suggests in his book *The God of the Bible*, "The whole point of the context of Hebrews 13:8 is that, in the New Testament, God has ceased doing many things that He did under the Old Testament. If it does not violate Hebrews 13:8 to believe that God ceased doing many works, including many miracles, why would it violate the verse to believe that He has ceased doing all miracles?" Pratte points out that Hebrews 13:8 says that Christ "*is* the same, not that He *does* the same." While his character has not changed, "His **deeds** and His **will** for men have changed. That is the point of the book of Hebrews: God ceased binding the Old Covenant because we now have the New Covenant. Likewise, He has ceased doing miracles, because we have the completed Scriptures."[43]

Regarding the call of God, which I introduced in the previous chapter and which I will discuss at much greater length in chapter 5, if individuals today are called, by the preaching of the gospel, to things spiritual—as the scriptures repeatedly teach—then to argue on the basis of some esoteric, unique, personal experience that God has called us to something physical, in a manner different from hearing his word proclaimed, would be a contradiction of the larger body of truth about the call of God as revealed in the scriptures. This is why one should never base one's theology either on a personal experience or on some sensational testimony of another person's encounter—including faith healers'. God has not entrusted us to know his will on the basis of some dramatic story that either faith healers or family and friends around us would like for us to believe, no matter how wonderful or sensational the story might sound to us or to them. If we want to know what the will of God is for us (or for any other individual, for that matter), we must simply read the Bible. The will of God will be the same from person to person.

Ernest Angley is one of the best examples of someone who has failed to understand the principle that verses in the Bible need to be interpreted against a larger picture of truth, when he talks about why he lays hands on people in his healing lines and elsewhere. Quoting from numerous passages in the Bible that discuss the apostle Paul and other apostles laying hands on individuals, Angley leaves his followers with the impression that he, too, has this supernatural ability given to him by God. Or as Angley suggests, "God has gifted me with His power; He directs me to touch those who are afflicted, those who are sick. His great miracles that are taking place by the hand of God are simply marvelous as He moves on me to touch people."[44] Yet Angley fails to understand that laying hands on individuals in the scripture (as I will show in greater detail in chapter 7) was done to impart a miraculous gift from the apostles—and only the apostles, who were empowered by God—to those in the first-century church who needed spiritual gifts to direct the church in absence of written revelation. Angley not only fails to understand that only the apostles, those foundational to the church in the first century (Eph. 2:20), were entrusted with the ability to share miraculous powers with others, but that miraculous powers were given for a limited season and for a limited purpose. Why would God, twenty-one centuries later, choose Ernest Angley—or any other individual—and empower them with miraculous abilities when such miraculous abilities are no longer needed? Now, in place of the miraculous, we have the written revelation "that the man of God may be complete, furnished completely unto every good work" (2 Tim. 3:16–17). Scriptures teach that we have sufficient spiritual resources for "every good work," not just for some good works. In other words, to borrow the words of the apostle Peter, we have been given "all things that pertain unto life and godliness" (2 Pet. 1:3). Nothing else is needed, including miracles. We certainly do not need Ernest Angley, or anyone else, to lay hands on anyone.

In an attempt to justify his "ability" to lay hands on the sick, Angley cites Mark 16:17–18, among others. Angley asks, "Who would lay hands on the sick?—The believers, Jesus' believers. Because the Bible tells us to lay hands on the sick, and they shall recover, I lay hands on the sick. Jesus said a believer would lay hands on the sick, and He would get them well."[45] If this were truly what Jesus meant—that all believers would be able to lay hands on the sick and heal them—then every believer today, not just Ernest Angley, should have this ability. Angley himself is not even willing to admit this. Rather, he uses this passage to justify himself as specially chosen by God. In doing so, he has failed to consider the larger picture of truth about why the apostles laid hands on people in the first-century church in the first place—to impart spiritual gifts to others.

UNDERSTANDING THAT THE BIBLE SOMETIMES USES FIGURES OF SPEECH

One of the most helpful principles of biblical interpretation to keep in mind is that sometimes the Bible uses figures of speech, which were never meant to be taken literally. A very common figure of speech often found in the Bible is metaphor or analogy, where one thing is compared to another. Jesus, for example, once referred to himself as "the door" (John 10:9). Elsewhere he referred to himself as "the bread of life" (John 6:48), "the true vine" (John 15:1), and "the light of the world" (John 8:12). On another occasion, when warned by the Pharisees that Herod Antipas was looking to kill him, Jesus told them, "Go and say to that fox. . . ." (John 13:32). Jesus was not suggesting that Herod had a bushy tail, but that Herod was a sly, cunning individual.

Modern-day exorcist Bob Larson (whom I will discuss in more detail in chapter 4, on demons and exorcisms) misses the metaphorical point of Hebrews 4:12, which says, "For the word of God is living, and active, and sharper than any two-edged sword." During his "exorcisms," Larson sometimes pokes his Bible under the chin of individuals who are supposedly possessed by demons. Sometimes he waves it behind a person's head or to that individual's right and left to corral while leading him or her to the front of an audience. He uses the Bible, in other words, as a metaphysical sword. In doing so, he actually quotes Hebrews 4:12. The author of Hebrews never wrote this verse to suggest that the Bible should be used the way Larson physically uses it. In fact, the writer of Hebrews is not talking about a literal, physical book at all, much less a literal sword. Instead, he is talking about the contents of the book. The contents are the "word of God." This is what is "living, and active, and shaper than any two-edged sword, and piercing even to the dividing of soul and spirit, of both joints and marrow, and quick to discern the thoughts and intents of the heart." Even when the apostle Paul commanded the Ephesians to take up "the sword of the Spirit, which is the word of God" (Eph. 6:17), he was speaking metaphorically, not literally. He was talking neither about a physical sword nor a physical book. Rather, he was talking about the contents of the book—its principles and ideas.

One of the most symbolic books of the entire Bible is Revelation. This book was written symbolically as code for first-century Christians who were undergoing heavy persecution. John, for instance, once referred to Christ as both a lion and a lamb in the same context (Rev. 5:5–6). Dozens, if not hundreds, of other metaphors can be found in Revelation. After reading Revelation 20, it would be a mistake, for example, to conclude that a literal chain could bind Satan or that he could be physically kept in an "abyss" (Rev. 20:1–3), because the Bible depicts Satan as a spirit, not as flesh and blood. There are any number of other examples from the book of Revelation that were never intended to be taken literally, such as the 144,000 virgin males in heaven, the mark of the beast upon a person's forehead or hand, a 1,000-year reign with Christ upon the earth, or the physical depiction of the "new Jerusalem," with its streets of gold and wall of jasper and other "precious stones," for instance (Rev. 21). John never intended his readers to interpret all of these symbols literally. In his commentary on Revelation, Summers suggests that many of the symbols in this book "are exaggerated symbols for the purpose of a dramatic effect. The meaning of the figure is to be discerned by viewing it in broad perspective as a whole and not by trying to determine the meaning of each minute detail."[46] Continuing, Summers correctly writes, "There are some symbols which are not so easily understood and where there is much room for diversity of opinion. About these one can ill afford to be dogmatic. The wise thing to do is to seek earnestly to find the most probable meaning of the symbol to those who first received the book and consider that as the most likely interpretation."[47] Even though Summers is talking specifically about the book of Revelation, his advice holds true for figurative language in other parts of the Bible as well.

Faith healer Ernest Angley, among others, has failed to grasp this concept. Drawing largely from Revelation 20, in his book *Raptured: A Novel on the Second Coming of the Lord*,[48] Angley tells a fanciful story of what he believes will happen before, during, and after the second coming of Christ, which involves, among other things, a period of tribulation in which God's wrath will be poured out on everyone who has accepted the mark of the beast to buy and sell. While a full-blown discussion and critique of this theory is beyond the scope of this book, I mention it here simply to suggest that sometimes faith healers literally interpret symbols in the Bible when these symbols were never meant to be taken literally. So, when faith healers refer from time to time to the indwelling of the Holy Spirit, which, according to them, empowers an individual with supernatural abilities, we should understand that the expression *dwells* or *dwelleth* was never really meant to be interpreted literally. As I will argue in greater detail in chapter 7, the idea of an indwelling is only a metaphor for the relationship that one has with God the Father, Christ the Son, and the Holy Spirit, as well as with other Christians. Faith healers have failed to understand that the indwelling of any part of the godhead is merely a metaphorical concept to describe a spiritual relationship.

Another figure of speech often found in the scriptures is hyperbole. Hyperbole is a gross exaggeration to prove a point. When I was a boy, my mother would occasionally say to me, "I've told you a thousand times" to do something. She did not mean that literally, nor did I ever think she did. Even as a boy I understood her point. In the story of Jesus talking to the woman at Jacob's well in John 4, after their conversation, the woman went into the city and proclaimed to the people, "Come, see a man, who told me all things that ever I did: can this be the Christ?" (John 4:29). In saying this, the woman was using hyperbole. Christ had not told the woman everything about her life, nor did the woman mean this. Instead he had told her enough about herself to make her think that he was a prophet. In her amazement, and in her attempt to share her excitement with others, she exaggerated the point. Essentially, she was saying, "He knew everything about me." We do the same today when we say things like "I know all about you" or "He knows everything." We do not mean this literally, but figuratively.

When Christ said that "all things are possible to him that believeth," a phrase that faith healers often seize on to prove that miracles happen today, he did not mean that everything was possible. He was using hyperbole. He wanted the father of the child with the unclean spirit in Mark 9 to believe who he was—the son of God—and if that father believed in Christ, great things would occur as proof of Christ's divinity. In fact, this was Christ's purpose for performing miracles in the first place: to prove his divinity. As I will show in chapter 6, faith healers like Benny Hinn and others have failed to grasp the concept of hyperbole in the context of Mark 9:23, choosing instead to use it to justify that people can and should expect to receive miraculous healings today because, after all, Christ himself said that "all things are possible." The reality is, throughout the Bible, the phrase *all things* frequently does not mean *everything*. When Paul said in Philippians 4:13, "I can do all things through Christ which strengtheneth me" (KJV), he did not literally mean that he could turn rocks into diamonds, for example. Instead, like Christ, he was using hyperbole. As I will demonstrate later on, there are actually some things that are not possible. If all things really were possible, literally speaking, as faith healers would have us believe, then glass eyes could be regenerated into functioning eyes of flesh and blood; missing appendages (e.g., ears) could be replaced; dead people could be resurrected. Moreover, these could be done in front of everyone to visually verify. Religiously speaking, the proverbial pig would be flying. But these do not really happen, nor do the scriptures teach that they will happen.

Hyperbole can be seen on another occasion when Christ told his apostles that "if you have faith the size of a mustard seed, you will say to this mountain, 'Move from here to there,' and it will move; and nothing will be impossible to you" (Matt. 17: 21). He wanted his disciples to have faith in him. If they would do so, they would be able to accomplish great feats. To explain to them just how great would be the feats they could accomplish, he chose the imagery of removing a mountain, something obviously impossible from a human perspective but so magnificent that they would understand the wonderful types of works that they could accomplish if they were to follow Christ. He never really meant for his apostles to literally move mountains. What need would there be for that? They were in neither the excavation business nor the construction business. There would, however, be a need for them to do great things spiritually in the kingdom that Christ would establish that, comparatively speaking, would be equivalent to moving mountains.

CONCLUSION

While many people today believe that the Bible is the inspired word of God that should be followed, evidence suggests that not many people are actually reading it, let alone studying it. Needless to say, this can lead to confusion, leaving one vulnerable to believe anything and everything that he or she hears preached. In this chapter, I have tried to suggest three principles to help us come to a better understanding of the scriptures if and when we study them. Moreover, these principles can help us to critique the discourse we hear, especially when listening to some of the sensational claims made by faith healers: (1) Exegete a verse within its context; (2) Never allow a verse to contradict clearer, broader principles of truth revealed elsewhere in the Bible, but interpret a verse in light of what the Bible says as a whole on a given subject; and (3) Realize that while there may be times to take a verse literally, there are other times when we should understand that the Bible is merely employing figurative language such as metaphor or hyperbole to teach a point. The context will often determine when and if something should be taken literally. Moreover, one should never interpret a verse literally if, in doing so, it would do violence to some other well established principle of truth. To do so would simply be short-sighted.

In all fairness, in the final analysis, there is really no such thing as purely objective exegesis. As Fee reminds us, "The exegete is a reader, whatever else, and as such we bring all of who we are to the reading of the text, apply-ing both known and unknown presuppositions of all kinds—theological, sociological, and cultural." This reality should cause us, according to Fee, to "be open to changing our minds about texts on a regular basis and . . . to cause us all the more to take a stance of humility before the text, rather than a heavy-handed, authoritarian ownership (mastery?) of the text."[49] This does not mean that we should flip-flop on issues depending on what day of the week it is, nor that we should not be confident in our positions. Instead, we should be willing to change if and when someone shows us the truth, realizing that we might not have had a full understanding of an idea previously. In short we should be like the Beroean Jews in Acts 17:11, who "were more noble than those in Thessalonica, in that they received the word with all readiness of mind, examining the scriptures daily, whether these things [i.e., the preaching of Paul and Silas] were so." Having said this, one should attempt to study the scriptures with an open mind, allow-ing them—indeed even struggling with them at times—to instruct us. Only then can we really understand what is being taught in the word. Not to do so would be nothing less than shortchanging ourselves. In the fol-lowing chapters, let us take a closer look at some of the various things that faith healers have taught, in an attempt to see how closely they stack up against the Bible and the principles I have set forth in this chapter.

3

❖

"That They May Believe"[1]: Distinguishing the Miraculous from the Providential

In October of 2005, the unthinkable happened to Shana West. In what must be every skydiver's worst nightmare, after she leaped from the plane, Shana's tangled parachute only partially deployed, leaving her to fall toward the earth at an astounding fifty miles per hour. The resulting collision broke multiple bones in her face and body but did not kill her. To complicate matters, unknown to her, Shana was two weeks pregnant. Amazingly, she not only survived what was almost a total free fall, but in time gave birth to a healthy baby boy. In reporting the story in March 2007, Robin Roberts, co-anchor for *Good Morning America*, called Shana's survival "miraculous."[2] It is doubtful that many people, especially people of faith, would have disagreed with Roberts' assessment.

A few days later, ABC News reported that Christa Lilly of Colorado Springs, Colorado, had slipped into a coma in October of 2001. After four years, though, she suddenly and unexplainably "woke up." Calling her ordeal "mystical," Christa's neurologist could not explain why. Family members, however, had a different take. They called it a "miracle" from God.[3] It is doubtful that many people would have disagreed with their assessment either.

A few weeks afterward, *Good Morning America* reported yet another story, in which a teenager by the name of Levi Draher survived after passing out for five minutes, during which time his brain was deprived of oxygen. Draher was participating in a fad known as "the choking game," in which teenagers intentionally choke themselves in an attempt to get high. Fortunately, Draher was resuscitated in time to save his life. Despite the fact that Draher suffered a dramatic loss of speech and motor skills and would have to spend the next two years in rehabilitation in order to fully recover, reporter Chris Cuomo hailed the young man's survival as "nothing short of a miracle."[4] In a speech to a group of high school students Draher himself said, "Do I consider myself a miracle? Yes, I do."[5] As in the previous two cases, few would probably disagree with Cuomo's and Draher's assessments either.

In early May of 2007, a tornado a mile and a quarter to a mile and a half wide, with winds greater than two hundred miles per hour, ripped through the small town of Greensburg, Kansas. It destroyed about 85 percent of the town and caused the deaths of what was reported at the time to be eight people. ABC News titled their story "Miracle in Kansas." Even though the town had been warned a few minutes earlier by the National Weather Service, the alleged "miracle" was the fact that more people were not killed from such a large and powerful storm.[6]

The above examples illustrate the fact that we are quick to label "miraculous" things that we cannot explain. But should we? Whenever an individual narrowly avoids what could have been a major automobile accident while traveling at high speed, or trapped coal miners are extracted alive from deep within the earth after several days without food and water, or individuals with terminal diseases who are given weeks to live suddenly go into remission, individuals of faith are quick to call these incidents miraculous. However, do any of the above examples actually qualify as miracles?

My purpose in this chapter is to address this issue from a biblical perspective. Specifically I want to examine how miracles are depicted in both the Old and New Testaments. Additionally, and equally importantly, I want to analyze what differences, if any, there may be between the miraculous and the providential. What role, if any, does God play in these two areas according to the Bible?

Before going further, let us pause to deal with a few preliminary issues. Why should we analyze miracles as depicted in the Old and New Testaments? The answer is relatively simple. As I suggested in chapter 1, many people who are quick to call miraculous those seemingly unexplainable events that defy the odds, are usually people of faith who have read at least portions of the Bible. In many cases it is *because* they have read stories of the miraculous in the Bible that they believe in the possibilities of miracles today in the first place. But should they?

Because people are quick to label unexplainable positive outcomes as miraculous, with little thought to what they are saying, this topic is important. Furthermore, as I pointed out in chapter 1, there are a number of televangelists and faith healers today who make the claim to an unsuspecting public that they can and should receive some type of miracle in their life, be it financial, physical, social, or emotional, provided they have enough faith. However, if miracles do not exist today, what faith healers are teaching is problematic. As I suggested earlier, unsuspecting individuals may decide that they have indeed received a miraculous healing. This in turn my lead them to stop taking badly needed medicine, or throw away essential medical apparatuses, and die. Even if these individuals do not die but never improve when they think they should simply because some preacher is telling them to believe in miracles, this is torturous. Boggs rightly points out that "It is a very serious thing to raise the hopes of multitudes of sick people with assurances that God will always reward true faith by healing diseases, and then to lead the great majority of these people through disillusionment to despair."[7]

Although Judaism traditionally has not practiced faith healing per se, Rabbi Harold Kushner takes a more radical stand. He argues, "I hope there is a special place in hell for people who try and enrich themselves on the suffering of others. To tantalize the blind, the lame, the dying, the afflicted, the terminally ill—to dangle hope before parents of a severely afflicted child is an indescribably cruel thing to do, and to do it in the name of God, to do it in the name of religion, I think, is unforgiveable."[8]

Joseph Hough, president of Union Theological Seminary in New York, likewise sympathizes with the afflicted who attend revivals of faith healers when he suggests, "And you look at their faces and you see their hands, lifted up, looking up toward the sky, praying, mumbling prayers, and you just hurt for them. It breaks your heart to know that they're being deceived because they genuinely are hoping and believing, and they'll leave there thinking that if they didn't get a miracle it's because they didn't believe."[9]

In analyzing the stories of miracles in both the Old and New Testament, my intention is not to argue one way or another regarding their veracity. I understand that there are a number of people who dismiss the Bible as mere myth. By doing so, one does not have to grapple with the issue of miracles in the first place—at least as the Bible portrays them. Such people can simply dismiss stories of biblical miracles as impossible. However, there are millions of people who accept the claims regarding the miraculous as revealed in the Bible. Moreover, as I suggested earlier, in most cases it is because individuals read stories about the miraculous in the Bible that they believe miracles occur nowadays. My intention is to provide a better understanding of miracles as they are depicted in the Bible, for people of faith today. I want to offer these individuals a clearer understanding of what constitutes the miraculous and what constitutes the providential, from a biblical perspective, without throwing God out of the picture.

Differentiating the miraculous from the providential is not merely a matter of semantics. Knowing what a miracle is, what providence is, and the differences between the two, is very important in helping individuals to have realistic expectations. I will argue that, whether or not an individual believes in God, according to the scriptures miracles do not occur today, because their original purpose has ceased. I will also suggest that the events that some claim to be miracles today, especially those related to physical healings, in no way resemble what one reads about in the Bible. However, despite the fact that it cannot be verified today, one may continue to believe in the providential, which is different from the miraculous. Let us turn our attention first to the miraculous.

MIRACLES

Miracles Violated Natural Law

One of the first things that we should understand about miracles as they are revealed to us in the Bible, which I introduced in chapter 1, is that they always violated or interrupted the laws of nature. Let us take a closer look at this notion. McCarron argues that it is one thing to pray on the way toward the ground that one's tangled parachute open, and it does so, and another to stop in midair and untangle it before proceeding further.[10] Stopping in midair would constitute a violation of the laws of gravity, making it miraculous.

In the Old Testament, when God called Moses to lead the Israelites out of Egypt some fifteen hundred years before Christ, Moses was not confident he could do the job. Part of his problem was that he was not convinced that the Jewish elders would believe him when he would go to them with the message that God had called him to lead.

Exodus 4 records how God gave Moses three "signs"—that is, miracles—to demonstrate to the Jews that he had chosen Moses as their leader. God first told Moses to cast his rod on the ground. When he did, it turned into a snake. When Moses picked the snake up by the tail, it turned back into a rod. The second sign involved Moses putting his hand into his bosom and taking it out—whereupon it turned leprous. God then instructed Moses to return his leprous hand to his bosom and to remove it a second time, at which point it was restored. For the third sign, God instructed Moses to pour water from the river onto the ground. When Moses did so, the water turned into blood. All of these involved a violation of nature. Rods left alone do not morph into snakes. Hands do not naturally change instantaneously from healthy to leprous and back to healthy again. In nature, when skin diseases heal, they take time—weeks, months, or even years—but they certainly do not heal immediately. Water does not change into blood in nature, if left on its own.

Another popular story from the Old Testament that illustrates that miracles were a violation of the laws of nature involved Elijah the prophet and his contest with the prophets of Baal on Mount Carmel. 1 Kings 18 records how Elijah, in an attempt to persuade the Israelites to believe in God, suggested that they build two altars on which to offer a sacrifice, one for Baal and one for Elijah's God. Elijah proposed that the God who "answers by fire" (1 Kings 18:24) would thereby demonstrate that he was the true God. He allowed the prophets of Baal to go first. Although these prophets invoked their god from morning until noon, nothing happened. Then came Elijah's turn. He commanded the people to douse his altar three times with water before he invoked his God to consume it. The narrative tells us that "the fire of Jehovah fell, and consumed the burnt-offering, and the wood, and the stones, and the dust, and licked up the water that was in the trench" (1 Kings 18:38).What makes this miraculous is the fact that in nature fire does not rain down from heaven or burn up stones.

One of the best examples of nature being violated is the conception of Christ by the Virgin Mary, as recorded in the New Testament (see Matt. 1). Christ's conception is considered miraculous because the laws of nature tell us that women, especially virgins, do not conceive children without being inseminated by a man. Before we go further, let us be clear that conception and birth are two different things. Births in any species are in no way miraculous, even though they are often speciously referred to as miracles.[11] The fact is, births occur every day in nature and have been occurring for thousands of years. As I argue elsewhere, they are as common in nature as thunderstorms.[12] So, while babies being born are glorious events, they hardly qualify as miraculous. However, among some Christians, at least, Mary's conception of Christ was a different matter. It was miraculous.

At least once in the Bible a miraculous conception occurred even with normal sexual intercourse: this was the case of Sarah, wife of Abraham. What made this conception miraculous was that the laws of nature do not allow women who have gone through menopause to conceive babies even though they may engage in sexual intercourse. Sarah was ninety years old when she conceived Isaac. When she overheard messengers from God tell her husband that she would "have a son," the Bible records how Sarah "laughed within herself, saying, 'After I am waxed old shall I have pleasure, my lord being old also?'" (Gen. 18:12). Sarah was fully aware of the laws of nature regarding conception for women of her age. She knew that left on their own, she and Abraham were not going to have any children at that stage in their life together.[13]

As stated earlier, while the conceptions of Christ and Isaac were miraculous, the physical births themselves were not. We assume that both Mary and Sarah, once they had conceived, carried their babies to full term and delivered them in the natural way that women give birth. The only way these births would have been miraculous would be if Mary and Sarah had delivered them through some mode that would have violated what the laws of nature dictate, or delivered them a day or two after conception, which would have violated the laws of human gestation and delivery. C. S. Lewis observes, "If God creates a miraculous spermatozoon in the body of a virgin, it does not proceed to break any laws. The laws at once take it over. Nature is ready. Pregnancy follows, according to all the normal laws, and nine months later a child is born."[14]

Other examples of the laws of nature being violated or suspended can be found in the New Testament. According to the synoptic gospels, Jesus, for example, walked on water (Matt. 14:25) and turned water into wine (John 2:1–10). On other occasions he stilled a storm on the Sea of Galilee (Matt. 8:26), restored the right ear of Malchus, which had been cut off by Peter in the Garden of Gethsemane (John 18:2–12; Luke 22:51), and even raised a dead person (John 11). These are just a few of the many types of miracles recorded for us in the Old and New Testaments that demonstrate a violation of natural law.

Miracles Were Unlimited in Scope

Throughout the Bible, miracles dealt with a wide variety of phenomenon. Perhaps this is most easily seen, though not exclusively, in the ministry of Jesus in the New Testament. Cogdill points out that Jesus demonstrated authority over nature when he calmed the storm on the Sea of Galilee. He also demonstrated authority over material things when he multiplied the loaves and fishes and fed five thousand people. In healing lepers as well as "all manner of disease and . . . sickness" (Matt. 4:23), Jesus demonstrated power over physical ailments. He also demonstrated power over demons by casting them out. Ultimately he showed his authority over death when, for example, he raised Lazarus from the dead. In short, nothing was impossible for Jesus. After arguing that contemporary faith healers would not attempt to do what Jesus did but, nonetheless, would have people to believe that nothing is impossible with God and that Jesus heals today through them, Cogdill persuasively asks, "If Jesus is doing the healing now why doesn't He heal now like He did then?"[15]

Miracles Caused Astonishment

Vine suggests that the word "miracle" as translated in the New Testament comes from two Greek words: *dunamis* and *semeion*. *Dunamis* carries the idea of power or "inherent ability," and "is used of works of a supernatural origin and character, such as could not be produced by natural agents and means." *Semeion* "is used of miracles and wonders as signs of Divine authority." Another word that is frequently found in the same context with signs and/or mighty works is the word "wonder." Vine points out that wonder in the New Testament is sometimes translated from the Greek *teras*. A wonder caused "the beholder to marvel." He suggests that while "A sign is intended to appeal to the understanding," and "power (dunamis) indicates its source as supernatural . . . a wonder appeals to the imagination."[16] Miracles, in other words, caused astonishment on the part of those who witnessed them.

There was a "wow" factor involved in beholding miracles as they are revealed to us in the Bible. For instance, when Jesus healed the man with palsy in Mark 2, the narrative tells us that those who looked on "were all amazed and glorified God" (Mark 2:12). When he healed Jairus's daughter, witnesses "were amazed . . . with a great amazement" (Mark 5:42). When many witnessed the healing of a man possessed with a demon, the Bible says that "amazement came upon all" (Luke 4:36). When Peter healed the lame man who was laid daily at the gate of the temple in Acts 3, Luke records how the people who witnessed it "were filled with wonder and amazement at that which had happened unto him" (Acts 3:8–10).

This particular incident caused many problems for Peter and John. When the authorities heard of the healing, they arrested them. In deciding what to do with Peter and John, the authorities huddled together. Their conversation is telltale: "What shall we do with these men? For the fact that a noteworthy miracle has taken place through them is apparent to all who live in Jerusalem, and we cannot deny it" (Acts 4:16, NASV). The point to be understood here is that even the enemies of Peter and John could not, nor did they try to, deny that a miracle had occurred. The

New Testament also tells us that when Jesus raised Lazarus from the dead, the religious leaders asked, "What do we do? For this man doeth many signs" (John 11:47). They could not and did not try to deny the miraculous event. A similar situation occurred in Matthew 12, when Jesus cast a demon out of a man. The Bible says, "the multitudes were amazed" (Matt. 12:23). Rather than try to deny the miracle, which they honestly could not, the enemies of Christ put the worst possible slant on it by saying that Jesus was able to do what he did only because he was himself in allegiance with the devil.

What I am trying to illustrate in this section is that whenever a miracle occurred in the Bible, people did not question it. Biblical miracles did not cause skepticism like many so-called miracles today do. In the words of McCarron, those "miracles" today claimed by many televangelists are "utterly mundane."[17] McCarron rightly points out that "the events today's televangelists see as miraculous have nothing to do with the notion of nature suddenly deviating from its discernible pattern."[18] Miracles in the Bible caused astonishment, even to the point that hardened critics could not deny what had occurred. While they may have been inconvenient for various religious leaders, miracles were nonetheless astounding. Moreover these miracles never occurred in an emotionally charged atmosphere where people had been whipped into a frenzy before they could believe in them.

Miracles Were Immediate

A fourth characteristic of miracles, particularly as they related to healings, is that, with one exception, which I will discuss momentarily, they were always immediate. In other words, there was no waiting period. A person who was healed miraculously, for example, did not have to go home, lie around the house for a few days or weeks, and experience ups and downs before gradually being cured. The healing occurred instantaneously. In the story of a man cured of leprosy, for instance, the New Testament records how he was healed "straightway" (Matt. 8:3). In fact, "straightway" is often used to describe individuals' miraculous healings. The scriptures say that when Jesus healed a paralytic man who had been let down through the ceiling "he arose, and straightway took up the bed" (Mark 2:12). The woman with "an issue of blood" was likewise healed "straightway" (Mark 5:29). The Bible records how Peter's mother-in-law was healed of a fever and "immediately . . . rose up" (Luke 4:39). This implies that there was no waiting period for her healing. Returning to the lame man of Acts 3, who had been laid daily at the gate of the temple, the scriptures suggest that when Peter healed him, "immediately his feet and ankle bones received strength" and he leaped up and ran around (Acts 3:7).

As I pointed out in chapter 1, in his book *Healing: A Doctor in Search of a Miracle*, medical doctor William Nolen analyzed over 80 cases of individuals who supposedly received a miraculous healing during one of the crusades of the world-renowned faith healer Kathryn Kuhlman, in Minneapolis. After following up these cases, Nolan concluded that not only had many of these people never received a healing, let alone an instantaneous cure, but many died from their life-threatening ailments. One case specifically that Nolen cites, of an individual who claimed to have received a miraculous healing but did not truly receive one, was 23-three-year-old Rita Swanson. Rita "had blemishes all over her face . . . that is a common consequence of severe adolescent acne," reports Nolen. He reveals how Kuhlman said, "In three days that skin problem will be cured." Even Nolen himself, upon future examination, agreed that Swanson's face "was very much improved." However, Nolen points out that "skin is highly subjective. You look in the mirror, and unless things are too shockingly obvious, you will see, at least in part, what you want." [19] Even though Rita's skin may have been improved, one can hardly call this miraculous. Nolen concludes that "none of the patients who had returned to Minneapolis to reaffirm the cures they had claimed at the miracle service had, in fact, been miraculously cured of anything."[20]

Popular contemporary faith healer Ernest Angley, like other faith healers, occasionally tells individuals who come through his healing lines to "Go and get well."[21] This is ironic due to the fact that, ostensibly, a person is in the healing line in the first place to immediately "get well," not to have to wait a period of time afterward. Where is the miracle in having to wait? What contemporary faith healers claim does not square with the Bible, that miraculous cures were always instantaneous.

The story of Jesus healing a blind man in Mark 8 is sometimes offered as evidence that not all miraculous healings had to occur instantaneously. The Bible says that, after Jesus "spit on his eyes, and laid his hands upon him," he asked the man whether he could see. The man responded that he could see men but that he saw them "as trees, walking," which suggests that he was not fully healed. Seconds later, Jesus again laid his hands upon the man's eyes, at which point the man "saw all things clearly" (Mark 8: 24–25). For reasons that we can only surmise, the blind man was not able to see clearly the first time.

Foster argues, "We cannot tell why the miracle was gradual: whether by the purpose of Jesus or because of the slow-moving faith of the man."

Christians would probably not concede that it was because Jesus did not have the ability to "get it right" the first time. Regardless of why the man was not able to see clearly the first time, the point that should be understood is that Jesus did not tell him to go home and gradually improve over time. The man was healed before he left the presence of Jesus—therefore, immediately. In no way should this example be used to justify the notion that miracles were not instantaneous. Foster argues, "it is absurd" to take this example "as the necessary model for all [miraculous healings] when the peculiarities are" an exception to the other examples "in the life of Christ." [22]

Miracles Were Always Complete

Closely related to the idea of immediacy is the fact that miraculous healings in the Bible were always complete. In other words, individuals' ailments were always made whole, the above example from Mark 8 notwithstanding. Never was an individual just a little healed and then sent on his way to get better, perhaps never to fully recover. The man in the Gospel of Matthew who had a withered hand, for example, was "restored whole" (Matt. 12:13). The lame man in Acts 3 did not need crutches or a cane after he was healed. There were no recurring side effects to anyone who received a healing in the Bible. Moreover, individuals never lost their miracle once they received it. [23]

Perhaps one of the best examples of individuals in our time who claimed to have received miraculous cures but clearly was not wholly healed is that of a young woman in one of Kathryn Kuhlman's crusades. This woman who had no kneecap came to the stage, claiming that, until she was just healed, she could not walk without her brace. In what was a noble attempt to demonstrate her "miracle" to the thousands of people in attendance, she had taken the brace off of her leg and hobbled badly, yet courageously, across the stage to thunderous applauds. Moreover, she hobbled off the stage as badly as she had hobbled onto it, without any obvious improvement, because she was still missing her kneecap. [24] This could hardly be called a miracle.

In one of contemporary faith healer Benny Hinn's crusades, a young woman came to the stage, claiming she had been healed of deafness. However, she could not speak. One of Hinn's assistants reminded Hinn and the entire auditorium that because the young lady had not been able to hear since birth, she would have to learn how to speak. [25] Ironically, in other words, the young lady was not whole. Why would she receive a miracle involving hearing but not speaking? This makes no sense.

Miracles Were Empirically Verifiable

One very important characteristic of biblical miracles, especially those involving physical healings, was the fact that they could be seen by everyone present. Individuals were never asked to rely on the testimony of another person before believing in miracles. Miracles could be seen with one's own eyes. This principle seems to be lost on many people today. In the Bible one could see, for example, Malchus's ear put back on the side of his head, withered hands restored whole (Matt. 12:9), totally blind men receive their sight, lame individuals leap for joy, lepers' skin completely made whole—even people brought back to life after having been dead for days. There were other types of miracles that were visually verifiable as well, such as water instantaneously turning to wine, a man walking on water, or a storm suddenly being calmed, to name a few.

So-called miracles today, especially "miraculous healings" cannot always be immediately verified with one's eyes. We are forced to take people's word that they were once infirm but now are healed. For example, the types of "miracles" that one witnesses in faith healing services today involve poor blood circulation, weak eyes, backaches, deteriorated disks, internal cancers, depression and other emotional problems, heart conditions, bursitis, arthritis, rheumatism, inability to smell, and even cigarette and drug addiction.[26] Body parts are never regenerated, like the cases in the Bible—which is one reason we will never see glass eyes or other prostheses in the trophy cases of faith healers. In short, none of the types of "miracles" one supposedly sees are visually verifiable on the spot like those recorded in the Bible. Therefore, they are non-falsifiable. In other words, merely from an empirical perspective, witnesses cannot always say, "No, you were not really healed." Audiences are simply asked to take the word of the person who is supposedly being healed. They cannot see for themselves, like audiences in the Bible could. Biblical audiences were never merely asked to take the word of anyone. They could see the healing with their own eyes. Even when people occasionally stand up from wheelchairs today during some healing service as proof of the miraculous, audiences still do not know to what extent the individual could or could not walk prior to coming there.

Miracles Preceded Faith

We are told today that faith is necessary to experience a miracle, especially a miraculous healing. However, in the Bible, miracles almost always occurred *prior* to belief. In other words, most of the time, faith was not a prerequisite to receive a miracle. In fact, quite often, it was because of the miracle that audiences developed faith. This is not to say that in every case where a miracle occurred, faith always followed. Rather, what I am suggesting is that miracles were designed to produce faith, not vice versa. For instance, in the case of God giving Moses three signs, these miracles were given "that they may believe" (Exod. 4:5). After Moses performed these miracles to the Israelites, "the people believed: and . . . bowed their heads and worshipped" (Exod. 4:31).

In Elijah's contest with the prophets of Baal in 1 Kings 18, he invoked his God to rain fire from heaven to consume the altar that he had built "that this people may know that thou, Jehovah, art God." The Bible suggests that "when all the people" witnessed the altar consumed with fire from heaven, "they fell on their faces: and they said, Jehovah, he is God; Jehovah, he is God" (1 Kings 18:37–39). Shortly before Elijah's confrontation with the prophets of Baal, the Old Testament tells us that he raised the dead son of the widow of Zarephath. Afterward, the woman said to Elijah, "Now I know that you are a man of God and that the word of the Lord in your mouth is truth" (1 Kings 17:24). Faith followed both of these miracles in the Bible. It did not precede them.

Jesus performed miracles to produce belief in those around him as well. When he told a palsied man that his sins were forgiven, after realizing that there were some who were skeptical of who he claimed to be, Jesus told his onlookers, "But so that you may know that the Son of man hath authority on earth to forgive sins"—then He said to the paralytic, "I say to you, get up, pick up your pallet and go home." When the crowd witnessed the healing, "they were all amazed and were glorifying God" (Mark 2:1–12, NASV). When John the baptizer was put into prison, he sent his disciples to inquire about Jesus. "Ask him," John instructed, "Are You the Expected One, or shall we look for someone else?" Jesus responded to John's disciples, "Go and tell John the things which you hear and see: the blind receive their sight, and the lame walk, the lepers are cleansed, and the deaf hear, and the dead are raised up" (Matt. 11:2–6; see also the NASV). Jesus was saying, in other words, "Go offer John the evidence. Tell him what you see for yourselves. Then he'll know who I am."

Nicodemus understood this idea when he said to Jesus, "We know that You have come from God as a teacher; for no one can do these signs that You do unless God is with him" (John 3: 1–3, NASV).[27] The apostle Peter articulated a similar notion when, in his inaugural address of Christianity on the day of Pentecost, he described Jesus as "a man approved of God unto you by mighty works and wonders and signs which God did by him in the midst of you, even as ye yourselves know" (Acts 2:22).

The apostles of Christ also performed miracles to produce faith. For instance, when the apostle Paul smote Elymus blind, Sergius Paulus "when he saw what was done, believed, being astonished at the teaching of the Lord" (Acts 13:12). Moreover, Acts records that the people became believers after having seen the "signs and wonders" performed by Peter and other apostles (Acts 8:12–16). The book of Hebrews explains how the apostles were validated as messengers of God "by signs and wonders, and by manifold powers, and by gifts of the Holy Spirit" (Heb. 2:3–4; compare to Mark 16:20). In fact the apostle Paul himself reminded the Corinthian church that the "signs of an apostle" were performed among them "by signs and wonders and mighty works" (2 Cor. 12:12).

In his article "What Is A Miracle?" Roberts argues that a miracle was not "just *any* divine intervention . . . It was a very special type of divine intervention that could serve as a *sign* that the person performing the miracle had the power of God behind him." Roberts contends that miracles "were a very special class of supernatural interventions of particularly astounding nature that were especially designed by God to serve as signs in the hands of certain men that he selected to be his messengers."[28]

To reiterate, miracles were designed to produce faith. Faith was not designed to produce miracles. It is true that on one occasion Jesus demanded faith on the part of two blind men before he healed them (Matt. 9:27–31). This was the exception to the rule, though. In the majority of cases, faith was not a prerequisite. This *was* the rule. In his text *Modern Divine Healing*, Miller points out that in the 31 cases of miraculous healings performed by Christ in the synoptic gospels, only once did Jesus require faith on the part of recipients before he healed them. Miller also reveals that in other cases faith may have been present but was not required.[29] It seems, then, that while Jesus may have rewarded faith, having faith was not necessarily a condition for one to receive a miraculous cure. Most cases of healing involved no faith whatsoever.[30]

In the Bible, sometimes those who were healed knew absolutely nothing about the healer (John 5:13). Hence, there could be no faith. Sometimes those healed were not even present with the healer when they were healed (Matt. 8:5–13). Sometimes those healed were not even alive; how could they have faith? Sometimes people were healed because of the faith of other people (Matt. 8:5–13; Matt. 17:14–21; John 4:46–49). If a miraculous healing failed, it was due to the faithlessness of the healer, not the person being healed (Matt. 17: 14–21). What faith healer today would admit to being the cause of someone not receiving a miraculous cure?

Before closing this section, permit me to deal with a narrative that is sometimes cited to prove that faith is necessary for miracles to occur.

Mark 6:5–6 states of Jesus, "And he could there do no mighty work, save that he laid his hands upon a few sick folk, and healed them. And he marveled because of their unbelief." The argument is that because the people did not believe (i.e., had no faith), Jesus could not perform miracles at that location.[31] Two observations are in order here: (1) the phrase "mighty work" is much broader than just performing miracles. It probably has reference to Jesus's general teachings and attempts to persuade people to accept him; (2) the phrase "mighty work" obviously does not include miraculous healings, because the very next phrase says that he laid hands on a few sick people and healed them. He apparently did this regardless of the lack of faith on the part of the people. So, the phrase "could there do no mighty work . . . because of their unbelief" does not suggest that faith is necessary for miraculous healings to occur. However, this passage does seem to suggest that one cannot be successful in a ministry if one is rejected by the faithless. Jesus's point about a prophet not being without honor except in his own country emphasizes that the people in his hometown rejected him. They knew him. They had grown up with him. Apparently, for whatever reason, they were not impressed with him. Hence, he could do no "mighty work" there.

THE PROVIDENTIAL

Having discussed the miraculous as depicted in the Old and New Testaments, let us now turn our attention to the providential, to see what differences there are between the two. If miracles do not occur today, does this mean that we should not believe in God or that we should not believe in his providential care? The answer to these questions, I believe, is no.

The word *providence*, per se, is used only one time in the entire Bible—in Acts 24:2. Here the orator Tertullus explains to Felix, the governor of Palestine, that it was by Felix's providence that "evils are corrected for this nation." When translated in the New Testament, the term *providence* comes from the Greek *pronoia*, which means "forethought." This is derived from *pro*, meaning before, and *noeo*, to think.[32] Corroborating Vine, Strong suggests that *pro* and *noeo* carry with them the idea "to consider in advance, i.e. look out for beforehand," to "provide (for)."[33] Citing McClintock and Strong, Jackson points out that providence comes from the Latin *providentia* which suggests "foresight." Jackson argues, "The word is used to denote the biblical idea of the wisdom and power which God continually exercises in the preservation and government of the world, for the ends which he proposes to accomplish."[34]

Citing Tenny, Jackson also reports, "Providence concerns God's support, care and supervision of all creation, from the moment of the first creation to all the future into eternity." According to Jackson, providence is the opposite of chance or fate, which suggests that events are "uncontrollable and without any element of benevolent purpose."[35] Bowman argues that the concept of providence, "whether in Greek, Latin, or English has to do with getting something ready, preparing something ahead of time, with equipping or furnishing what is needed."[36]

Although the word *providence* appears only once in the Bible, the concept of God looking out for or providing for his people can be found throughout the Bible. In Genesis 37–46, for instance, we read about how Joseph's brothers sold him into Egyptian bondage but how Joseph eventually rose to second in command of Egypt and saved his family from a famine, including the very brothers who sold him. Ostensibly, at least, it appears that God was operating behind the scenes providentially to care for both Joseph and the Israelites. In Exodus 2:1–10 we read about the Egyptian pharaoh's daughter finding baby Moses floating in a basket in the crocodile-teeming Nile river and giving the baby back to his Hebrew mother to nurse him. This may have been the irony of ironies. The mother who had to give up her son in order to save him was now nursing him. Was this by coincidence or by the providence of God? People of faith would suggest that God was probably behind this action, too.

In the book of Esther, we read about the Persian King Ahasuerus (Xerxes) granting permission to his servant Haman to issue a decree to kill all of the Jews in his kingdom. When Mordecai, Queen Esther's cousin, found out about Haman's plot, he asked Esther (a Jewish woman herself) to risk her life and appear before her husband's throne to intercede for the Jewish people, which she reluctantly did. Haman was ultimately hanged on the very gallows that he had built for Mordecai, and the Jews were allowed to resist their attackers, thus saving them from annihilation.

In Esther 4:14, Mordecai persuaded Esther with these words, which suggest, on their face, possible providential intervention by God for His people: "For if you remain silent at this time, relief and deliverance will arise for the Jews from another place and you and your father's house will perish. And who knows whether you have not attained royalty for such a time as this?" (NASV). Mordecai is saying, in other words, "Esther, God will take care of us Jews. But how do you know that it was not God's providence that made you queen and put you here for a reason?" The idea behind the above examples is that God dwelt in the affairs of humans.

In the New Testament we are reminded that God continues to be active in the lives of people.[37] But how? Miraculously or providentially?

Prayer and Providence Are Inextricably Bound Together

People of faith pray today because they believe that God will respond in some way to their prayers. Bowman suggests, "If I didn't believe in providence, I would not take the trouble to pray."[38] The apostle John taught that "if we ask anything according to his will, he heareth us" (1 John 5:14). The apostle Peter suggests that "the eyes of the Lord are upon the righteous, And his ears unto their supplication" (1 Pet. 3:12). James suggests that "The supplication [i.e., prayer] of a righteous man availeth much" (James 5:16). Jesus himself taught, "Ask, and it shall be given you" (Matt. 7:7). He also reminded his disciples, "If you abide in Me, and my words abide in you, ask whatsoever you wish, and it shall be done for you" (John 15:7, NASV). The whole idea behind prayer is that there is a supernatural being behind the universe, who hears the requests and groanings of his people. However, when God grants the requests of an individual, does this mean that he has to do so miraculously? In other words, is everything that God brings about in the lives of individuals who pray a violation of natural law? Stated differently, should we call these events miraculous? I think not, for reasons which follow.

The Providential Involves God Working through Nature

Jackson rightly points out that whereas "A miracle is God's working on a plain [*sic*] that is above that of natural law; providence is his utilization of natural law." In the miraculous, God operates "directly," while "in providence, He operates indirectly, employing means to accomplish the end."[39] Let us be careful here to understand that both the miraculous and the providential involve supernatural intervention. However supernatural intervention can come through nature, not necessarily through a violation or interruption of nature. Let us look at some examples from the Bible to illustrate these points.

Jackson argues that while Mary's conception of Christ was miraculous, Hannah's conception of her son Samuel was providential. First Samuel 1:6 narrates that "Jehovah had shut up her [Hannah's] womb." However, she prayed to God to give her a son. The scriptures say that her husband "Elkanah knew Hannah his wife; and Jehovah remembered her." The meaning of "knew" here is that they had sexual relations. Later, "Hannah conceived, and bare a son; and she called his name Samuel, saying, Because I have asked him of Jehovah." Hannah's prayer had been answered. Jackson suggests, "Here by means of the law of procreation, God intervened and sent a child into the world."[40] One child (i.e., Jesus) came into the world through a miracle. Another child (i.e., Samuel) came into the world providentially. Nonetheless, God was behind both events.

One might ask, "How is it that Hannah's conception was providential, but Mary's (and Sarah's) were miraculous?" Mary's and Sarah's conceptions were miraculous because both clearly violated natural law in their own way, as stated earlier. However, there is no indication that any natural law was violated with Hannah. Occasionally in nature, even when God may not be involved, women can go for years thinking that they cannot have any children, when suddenly, seemingly out of nowhere, they become pregnant with the help of their male mate. This is certainly not miraculous. We do not really know why Hannah could not conceive, other than that the Bible tells us that God had "closed her womb." What God had closed, God could open through natural means. The point to be understood here is that providence still involves supernatural intervention. However, supernatural intervention does not necessarily come miraculously.

Jackson offers other examples of the providential.[41] When the Jewish King Hezekiah prayed to God to deliver him from the Assyrian King Sennacherib, who had besieged Jerusalem, the Bible tells us that "an angel of Jehovah" smote 185,000 Assyrian troops. Sennacherib was then forced to withdraw to his capital Nineveh. This was miraculous because an angel, a supernatural being, was responsible for single-handedly slaying thousands of enemy soldiers—something impossible to do naturally. Earlier, God had told Hezekiah that God would "cause him [Sennacherib] to fall by the sword in his own land." But how would God accomplish this? When Sennacherib returned from Jerusalem, two of his sons slew him in the temple as he was praying at the altar (Isaiah 37:5–7, 36–37). Sennacherib's death came about through natural means, but God was behind his death, making it providential.

In the New Testament, when King Herod jailed Peter, the Bible tells us that Peter had been "bound with two chains" and was asleep between two guards. Two other soldiers were guarding the doors of the prison. However, "an angel of the Lord stood by him [Peter] and a light shined in the cell: and he smote Peter . . . and awoke him . . . and his chains fell off from his hands." The angel proceeded to miraculously lead Peter out of the prison, past all of the guards and the locked door. Eventually he came to "the iron gate that leadeth into the city." This gate "opened . . . of its own accord," allowing Peter to flee from his captors. This all occurred miraculously

(Acts 12:1–10). In the natural realm, chains and locked doors do not automatically fall off or unlock themselves.

There was another escape that one could argue occurred providentially. In Acts 19, the apostle Paul had gone to Ephesus to preach. Demetrius, a silversmith who made shrines to the goddess Diana, took offense at Paul's preaching and stirred up an insurrection against him and his traveling companions Gaius and Aristarchus, who had been "seized." Eventually a man named Alexander quieted the mob and persuaded them to take up their cause peacefully in the courts, thus allowing Paul, Gaius, and Aristarchus to leave (Acts 19:23–41). One could argue that it was God who allowed Paul and his companions to escape. However, no laws of nature were violated, as in the earlier case with Peter.

In the Bible we read that God destroyed two cities, one miraculously and one providentially. The scriptures say that "Jehovah rained upon Sodom and . . . Gomorrah brimstone and fire from out of heaven" (Gen. 19:24). This occurred miraculously, for roughly the same reason that Elijah's altar catching fire was also miraculous: because fire and brimstone do not fall from heaven according to any laws of nature. On the other hand, Matthew 24 reveals how God would come in judgment against the city of Jerusalem. This was accomplished in AD 70 by the Romans. One can argue that God was behind this act; however, the destruction of Jerusalem was not miraculous. God operated through the realm of nature— in this case, using a foreign army to destroy the city—making the event providential.

One last example of the providential as compared to the miraculous should suffice. It is one thing to miraculously rebuke "the winds and the sea" and bring about "a great calm" (Matt. 8:26), thus showing power over nature—but it is another thing to pray to God to send rain. This is exactly what Elijah did after Israel had endured a three-and-a-half-year draught. The scriptures say that "the heavens grew black with clouds and wind, and there was a great rain" (1 Kings. 18:44–45; James 5:16–18). There was nothing miraculous about rain clouds, even though God had answered Elijah's prayer and brought about the change. God had operated providentially through nature.

This discussion about the miraculous versus the providential means, practically speaking, that God has not performed a miracle even though he may have supernaturally intervened in the lives of people. This is a point that many people today fail to understand, especially when it comes to praying for the sick and afflicted. If a sick or ailing individual recovers, it might be because God effected a change through natural law. In other words, God may have operated providentially. However, we should not make the mistake of calling it a miracle. Nevertheless, we have not thrown God out of the picture simply because we deny that a miracle occurred.

But what role, if any, does faith play in all of this? It is true that God could, at any time, make something happen providentially without anyone invoking him. In other words, no prayer or faith on the part of anyone whatsoever need be involved. Often, though, individuals beseech God through prayer. It is during these times that faith is required. In fact it would not make sense for a person to pray unless he or she had faith in the first place. The author of Hebrews asserts that "without faith it is impossible to be well-pleasing unto him; for he that cometh to God must believe that he is, and that he is a rewarder of them that seek after him" (Heb. 11:6). James states that those who pray "must ask in faith without any doubting . . . For that man ought not to expect that he will receive anything from the Lord" (James 1:6–7, NASV).

Even though faith may be necessary to bring about change under the providential, one must understand that realistically there are limitations here. Individuals who have lost a limb or some other bodily member, for example, may pray with all the faith they can muster that their body parts will grow back, but they will never regenerate themselves, because this never occurs for humans in nature. Furthermore, some individuals have gone through multiple surgeries and have such ailing bodies that nothing will ever change organically, no matter how full of faith their prayers are. As in the case of the apostle Paul's "thorn in the flesh" (2 Cor. 12:7)—whatever that might have been—the best that they can hope for is what Paul could hope for: strength to endure it. At the beginning of this chapter, I pointed out that the difference between the miraculous and the providential is not merely a matter of semantics but has everything to do with expectations. Knowing the differences between the two allows us to understand that some things we may be inclined to pray for will never occur, and we should not expect them to. The fact is, we can pray until we are blue in the face, with all the faith in the world, but still not see any organic change in our defective bodies. Instead what individuals ought to be praying for is strength to overcome. This is realistic.

Providence Cannot Be Proven Factually

Often events happen in our day and age that appear on the surface to be the workings of God. The fact is, though, we cannot be so sure. Bowman argues, "We strongly suspect that in certain instances, God has altered circumstances, changed situations so that our best interests were served, perhaps even in what seems to be the answer to our prayers. But we cannot know for sure; we can be certain only if God has revealed [it]."[42] Similarly, Hagewood warns against being "dogmatic about our interpretation" of God's providence. "Accept the fact that God has simply not made us privy to His providence," he concludes.[43] Likewise, Jackson contends that "no person can point to particular circumstances of his or her life and confidently assert, 'I know that this was the providential intervention of God at work!'" Jackson concedes that an event may very well be the result of the providence of God at work, but our "subjective assertions . . . prove nothing." He goes on to point out that, "while it is true that God does work in the lives of men, they are frequently unaware of it. We may suspect it, believe it, hope it to be the case, and even act in such a way as to accommodate it; but, in the final analysis, 'we walk by faith and not by sight' (2 Cor. 5:7)."[44]

Turner, too, warns against "thinking a certain event or set of circumstances *definitely* means that God has done this or that or wants this or that to happen." He rightly points out that "an event can happen because God wants it to happen and causes it to happen or it may happen for various other reasons," neither of which we can really know for sure. Citing Mordecai's words to Queen Esther (i.e.,"Yet who knows whether you have come to the kingdom for such as this?"), Turner argues that Mordecai was not demonstrating a lack of faith. Instead, he was merely being careful not to assume something he should not be assuming.[45] The fact is, people of faith should be careful about what events, whether good or bad, they attribute to God. It just might be that God had absolutely nothing to do with them.

CONCLUSION

In this chapter, I have tried to demonstrate that there are significant differences between the miraculous and the providential as they are portrayed in the Bible. Miracles involved a suspension of the laws of nature, were unlimited in scope, caused astonishment on the part of onlookers, were always immediate, were always complete, were always empirically verifiable, and almost always occurred without faith on the part of onlookers or recipients. Providence, on the other hand, is linked to faith and prayer, and involves God working through nature, but cannot be proven factually. While both involve supernatural intervention in the lives of people, they are not the same things and, therefore, should not be confused.

Having a proper understanding of each has everything to do with what a person can realistically expect to receive when he or she prays to God, or even what he or she should be praying for in the first place. While God is "able to do exceedingly abundantly above all that we ask or think" (Eph. 3:20), there is a limit to what we can and should expect him to do. This does not represent a lack of faith, however. This is the reality that is presented for us in the Bible. Specifically, with regard to miraculous healings, Miller points out that "the issue" is not "whether we believe God capable of healing the sick today. He most certainly is able to heal the sick today, and possesses abundant power to do so miraculously now if this were his will. . . . The issue is not what God is able to do, but what he wills to do today."[46]

In the infant church, miracles were designed to produce faith and guide it in the will of the Lord during a particular period in history, not to serve as God's way of leading people to him forever, and certainly not to benefit society as a whole.[47] In other words, miracles were not intended for all people of all ages for all purposes, Hebrews 13:8 ("Jesus Christ is the same yesterday and today and forever" [ASV]) notwithstanding. At least one key biblical context demonstrates this for us: 1 Corinthians 13:8–13.

In 1 Corinthians 13:10, the apostle Paul argues that we would no longer need the miraculous after "that which is perfect is come." As we have discussed, *perfect* in this verse does not mean sinless. Nor is it referring to Christ's second coming or heaven itself. Instead, *perfect* means complete, fully grown, or mature, (in this context from the Greek *teleios*).[48] It refers to the completed revelation of God's will. The apostle James argues that "he that looketh into the perfect [*teleios*] law, the law of liberty and so continueth . . . shall be blessed in his doing" (James 1:25).

In the context of 1 Corinthians 13, "that which is in part" (i.e., miraculous gifts such as prophecies, speaking in tongues, knowledge, etc.) is contrasted to that which is "perfect" (i.e., something that is completed). "Childish things" are juxtaposed to the mature. The dim is contrasted to the clear. There would come a time when spiritual gifts and other miracles (i.e., things done "in part," "childish things," or dim things) would give way to the "perfect" (i.e., the complete or mature).

Moreover, even when miraculous gifts pass away when the perfect has come, three things would still remain: faith, hope, and love. If "that which is perfect" refers to the second coming of Christ, then faith would no longer be faith; it would change to sight. Hope would no longer be hope; it would become reality. Thus, "that which is perfect" could not possibly be referring to the second coming of Christ, because faith and hope would no longer "abide." However, Paul said they would. On the other hand, faith and hope could still abide if "that which is perfect" refers to the completed revelation of scriptures.

Morehead argues that the "gist of 1 Corinthians 13:10 is that gifts [miracles] would cease in relation to the universal attainment, or coming of the canon." This has been accomplished today. "The community of faith gathered for edification via the Scripture is God's plan for the edification of the church today,"[49] not through signs, miracles, or spiritual gifts.

Moorhead also points out that the miracles mentioned in 1 Corinthians 13 "enabled the Christian to minister beyond human capacity during transition from [the] old covenant to the new covenant program." Their purposes "were to glorify God by equipping and edifying the body of saints in sound doctrine toward maturation and to serve as a sign to unbelievers." Moorhead freely admits that the "exact time of the cessation of spiritual gifts is up for debate," but there are at least four "prevailing views" of when this occurred: (1) after the book of Revelation was complete; (2) "after the last Apostle died; (3) after the last gifted person died following the close of the canon; and (4) upon the dissemination of the canon throughout the region."[50] Most of these probably occurred sometime during the second century. And while the "official" canon of the scriptures was not recognized until the fourth century, the books of the New Testament were already in use by the early church and were already accepted by many as authoritative by 200 AD, if not sooner. In this sense, they were already canonical.

Unfortunately, as Moorhead cleverly notes, "In too many churches [today] the partial has done away with the complete, the adult has stood aside for the child, the dim mirror is in high demand over a clear vision, and full knowledge is jettisoned for incomplete musings. The total cessation of all spiritual gifts in the apostolic era draws attention away from gifts of a bygone era to that which far surpasses them."[51] In other words, rather than flirt with childish, dim, immature, and incomplete things such as the spiritual gifts discussed in 1 Corinthians 12–14, the church today should immerse itself solely in a study of scriptures preserved for us—what has come to be known by the Latin phrase *sola Scriptura* ("scripture alone"). After all, the apostle Paul, in writing to his young friend Timothy (2 Tim. 3:16–17), reminded him that it was "scripture"—not spiritual gifts—that was to make "the man of God" "perfect" (KJV), "complete" (ASV), or "adequate" (NASV).

There are those who claim that, if we do not have miraculous, spiritual gifts today like we read about in the early New Testament church, then God is being unfair to us. In his book *The God of the Bible*, Pratte cleverly deals with this objection:

It is true that we don't have gifts as those people did; but it is also true that we do have the **completed Scriptures** [boldface in original], which they did not. In fact, the reason the gifts ceased is that we now have the Scriptures, so the gifts are not needed.

We are at no disadvantage to the people who received miracles, so God has shown us no lack of love nor any respect of persons. To say otherwise is to belittle the blessing of the Scriptures. This argument simply proves again that those who want miracles today do not appreciate the Bible. They think that which is "in part" (gifts) is better than "that which is perfect" (the Bible).[52]

Although the miraculous has ceased, this should in no way alarm people of faith, because the providential continues. Nothing in the Bible suggests that God has stopped providing for his people. So, while we should be careful about what we label a miracle—even be so bold as to say that miracles no longer exist—this is not to suggest that God does not exist, nor that he does not intervene in the lives of humans. But supernatural intervention does not necessarily equate to the miraculous. Here is where many people err in their thinking.

Although Shana West's story, like that of Christa Lilly and Levi Draher, may be amazing, they hardly qualify as miracles. Certainly they do not violate any laws of nature. The truth is, many people before them have had similar experiences. And just because we may not fully understand them from a scientific point of view, this does not give us the liberty of labeling them miraculous. Whenever an individual escapes a tornado, a car wreck, a mine cave-in, or a life-threatening illness, although they may be wonderful outcomes, they do not qualify as miracles in the biblical sense of the word. Was God looking out for all of these people? Perhaps he was. Perhaps he was not. It could be that sometimes God simply allows nature to run its course without intervening whatsoever; in other words, allowing "time and chance" to occur "to them all" (Ecc. 9:11). This is quite possible, even though some may not want to admit it. We can never know about every situation with absolute certainty. Even though we may not always know when God is at work, we can still believe in a God that dwells in the lives of people today. We do not have to throw the baby out with the bathwater.

4

Exorcising Evil: The Bible and Psychology on Demon Possession

Several years ago, an old friend came to visit me. Because we had not seen each other in a couple of years, he was eager to catch me up on all that had been going on in his life since we had last spent time together. Very early in the conversation, my friend paused. With a serious look on his face, he eagerly announced to me, "Stephen, we finally found out what was wrong with Martha," his wife. Not remembering that anything serious had ever been wrong with her, I played along. "Oh, and what was that?" I asked. Before giving me the answer, he warned me, "This is going to rock your theology." Now I was really puzzled, wondering what on earth he was about to disclose. And then came his reply—stern, sober-faced, adamant. "She was demon possessed," he boldly announced. Not wanting me to be overly worried, though, he quickly attempted to calm whatever trepidations he thought I might have had. "But she's okay now," he assured me, "because we had it exorcised." At the time, I remained detached. I offered no rebuttal, nor did I ask any other questions, choosing rather to allow him to bask in the relief that his wife was finally well. In other words, I just listened. Whatever problems my friend's wife might have suffered and for whatever reason, I was certainly glad that she was now okay, and I communicated this to him.

My friend's story is not unlike many individuals'. Though the specifics may differ, untold numbers of people over the last five decades have claimed similar experiences. Many of these stories have been chronicled in books. Perhaps the best-known set of stories is found in Malachi Martin's book *Hostage to the Devil*.[1] Appearing three years after William Peter Blatty's enormously influential movie *The Exorcist*,[2] which was based on his 1971 book by the same title, *Hostage to the Devil* tells the story of "the possession and exorcism of five living Americans."[3] Other books that recount exorcisms include Carl Vogl's *Begone Satan*,[4] Gerald Brittle's *The Demonologist: The Extraordinary Career of Ed and Lorraine Warren, the World-Famous Exorcism Team*,[5] and Felicitas Goodman's *The Exorcism of Anneliese Michel*.[6]

One of the most influential books attesting to demon possession, *People of the Lie*, was written by psychiatrist and best-selling author M. Scott Peck.[7] Then there was Gabriele Amorth's two books, *An Exorcist Tells His Story*[8] and *An Exorcist: More Stories*,[9] as well as John Zaffis and Brian McIntyre's *Shadows of the Dark*.[10] Other, more recent books testifying to the validity of demon possession include Jose Fortea's *Interview With an Exorcist*,[11] David Kiely and Christina McKenna's *The Dark Sacrament: True Stories of Modern-Day Demon Possession and Exorcism*,[12] Anne Palagruto's *Deliver Us From Evil: A Guide to Spiritual Warfare and Exorcism*,[13] Stephen Conn's *The Devil Called Collect*,[14] and journalist Matt Baglio's *The Rite: The Making of a Modern Exorcist*.[15] All of these works support the notion that demon possession is as common today as dog tracks in a kennel. These are only a few of the scores of books written to convince people that demon possession is not only possible but also more probable than one suspects, and that people can and should take steps to free themselves from such evil spirits.

Aside from books on the subject, we are constantly bombarded nowadays with the rhetoric of televangelists and faith healers testifying that demons possess people. Longtime resident and faith healer of Akron, Ohio, the well-known Ernest Angley, for example, reveals in his book *The Deceit of Lucifer* that during his ministry, "The Lord would bring the demons . . . and let me look at them. They're hideous to behold. If you knew how they looked in the devil-possessed people you associate with, you would not want to be around those people at all."[16]

Angley claims that "seeing the devils—their eyes, ears, noses, teeth—is absolutely horrifying."[17] Claiming that he sometimes sees demons "the way God sees them," Angley describes them as having "'horses-eyes' lit with fire."[18] On one occasion, Angley writes that while dining one day in a "mission field," just before he was going to give thanks for the meal, a demon manifested itself to him: "All of a sudden the most repulsive head I have ever seen—no body, but great eyes, beard and all—came rolling down that table toward me. I just gasped!"[19] Moreover, Angley points out that demons talk in "a raspy, harsh, satanic voice."[20]

In his book *Faith in God Heals the Sick*, Angley relays the story of praying alongside an individual one day. When he looked at the individual kneeling next to him, he claims he saw a demon over that person's head that "wasn't much larger than a bumblebee and its wings, eyes and feet resembled a bee." One type of demon in particular, a "trouble demon," suggests Angley, "just looks sometimes like a number of bees rolled into a ball. It has wings and eyes similar to a bee." Angley recalls, "One morning I went out of my house and I saw the awfullest looking mass of trouble demons floating in the air between my house and the next door neighbor."[21]

Contemporary faith healer Benny Hinn also attempts to persuade his audiences that demons possess people today. As I pointed out in chapter 1, on one occasion, Hinn claimed that he cast a demon out of the sole of a woman's foot and that it slithered off the stage in the form of a serpent.[22] On another occasion, Hinn tried to convince a Portland, Oregon, audience that he saw a demon leave the auditorium after he commanded it, "Go out of this place!" Mustering all of the rhetorical drama he could, Hinn announced, "I see an animal—half-man, half-animal—literally walking out of this building in fear and trembling."[23]

As I suggested in chapter 1, historically other faith healers—such as Oral Roberts, A. A. Allen, and Jack Coe, to name a few—believed that physical afflictions such as cancer, deafness, and the inability to speak were due, in part, to demon possession. Moreover, they believed that habits such as cigarette smoking, drug addiction, illicit sexual conduct, and lying were caused by demons possessing people. Well-known faith healer Kenneth Hagin tells of healing a young girl who had lung cancer, which was caused by a demon. "As I looked at her," recounts Hagin, "I saw fastened to the outside of her body, over her left lung, an evil spirit, or an imp. He looked very similar to a small monkey." After casting out the demon, according to Hagin, it fell to the floor before running down the aisle and out of the building. Hagin also reported a demon sitting on a man's shoulder, holding the man in a headlock with both arms.[24]

Writing in 2001, sociologist Michael Cuneo cogently argued that demon possession and exorcisms were very common among "Christians of various persuasions."[25] They could be found among Catholics, Charismatics, and Evangelicals alike. "By conservative estimates," suggests Cuneo, "there are at least five or six hundred evangelical exorcism ministries in operation today, and quite possibly two or three times this many."[26] He concludes, "Over the past thirty years plenty of people have needed or wanted an exorcism badly enough to go looking for one."[27]

Cuneo argues that, after "decades of near-invisibility," exorcisms became a "raging concern" in the United States during the mid-1970s, as the result of the entertainment industry. He contends that "fears of demonization" became "widespread" only after the release of the Hollywood blockbuster *The Exorcist* and the publication of Malachi Martin's book *Hostage to the Devil.* "Almost overnight," writes Cuneo, "untold numbers of people were complaining of being afflicted by demons, and new exorcism ministries couldn't spring up fast enough to meet the soaring demand."[28] Cuneo remarks that throughout the 1970s, "Tens of thousands of people (the number is only a rough approximation) who previously wouldn't have given a thought to demons now seemed obsessed with extricating themselves from demonic influence."[29]

Suffice it to say that belief in demon possession, along with its counterpart, the exorcism, is alive and well today. But what exactly do individuals mean when they say they are demon possessed? Moreover, what is an exorcism? Perhaps the best person to answer these questions is one who believes in and participates in these practices. Contemporary exorcist Bob Larson, the United States' "foremost exorcist," who flies around the country casting out demons in auditoriums and rented hotel conference rooms, is just the man to provide the answer. He defines an *exorcism* as "the expelling of a demon, an evil spirit that has entered into a person." Larson states, "Sometimes the term deliverance is used. I prefer to refer to deliverance as the process of healing that leads to the expulsion of a demon."[30] According to sociologist Michael Cuneo, those who believe in demons possessing people do not believe in them in some "metaphorical" sense. Instead, they believe that demons are "real supernatural entities, with their own identities and missions, their own strengths and foibles, and sometimes even their own telltale odors" that literally inhabit people.[31]

Given the fact that, ostensibly, so many people believe in demon possession, this is an important subject of investigation. The argument can be made that exorcisms and belief in demons today would not be as widespread had it not been for the entertainment industry in the early 1970s. This is probably true. However, the reality is that had there been no Bible, which recounts numerous stories of exorcisms by Jesus and/or his disciples, there probably would not have been movies and books on the subject to fuel the fire that rages nowadays, in the first place. Just as I suggested in chapter 1, about the way faith healers have incorrectly interpreted the Bible to believe in modern-day miraculous healings, they have also incorrectly used the Bible as a basis to believe in demon possession. After all, as Cuneo rightly points out, miraculous healings and exorcisms are "two sides of the same coin."[32]

Let me be clear here. I am in no way blaming the Bible. Rather, I am merely trying to point out why people believe in demon possession in the first place. After all, people believed in demon possession even before there were movies. Outside of Hollywood, there is nothing that I know of in our present experience, other than what is recorded in the Bible, that would cause us to believe in either miracles or demon possession by themselves. What has happened is that uninformed and misguided people today think there are demon possessions *simply because* they can read about them in the scriptures. But the matter is a little more complicated than that. The reality is, what people see today in no way resembles what one reads about in the Bible, as I will point out momentarily.

Although many Charismatics, Pentecostals, Evangelicals, and Catholics draw on personal experiences to prove the miraculous, frequently they will corroborate their stories by turning to the Bible in an attempt to legitimize their beliefs and practices, especially when talking to other people of faith, at least insofar as they think they can. And why not? After all, appealing to a credible source—one held in high esteem by nearly everyone who shares similar worldviews—is a common persuasive strategy. Rhetorical theorist Richard Weaver, for example, suggests that one way of proving an argument is to rely on a source external to the argument itself. In other words, the strength of one's argument is derived from the credibility of the source cited. Weaver points out, "If a proposition is backed by some weighty authority, like the Bible, or can be associated with a great name, people may be expected to respond to it in accordance with the veneration they have for these sources." Continuing, Weaver argues that "if [an individual] has been confronted with testimony or authority from sources he respects, he will receive this as a reliable, if secondary, kind of information about reality."[33] Charismatics, Pentecostals, Evangelicals, and Catholics—for that matter, anyone within the broader scope of Christianity—will most likely at some point cite the Bible to bolster their claims, because they realize the veneration that the Bible contains for people of faith, including themselves.

But herein lies the problem. If one is going to use the Bible to prove a case, one must understand its teachings on a given subject. Otherwise, it will be misapplied, which leads us to the purpose of this chapter. Four questions, I believe, are in order regarding the subject of demon possession as it relates to the Bible: (1) What does the Bible have to say about the origin of Satan? (2) What does it tell us about demon possession in general? (3) Do demons really possess people today according to the Bible? And (4) if demons do not possess people today according to the Bible, to what might we attribute the behavior of individuals who claim they are possessed? My intention is to help us to understand from a biblical perspective what I believe heretofore has been an often misunderstood subject, not only by faith healers, but by the average churchgoer, priest, and minister alike. Let us turn to our first question.

WHO IS SATAN, AND WHERE DID HE COME FROM?

In his *Expository Dictionary of New Testament Greek Words*, Vine tells us that the name Satan comes from the Greek *satanas*, which means "adversary."[34] Not only does the word occur frequently in the New Testament, but it is used around 17 or 18 times in the Old Testament as well. Another term used interchangeably with Satan is *devil*. According to Vine, *devil* comes from the Greek *diabolos*, meaning "an accuser, a slanderer." [35] Clinton Hamilton points out that although "Satan and Devil refer to the same being in the Bible," he is also referred to as "prince of the powers of the air" (Eph. 2:2), "prince of this world" (John 12:31; 14:30; 16:11), and "prince of the demons" (Matt. 9:34, 12:24; Mark 3:22; Luke 11:15). "Prince" comes from the Greek *archon*, meaning "chief ruler." Therefore, suggests Hamilton, "Satan is the chief or the ruler of the beings that seek to control men in this world and are also of 'the power of the air.'"[36]

In addition to the above terms, Darrell Conley reveals that the devil "is variously known in the Bible as 'Satan' . . . 'Beelzebub,' 'the prince of this world,' 'the prince of the power [*sic*] of the air,' 'the dragon,' or 'the old serpent.'"[37] Other descriptions include "enemy" (Matt. 13:39), "ruler of demons" (Matt. 12:24), "strong man" (Matt. 12:29), "murderer" (John 8:44), "liar and the father [of lies]" (John 8:44), "god of this world" (2 Cor. 4:4), "Belial" (2 Cor. 6:15), "tempter (1 Thess. 3:5), "adversary" (1 Pet. 5:8), and "accuser of the brethren" (Rev. 12:10).[38] These are some of the many terms that one will find in the New Testament that refer to the devil or Satan.

Demon is another term found in the Bible. Vine states that this name is translated in the New Testament from *daimon*, which "denotes an evil spirit" or "one that knows."[39] The Bible points out that although there is only one "devil" (i.e., Satan), there are many demons, or unclean spirits (James 2:19, Mark 3:11). These demons are depicted in the New Testament as evil beings who do the work of their leader, the devil (Rev. 16:13–14, Matt. 25:41).

Occasionally we hear various individuals within Christianity use the name Lucifer in reference to Satan. One need look no further than Ernest Angley's book *The Deceit of Lucifer*, for example.[40] In this book Angley assumes that Lucifer is the devil and expects all of his readers to believe the same. Not once, however, does he explain the etymology of "Lucifer" or why the reader should believe that Lucifer and the devil are the same being. The fact is that the word Lucifer is found only one time in the King James Version of the Bible—in Isaiah 14:12. In this context, Lucifer refers to an unnamed "king of Babylon" (vs. 4), not to Satan. Isaiah is writing against an arrogant king who, at one time, "smote the peoples [Jews] in wrath" and "ruled the nations in anger, with a persecution that none restrained" (vs. 6). The time would come, however, when this king would be defeated. Isaiah depicts the king of Babylon as a "day-star" "fallen from heaven" and "cut down to the ground" (vs. 12). In his humiliated state, those who look upon him would ask, "Is this the man that made the earth to tremble, that did shake kingdoms . . . and overthrew the cities thereof; that let not loose his prisoners to their home?" (vss. 16–17). In short, this text depicts an ignominious ending—the shameful death of a decrepit king who once ruled with the glory of a shining star. Nowhere in this text, however, does it refer to Satan. Any references to Satan as Lucifer, according to the Bible, are therefore unfounded.

But where did Satan come from? Frankly, the Bible does not have much to say about this subject. There have been a number of theories put forth, though. Some have suggested that Satan came from a "pre-Adamic race of men who lived upon the Earth in a 'gap period' that allegedly fits between Genesis 1:1 and 1:2."[41] Relying on Genesis 6:2–4, others, such as the early Church Patriarch Justin Martyr, suggest that demons were the offspring of angels that cohabited with women prior to the time of Noah. (One is tempted to ask how a spirit being can have physical intimacy with a woman.) A third theory suggests that demons were little more than the spirits of deceased wicked men who were allowed to returned to earth. Such was the belief of the Jewish historian Josephus.[42]

Perhaps the most reasonable explanation, according to the Bible, is that Satan was probably a created being, an angel that fell from heaven. Evidence to support this position can be found in 2 Peter 2:4, Jude 6, and Revelation 12:7–9. Second Peter 2:4 suggests that God "spared not angels when they sinned, but cast them down to hell." Jude 6 teaches that "angels that kept not their own principality, but left their proper habitation, he hath kept in everlasting bonds." Revelation 12:7–9 discusses a war in heaven between "Michael and his angels" and "the dragon . . . and his angels." The dragon lost the battle and was consequently "cast down . . . and his angels were cast down with him." According to Rudd, these verses suggest "that demons are most likely angels who sinned."[43] Likewise, Hamilton argues that Satan, the "prince of demons" (Matt. 9:34), was one of these angels who were cast out of heaven. "The inference appears to be inescapable," suggests Hamilton: demons "are fallen angels about whom Peter and Jude wrote . . . In fact, the inference that they are fallen angels appears to be incontrovertible."[44] Jackson, on the other hand, is not so sure. He argues, "In the final analysis, no dogmatic conclusion can be drawn with reference to the origin of demons. That they existed admits of no doubt to anyone who takes the Bible seriously; as to their origin, the Scriptures are silent."[45]

WHAT DOES THE BIBLE TELL US ABOUT DEMON POSSESSION?

That demons possessed people in the New Testament is clearly taught. In what sense, though, were they "possessed"? Some have suggested that Jesus did not actually cast out demons or perform any other miraculous healings, for that matter. Instead, acting as the "village psychiatrist,"[46] he merely went about trying to help people psychologically—especially males who had been "demasculinized"—to deal with the stresses and anxiety of everyday life, compounded by the occupation of the Roman forces in the land of Palestine.[47] In other words, Jesus as the "village psychiatrist" merely tried to empower people to cope with life's stressors rather than literally cast out evil spirits. Any "demons," therefore, were merely metaphorical.

Similarly, others have suggested that when Jesus either healed or cast out demons, he was merely seeking to accommodate the "popular ignorance and superstition" of his day. In other words, those who were believed to be demon possessed were actually suffering from "natural diseases" of the day such as epilepsy or mental illness. Gould, for example, suggests, "It was the unscientific habit of the ancient mind to account for abnormal and uncanny things, such as lunacy and epilepsy, supernaturally."[48]

Still others suggest that "demons" were only symbolic representations of evil. When Jesus cast out a demon, according to this theory, he was casting out mythological characters, which "represent[ed] His conquest over evil by His doctrine and life."[49]

There is a fourth approach, however: the view that demons literally possessed people and were literally cast out. It is this literal view that those today who believe in demon possession tenaciously hold. But should they? In other words, does a literal interpretation of the Bible regarding demons in the first century give us a license to believe in literal demon possession today? In the remainder of this section, I will attempt to show that although some characteristics of what some people today think is demon possession coincide with what one reads about in the synoptic gospels, what is actually believed and practiced nowadays differs significantly, even if one takes a literalist view.

As described in the New Testament, demon possession during the time of Christ was not merely a mental or physical illness (Mark 1:32–34; Matt. 10:1; Acts 8:7, 19:12). Instead, demons were depicted as spirit beings who were cognizant of their surroundings and capable of holding conversations (Luke 10:20; Matt. 8:28–34; Mark 5:7; Luke 4:34), something that mere illnesses cannot do. Although people today who believe in demon possession understand this dichotomy, there are several significant differences between what is believed today and what is revealed in the New Testament.

First, in the synoptic gospels, when demons talked to Christ (sometimes he made them keep quiet, as in Mark 1:34), they spoke to him with the utmost respect. As Jackson suggests, "There is not a single case of a demon blaspheming either God or Christ in the biblical narrative."[50] Demons did not insult Christ, nor did they fight against him physically. This is very ironic. How can a demon be so evil yet be so civil? In Matthew 8:29, for example, demons once respectfully asked Jesus, "What business do we have with each other, Son of God? Have You come here to torment us before the time?" (NASV). Knowing that they were about to be cast out, they begged Christ to send them into a heard of swine. Realizing their inferiority to Christ—that they were in no position to bargain—in essence, they begged Jesus to take it easy on them. Elsewhere a demon respectfully said to Christ, "I know who You are—the Holy One of God!" (Luke 4:34, NASV). The demons who confronted Paul, Luke, Timothy, and Silas in the city of Philippi in Acts 16 admitted, "These men are servants of the Most High God, who proclaim unto you the way of salvation" (vs. 17).

Juxtapose this to what one sees today. In William Peter Blatty's movie *The Exorcist*, the demons that possessed twelve-year-old Regan were combative and used the vilest language imaginable. Although, admittedly, this is merely Hollywood's take on the subject, this type of behavior often can be found in real-life exorcisms as well.[51] And why not? Cuneo argues that people who want to "deliver a convincing rendition" of demon possession have really nothing more to go on than Hollywood's depiction.[52] The problem, however, is Hollywood has it wrong. Although demons in the Bible sometimes caused people to flail around, foam at the mouth, and grind their teeth (Mark 9:17–27), much like one might see today in a person who claims to be possessed, demons ironically did not use foul language, insult the one doing the exorcising, or behave as recalcitrants. Instead, they spoke with respect and obeyed immediately when they were commanded to leave (Mark 1:34).

One might be quick to cite the example in Acts 19:13–16 as a counterargument. In this context, seven sons of a Jewish priest named Sceva tried to exorcise "evil spirits." In what I believe is one of the most comical stories told in the entire Bible, after the exorcists cried out, "I adjure you by Jesus whom Paul preacheth," one of the demons responded, "Jesus I know, and Paul I know; but who are you?" This is hardly a response of respect. Afterward, the sons of Sceva were "mastered" by the man with the evil spirit and "fled out of that house naked and wounded." The argument is, "See, here is an example of demons being uncooperative with the exorcist." Obviously this is an anomaly in the pattern revealed in the synoptic gospels. The response from the demon occurred because the sons of Sceva had no right to invoke the name of Christ. In other words, they had no authority to attempt the exorcism in the first place. They were not men of God; they were charlatans. In the New Testament, whenever the person attempting to cast out demons had the authority to do so, demons never insulted them.

A second characteristic of exorcisms in the New Testament is that they were performed with minimal effort on the part of the one casting out the demon. In short, demons were exorcised "with a word" (Matt. 8:16). There was no blood, sweat, or tears shed in the casting out of demons in the New Testament, unlike what one sees in modern exorcisms. Nowadays the exorcist may get down on his or her hands and knees and roll around on the floor with the victim before coming up physically exhausted, often with nothing to show for his or her efforts.

Third, and closely related to the second point, the effect of an exorcism was immediate. In the story of the two Gadarenes possessed by demons in Matthew 8:28–32, for example, Jesus merely told the demons to "go," and "they came out." In fact, the process seemed to be so easy that when the seventy on whom Christ had bestowed the ability to cast out demons returned to him, they were joyous, "saying, Lord, even the demons are subject unto us in thy name" (Luke 10: 17–20). When the apostle Paul cast the demon out of the maid in Acts 16:16–18, the Bible says that Paul "turned and said to the spirit, 'I command you in the name of Jesus Christ to come out of her!' And it came out at that very moment" (NASV). The idea is that it occurred immediately and with what appears to have been minimal effort on Paul's part. In the New Testament, whenever demons were cast out, there was certainly no need for future sessions, nor was there any need for constant cajoling and badgering of the demon on the part of the one doing the exorcising. The point is, the New Testament does not characterize exorcisms as a laborious task that takes hours and hours to accomplish.

Contrast this to the approach taken today. In his book *Interview With an Exorcist*, Catholic priest Jose Fortea suggests that both in "Orthodox Christianity" and among Pentecostal churches, a normal exorcism consists of a group of people surrounding the possessed individual and ordering the demon "again and again to leave the person in the name of Jesus."[53] In the movie *The Exorcist*, as well, the two priests exorcising the demons from Regan said no less than fifteen times in a row, "The power of Christ compels you." Even so, the demon refused to budge. In fact, the ordeal was so arduous that the priests had to take a break before beginning again. Mike Thierer, pastor and head exorcist for the Hegewisch Baptist Church in Highland, Indiana, whose approach is similar to that of many exorcists today, reveals, "We like to get into the pit with the people" who are demon possessed. This involves taking "the tie off" and having to "get down in the floor and roll around with them." Thierer learned his craft from his father-in-law Win Worley, the pioneer deliverance minister of the 1970s, whose exorcisms were described by Cuneo as "wild marathon, puke and rebuke" sessions.[54] There is only one problem with this approach: these methods are foreign to those that one reads about in the New Testament.

Sometimes the counterargument is made that in the New Testament, demons did not always come out of individuals when they were commanded to. Although it may be argued that even Christ's apostles occasionally could not perform the task of casting out demons, the problem was not that the demons had to be cajoled and browbeaten into submission. The problem was lack of faith on the part of the apostles, for which Christ rebuked them (Luke 9:40–41). Had the apostles had the necessary faith to do the job, it could have been done relatively easily.

In Mark 9, Christ's disciples were unable to cast the demon out of a boy. Christ called them a "faithless generation" and commanded that they bring him the boy to be exorcised. Eventually, the disciples asked Christ why it was that they were not able to cast out the demon. Jesus responded, "This kind can come out by nothing, save by prayer" (vs. 29). The idea is not that some demons are more powerful than other demons, as Fortea suggests,[55] but that the disciples—although they had the authority to cast out all demons—lacked the necessary faith. Jesus called them "faithless" and suggested that one way for them to increase their faith was through prayer. If the disciples had had the necessary faith, they could have performed the task relatively easily, regardless of the demon.

A fourth characteristic of exorcisms in the New Testament is that, like miraculous healings in general, which I discussed in the previous chapter, they caused amazement, not skepticism and disbelief. For instance, in Matthew 9:32–33, Christ healed a mute man possessed with a demon.

The Bible says, "The multitudes marveled, saying, It was never so seen in Israel." After Christ cast out a demon from one of the men in the country of the Gerasenes in Mark 5:2–20, the Bible says that "all men marvelled." When Christ healed a demon-possessed man in a synagogue in Capernaum, Luke records that "amazement came upon all, and they spake together, one with another, saying, what is this word? For with authority and power he commandeth the unclean spirits, and they come out" (4:36). In Matthew 12:22–23, we are told that after Christ healed a man "possessed with a demon," among other problems, "all the multitudes were amazed." Even the enemies of Christ did not deny that the demon had been cast out. As I argue in chapter 3, although on occasion they tried to put the worst interpretation on Jesus's work—saying that he cast out demons by the power of Beelzebub—they never actually denied the fact that he had, nonetheless, cast out a demon.

After having personally experienced over fifty different exorcisms in researching his book *American Exorcism*, Cuneo came away unimpressed. He reports seeing "nothing startling" whatsoever. There were no levitating bodies, no heads that spun around, or voices that talked from the grave. In short, there were no "fireworks" at all.[56] In fact, Cuneo was not even convinced that people had been possessed by demons in the first place, let alone set free from them. Simply put, Cuneo was not amazed like those who witnessed exorcisms in the synoptic gospels.

A fifth argument to be made against modern-day exorcisms is that there is no evidence whatsoever in the New Testament that demons withered or writhed in pain when a person possessed by a demon came into contact with holy water, Bibles, crucifixes, or any other physical object, for that matter—Acts 19:12 notwithstanding. In fact, none of these devices were ever used in New Testament exorcisms. These are obviously artifacts of the Catholic Church, which have been perpetuated to a great extent by William Peter Blatty's book and movie—clearly the stuff of Hollywood imagination. Apparently these paraphernalia have been handed down through the centuries by the Catholic Church, but there is no evidence whatsoever that they were ever used by either Christ or his apostles.

A sixth point to be made about demon possession is that in the New Testament, Christians were never possessed. Other people were, but Christians were not. Had this occurred, it would have suggested that demons were stronger than the Spirit of God, with which Christians were commanded to be filled (Eph. 5:18). I know of no Christian today who would be willing to grant this possibility. In fact, there are no cases of anyone in the early New Testament church who was ever possessed by a demon. In our day, exorcisms occur almost exclusively (the overwhelming majority of cases) among people of faith, so-called Christians. If a person is not religious in the first place, it is highly unlikely that he or she will admit to being possessed by a demon, let alone allow someone else to lay hands on him or her to exorcise an evil spirit, which he or she does not even believe exists.

It is important to note at this point that we should not confuse demon possession with being tempted by the devil. The two are not even remotely related. Although it is true that the Bible teaches that Satan tempts Christians (Eph. 6:10–13; 1 Pet. 5:8) just as Christ himself was tempted (Matt. 4:1–11), being tempted is a far cry from being possessed. Conley notes, "The influence of the devil today is real, but it is persuasive, not possessive."[57] One could even add that although the devil may be pervasive (1 Pet. 5:8), he is not possessive. The apostle James suggests that individuals are not tempted by God but are tempted when they are "drawn away by [their] own lust, and enticed" (James 1:13–14). James goes on to tell us to "resist the devil, and he will flee from you" (James 4:7). What James is teaching does not remotely sound like even the possibility of demon possession. The fact is, the Bible teaches, "There hath no temptation taken you but such as man can bear; but God is faithful, who will not suffer you to be tempted above that ye are able; but will with the temptation make also the way of escape, that you may be able to endure it" (1 Cor. 10:13).

The Bible teaches that not only are Christians not possessed by demons, as I will attempt to illustrate further in the following section, but also they are not even tempted beyond their abilities to resist the devil.

DO DEMONS POSSESS PEOPLE TODAY?

As I have already pointed out in the previous section, I do not believe that the Bible teaches that demons possess people today as depicted in the New Testament. Although individuals may be tempted, this is a far cry from being possessed. If demons do not possess people today as they did in the synoptic gospels and Acts, why do they not? Moreover, why did God allow demons to possess people in Jesus's day in the first place? Let us begin by answering the second of these two questions. Then we will be in a better position to understand the answer to the first.

Conley articulates three reasons why God allowed demons to possess individuals during the time of Christ: (a) "to demonstrate the power of Christ and His apostles over Satan and his cohorts"; (b) to prove to Christ's enemies that he received his power from God, not from Satan; and (c) "to demonstrate for all time the nature and reality of evil."[58]

There are a few verses in the synoptic gospels that suggest that demons were allowed to possess people so that Christ might demonstrate his power. Luke 11:20 quotes Christ as saying, "But if I by the finger of God cast out demons, then is the kingdom of God come upon you." A similar idea can be found in Matthew 12:28, where Jesus is quoted as saying, "But if I by the Spirit of God cast out demons, then is the kingdom of God come upon you." Regardless of terms used (i.e., the "finger of God" or the "Spirit of God"), Christ cast out demons. Therefore he has conquered the devil, he is more powerful than the devil, and he has the authority and the power to establish his kingdom. In effect, Christ has bound "the strong man" (Matt. 12:29). Christ wins; Satan loses. Jackson contends that Christ's argument is as follows: "I have cast out demons, the servants of Satan. I could not have done so if I were not stronger than he. My power thus is superior to his."[59] As I pointed out in the previous chapter, during his ministry, not only had Christ demonstrated power over diseases and physical ailments (Matt. 9:20-22; John 4:46–54, 9:1), power over nature (Matt. 8:23–27, 14:22–23), power over material things (John 6:1-14), and power over death (Matt 9:18–26; John 11:1–45), he also demonstrated power over demons. Jackson notes that just as Christ had demonstrated his power in the realms of diseases, nature, material things, and death, "it likewise was appropriate that he be able to demonstrate his authority in the *spirit* [emphasis Jackson's] sphere as well."[60] Similarly, Hamilton suggests, "Demons possessed men in the period between the testaments and in the New Testament period . . . evidently for the reason of presenting the occasions for Jesus to show his power over Satan and his angels in the world of the invisible spirits."[61]

In demonstrating his power over evil spirits, Christ also showed that he did not receive his abilities from Satan, as we have noted above that Conley suggests. When Christ's enemies accused him of casting out Satan by the power of Beelzebub, Jesus pointed out to them the silliness of their argument: "Every kingdom divided against itself is brought to desolation; and every city or house divided against itself shall not stand," he reminded them. No one would disagree with this logic. Reasoning by analogy, Christ went on to conclude, "and if Satan casteth out Satan, he is divided against himself; how then shall his kingdom stand?" (Matt. 12:25–26).

In casting out demons, suggests Conley, Christ also demonstrated "the nature and reality of evil." "No one who has read the gospel records," asserts Conley, "would be able to say that evil is abstract and impersonal. It is both real and personal." Conley concludes, "By allowing demon possession, God provided a glimpse into the demonic world that should sober all of us."[62]

The question remains, why do demons not possess individuals today? Conley writes that he does not believe in demon possession today because he does "not believe in present-day miracles." "Belief in demon possession and belief in miracles . . . are inextricably linked. To believe in demon possession today, logically and psychologically, requires belief in modern-day miracles."[63] As I suggested in the previous chapter, miracles ceased probably near the end of the first century or within the first half of the second century, with the coming of written scriptures, because their purpose had been fulfilled—to demonstrate that the person doing the preaching had the mantle of God upon him (Heb. 2:3–4; Mark 16:20; 2 Cor. 12:12) and to teach and edify the early church in the absence of scripture.

Gwinn argues that "at least two approaches can be used to show that evil spirits *do not* possess individuals in our day" (emphasis in original). First, he observes that Christ's disciples had the ability to cast out demons (Mark 16:17–20). "Add to this the knowledge that such gifts have now ended (1 Cor. 13:8–10), and we have the basis for a conclusion about these evil spirits." Concluding, Gwinn makes a compelling argument: "If men today were possessed, what method might be used to expel the devil? Since miraculous spiritual gifts have ceased, this would leave a person under the influence of a devil, with no possible means to escape."[64] In other words, there would be no defense or remedy.

There is a final line of reasoning I wish to pursue in showing from the Bible that demons do not possess people today: the second argument set forth above by Gwinn. The Old Testament prophet Zechariah told of a time when "the unclean spirit" would "pass out of the land" (Zech. 13:3). This would occur in "that day" when "a fountain [is] opened to the house of David and to the inhabitants of Jerusalem for sin and for uncleanness" (13:1). Zechariah is one of the most Messianic prophets in the Bible. In fact, Robinson suggests that the book of Zechariah "is the most Messianic, the most truly apocalyptic and eschatological, of all the writings of the O.T."[65] Just as "the spirit of grace and supplication" was to be poured out, just as there was to be a mourning for the one who was to be "pierced," a "fountain" was to be opened for "sin and uncleanness" (Zech. 12:10, 13:3). Hailey suggests that "the time under consideration in these two chapters" is "clearly Messianic."[66]

Zechariah was referring to the time of Christ when the unclean spirits would begin to depart. Hailey concludes, "In the conquest of Christ over Satan and his forces, unclean spirits have ceased to control men as they did in the time of the ministry of Christ and the apostles."[67] Jackson points out, "While this is not a common view of Zechariah's prophecy, and certainly not one upon which an entire case can be built, it is not without possibility."[68]

If demons do not possess people today, according to what we read about in the Bible, then how do we account for the behaviors of individuals who say they have been possessed? I believe we can find the answer to this question—at least in part—by turning to psychology.

WHAT DOES PSYCHOLOGY HAVE TO SAY ABOUT DEMON POSSESSION?

When one turns to the psychological literature on demon possession, one is quickly introduced to the concept of dissociative identity disorder (DID) as a possible explanation as to why individuals claim to be possessed. Formerly referred to as multiple personality disorder (perhaps "Sybil" is the best-known case of this), Carson and Butcher define this disorder as "a dissociative reaction . . . in which a patient manifests two or more complete systems of personality. Each system has distinct, well-developed emotional and thought processes and represents a unique and relatively stable personality. The individual may change from one personality to another at periods varying from a few minutes to several years."[69]

Bull points out that in "a survey of 236 cases of multiple personality disorder (MPD) by DSM-III-R criteria, 28.6% reported an alter personality identified as a demon."[70] In fact, Crabtree's 1985 book *Multiple Man: Explorations in Possession and Multiple Personality* is devoted "to a history of [demon] possession experiences as it relates to multiple personality disorder (now called DID)."[71]

In addition to DID, Ferracuti, Sacco, and Lazzari suggest that individuals who claim to be demon possessed may be suffering from dissociative trance disorder (DTD). DTD is "a distinct clinical manifestation of a dissociative continuum" that shares some of the same characteristics as DID.[72] Citing the *Diagnostic and Statistical Manual of Mental Disorders* (DSM-IV), Ferracuti, Sacco, and Lazzari suggest that DTD requires "the presence of either a trance state or a possession trance state."[73] According to these researchers, "A possession trance state is . . . the presence of a single or episodic altered state of consciousness, in which a person's customary identity is replaced by a new identity attributed to the influence of a spirit or deity."[74] In their study of ten individuals who claimed to be possessed by a demon and who met the criteria set forth above for DTD, Ferracuti, Sacco, and Lazzari conclude that most of their subjects suffered from a "severe distortion of reality."[75]

In a study of four cases of exorcism "performed at a Trinidadian Pentecostal Church," Ward and Beaubrun discovered that "these individuals had neither been institutionalized nor previously referred for psychiatric consultation, but their histories reflect[ed] maladaptive behavioural patterns." Although "no consistent clinical picture of psychopathology [was] apparent," suggest Ward and Beaubrun, these individuals showed "a tendency toward hysterical features, both conversion and dissociation."[76]

Not only might individuals who claim to be demon possessed be suffering from DID, DTD, or hysteria, also quite possibly they may suffer from some other psychological pathology such as schizophrenia. According to Dr. Alex Kopelowica, a clinical psychiatrist, schizophrenia "is probably the most severe and pernicious of the psychiatric disorders" and causes its victims to suffer "delusions, auditory hallucinations, and paranoia."[77]

Such was the case of twenty-five-year-old schizophrenic Holly Spence, who claimed to hear voices, especially from her deceased father. Believing that her illness was caused by a demon, she met privately with former Southern Baptist minister Brian Conner of Richmond, Virginia, to be exorcised. Conner believed that demons can come into people and impersonate dead relatives. Referring to the Spence case, Kopelowicz suggests that "the feeling of being possessed by a devil or a demon is not unusual in people with schizophrenia, especially folks who have a religious upbringing. They're trying to understand as best they can the experiences that they're having."[78]

Citing numerous psychological studies, Ward and Beaubrun argue that stress can also "precipitate [demon] possession" in individuals with psychological problems. They suggest that "possession is a basic condition in response to an individual's intrapsychic tension and a precipitating situation due to an event involving unusual stress or emotion."[79] Citing Ludwig, they report that "incestuous conflicts as well as emotional crises, guilt, feelings of rejection, strong unmet dependency needs, or feelings of inadequacy also act as precipitating factors."[80] According to Ward and Beaubrun, claiming to be possessed by a demon provides an individual with two benefits: He or she can (a) "escape from unpleasant reality" and (b) be set free from "guilt through a sense of diminished responsibility."[81] In other words, all the blame for a person's evil thoughts and behaviors can be placed squarely on a demon—an external force.

Corroborating the above findings, Ross and Joshi suggest, "Like dissociation in general, paranormal experiences [such as demon possession] can be triggered by trauma, especially childhood physical or sexual abuse."[82] In critiquing the work of contemporary exorcist Bob Larsen, Walter Brakelmanns, professor of psychiatry at UCLA's School of Medicine, suggests that "repressed impulses" are in all of us and that Bob Larson is giving subjects in his audiences permission to "vent" those repressed impulses and emotions "under the guise of the devil" causing them. Brackelmanns argues that Larson has a great talent for (a) "picking out people who are highly suggestable" and (b) "putting in their minds what it is he wants from them." "What he's really doing," suggests Brackelmanns "is tapping into a lot of the fears and unresolved issues and conflicts that people have."[83]

Besides the above psychological possibilities, individuals who claim to be possessed by a demon may, in some cases, actually be faking. Although this may occur only in extreme cases, it is certainly a possibility. Evangelist Ney Rieber, for example, tells of an instance in 1995 during a prison visit, when an inmate tried to trick Rieber into believing that he was demon possessed. As Rieber looked into his cell, he saw a man sitting in the floor with a "crazed look," drooling from his mouth. Not believing in demon possession, Rieber confessed, "I looked at him a moment, and began to laugh." As the man screamed louder and louder and "banged his fists against the door" in an attempt to be convincing, Rieber reveals that he kept laughing and eventually said to him, "Good show. How long have you been practicing?" The inmate quickly "broke into a laugh" himself and asked, "How did you know? How come I couldn't fool you like I have everyone else?"[84] Although this example may be atypical, I cite it here simply to support the possibility that, for whatever reason, individuals may claim to be demon possessed when, in reality, they are only trying to fool others around them.

CONCLUSION

In this chapter I have attempted to address four questions: What does the Bible have to say about the origin of Satan? What does the Bible have to say about demon possession? Do demons actually possess people today, not metaphorically but literally, as so many people believe? If not, to what might we attribute this belief and its concomitant behaviors?

Although the Bible does not have much to say about the origin of Satan, there are a few passages that suggest that he may have originally been an angel who rebelled. Known by such names as the devil, Satan, the prince of this world, and so on, the Bible depicts him as the chief devil who rules over many demons. The New Testament books Matthew, Mark, and Luke suggest that these demons occasionally inhabited people during the time of Christ and his disciples. It is, in part, because demon possession is recorded in the synoptics that people today believe in this phenomenon.

There are at least six characteristics that we can extrapolate from the synoptic gospels regarding demon possession: (1) Demons always spoke with respect when addressed by Christ. Never did they use foul language, nor did they talk impudently when being exorcised, with the exception of the example of the seven sons of Sceva—and they did so there because the men who were trying to exorcise them were frauds. Unfortunately, when one observes an exorcism today—either a real-life exorcism or one portrayed in the movies—respect for the exorcist is the last thing a person will see. (2) Exorcisms in the New Testament were performed with minimal effort and were often cast out "with a word" (Matt. 8:16). (3) Moreover, exorcisms were always immediate, like all other miracles recorded in the Bible. Nowadays, exorcisms are arduous, hours-long, multiple-day ordeals that leave both the exorcist and the victim physically exhausted. (4) Like other miracles recorded in the synoptic gospels, exorcisms caused amazement, not skepticism, on the part of onlookers. (5) Nowhere do we read about demons writhing in pain when their victims were touched by crucifixes, holy water, or Bibles used as metaphysical swords. The fact is these items were not employed in the exorcisms of the synoptic gospels. Instead, demons were cast out verbally. This raises the question of why crucifixes and the like are being used today if they cannot be found in the New Testament. (6) Finally, Christians were never possessed with demons in the New Testament. In fact, if anything, the Bible is clear on the idea that if Christians resist the devil, he will flee from them (James 4:7).

The truth of the matter is, according to the Bible, demons do not inhabit individuals today because, like miracles, possession was limited to a particular time and place. To suggest that demons possess people today without the supernatural ability to cast them out would leave individuals defenseless. What may be occurring today among individuals who claim to be possessed by demons is not really demon possession at all but behavior brought on by dissociative identity disorder (i.e., multiple personality disorder), dissociative trance disorder, hysteria, schizophrenia, or some other psychological pathology. In very rare cases, one could even argue that individuals may be, at worst, faking or, at best, self-deluded.

Despite what I believe the New Testament has to say about this subject, I have no delusions that belief in demon possession is likely to abate anytime in the near future. As long as individuals continue to read the myriad popular books on the subject, as long as there are movies made like *The Exorcist, The Exorcism of Emily Rose*,[85] or *The Last Exorcism*,[86] and as long as individuals fail to understand what the New Testament has to say about the miraculous in general and exorcisms in particular, we will continue to hear about people in our day and age being possessed. This in no way is to castigate these individuals.

Quite frankly, I am willing to grant that many people—perhaps even the majority—who believe in demon possession do so sincerely. This does not mean, however, that we should take them at their word. In other words, we do not have to believe them. Nor should we be enamored with their testimonies. Instead, we need to offer people who claim to be possessed psychiatric and psychological assessment and therapeutic interventions along with theological education. Having said all of this, one thing seems clear to me from reading the New Testament: demons do not possess people today, at least not the supernatural kind. Despite the thousands of claims made about demon possession, when they are examined against the Bible—the very book used to validate them—we are forced to the same conclusion made by the little boy who gazed at the ruler in his newly tailored birthday suit: "The emperor is wearing no clothes!" Simply put, things are not, in reality, as people say they are.

5

---❖---

Burning Bushes, Talking Donkeys, and Still, Small Voices: The Call of God in the Present Age

After he graduated from the Army Academy at West Point in 2002, Second Lieutenant Omari Thompson deployed to Iraq with the Army's Armored Division. In 2004, as a tank commander, he found himself in Fallujah, embroiled in a bloody, two-day battle with insurgents. In the middle of the night as he sat in his tank on the outskirts of the city, deep in thought and listening to the low rumble of his engine, he began to pray. As he did so, he looked up at the star-lit sky when he claims he heard it—audibly. According to Thompson, it was the voice of God calling him to preach. At first, Thompson thought it was one of his fellow soldiers talking to him, but then he realized "they were all asleep." Thompson recalls, "I looked up at the stars and heard a voice. It was the middle of the night . . . and as I sat in my tank . . . I received the audible voice of God saying that it was time to go into the ministry."[1]

In his book *Heaven Is For Real,* author Todd Burpo recounts how when he was attending a summer camp at John Brown University in Siloam Springs, Arkansas, God called him to preach when he was only thirteen years old. Burpo reveals how, while attending an evening meeting with some one hundred and fifty other young people, the preacher "challenged" the group to become "pastors and missionaries." Retelling the story as if it had happened yesterday, Burpo explains, "I remember that the crowd of kids faded away and the reverend's voice receded into the background. I felt a pressure in my heart, almost a whisper: *That's you, Todd. That's what I want you to do.* There was no doubt in my mind that I had just heard from God."[2]

On January 2, 2013, Ray Lewis, all-pro linebacker for the Baltimore Ravens, surprised the sports world by announcing his retirement from the National Football League after seventeen seasons. When asked why he was retiring, Lewis simply responded, "God is calling. God is calling in so many other areas of life." Leaving the impression that the decision was out of his hands yet not really disclosing what he would do after football, Lewis was unequivocal: "When God calls, he calls. And he's calling." There was really little more to explain. To hear him tell it, Lewis was merely following an injunction from the Lord.[3]

In 1986, the public was shocked when longtime faith healer Oral Roberts announced that unless he raised eight million dollars to educate and support medical missionaries, God was going to "call him home." Shortly after the media had broken the story, some people could be heard snickering, "Hey, did you hear that God was going to kill Oral Roberts if he didn't raise eight million dollars?" Suddenly, the phrase "call him home" had given way to "kill." Such public talk and speculation irritated Roberts. A year later, incapable of remaining silent any longer, Roberts addressed the subject head-on in an issue of his bi-monthly magazine *Abundant Life*.[4]

He disclosed that on January 25, 1986, the morning after his sixty-eighth birthday, "God awakened me with a stirring of my heart and spoke to me as He's spoken to me many times in my life." After God supposedly chastised him for not sending medical students into the field as Roberts claimed he had called him to do earlier, he recounts how God said, "I didn't call you to try; I called you to do it." According to Roberts, when he asked God how to do it, God responded, "You raise eight million dollars a year."[5]

But the story didn't end there. Roberts recalls that three months later, as he was sitting in his bedroom reading a spy novel, God spoke to him yet again. Among other things, God reportedly said to Roberts, "I want My medical presence in the earth . . . [sic] I want you to get this going in one year or I will call you home. I've got to do something to get the attention of My people. If I have to call you home I'm going to do it."[6]

To many people who knew Oral Roberts, this was just one more instance in a long line of callings by God, dating all the way back to 1947 when he began his independent ministry. In fact Roberts was so confident that God had specifically called him through the years for one project or another, that on one occasion he boldly asserted, "My faithful Partners, I want to take you back to 1947 when God began to deal with me in an unusual way, and to give me revelations never given to another man in the history of the Christian church."[7] To hear Roberts tell it, God often talked to him in ways that he had not spoken to other men before.

Reported callings like these have been commonplace among Christians and evangelists for decades if not centuries. In fact, Marjoe Gortner revealed in his 1972 documentary *Marjoe* that God had called him to preach even as a four-year-old while splashing around in the bathtub.[8] As I suggested in chapter 1, one of the rhetorical strategies that faith healers have traditionally employed to justify their existence is their claim that they have been personally called by none other than God himself. Moreover, in many of these cases, this calling has reportedly been audible.

In his article "Charisma and Media Evangelists: An Explication and Model of Communication Influence," Lewis argues that one thing that makes media evangelists attractive to audiences in crisis is that they claim a "special calling" from God.[9] These callings, according to Lewis, "can imbue a charismatic leader with a feeling of destiny or fate."[10] And what is more, these types of claims can often paralyze an audience's ability to critically evaluate both the messenger and the message. The reasoning goes, "After all, if God has called you, who am I to question your authority?"— end of discussion.

Years ago when I was in graduate school, I met a person who lived in the same apartment complex with me. I frequently would run into him on the sidewalk, where we would strike up a conversation. I was surprised to hear him tell me one day that not only had God called him to participate in the "March on Washington for Christ" campaign, but that God had also called him to study at the university where we were attending. As if these were not enough, he boldly announced that God had even called him to a specific major. I mention this example only to observe that alleged callings from God are not limited to either faith healers or those who claim they have been called into some type of ministry. Some individuals claim that they have been called into other areas. In fact, according to psychological anthropologist Tanya Luhrman, "26 percent of all Americans" say they have received "a direct revelation from God" at some point in their life to do one thing or another.[11]

While not everyone who claims to have experienced a call of God maintains that he or she has heard something audibly (indeed, some claim that God merely laid an impression upon their heart), the mere fact that they claim a calling at all raises a number of questions, especially from those who have never had such an experience and are curious to know what they may have missed out on. "Why is it," they ask, "that some people have received a direct revelation from God, but I have not?"

What does the Bible really say about this topic? Does God call people today like we read about in the Bible when God called Moses from a burning bush to lead the Israelites out of Egyptian bondage (Exod. 3:4), or when God spoke to Balaam through a donkey (Num. 22:28)? If God does call us, to what has he called us? Moreover, how has he called us? An equally important question is, how do we know if and when we have answered his call? My purpose in this chapter is to address these questions, in an attempt to take some of the mystery out of this often-misunderstood and, dare I say, abused subject.

DO THE SCRIPTURES TEACH THAT GOD HAS CALLED US?

To be fair, the fact that God has called his people is clearly taught in the Bible. A quick look at the New Testament, for example, reveals a number of verses that support this idea. In Romans 8:30, for example, the apostle Paul points out that those who were "foreordained, them [God] also called: and whom he called, them he also justified." In 1 Corinthians 1:24–26, Paul also suggests, "but unto them that are called . . . Christ [is] the power of God. . . . For behold your calling brethren." In Ephesians 1:18, Paul reminds his readers to have "the eyes of your heart . . . enlightened, so that you will know what is the hope of [God's] calling" (NASV). Later in Ephesians he exhorts them to "walk in a manner worthy of the calling with which you have been called" (Eph. 4:1, NASV). Moreover, he tells the Ephesians that "you were called in one hope of your calling" (Eph. 4:4, NASV). In 2 Timothy 1:9, Paul reminds his young protegé Timothy that they were "called . . . with a holy calling." The writer of Hebrews suggests that the "holy brethren" were "partakers of a heavenly calling" (Heb. 3:1). The apostle Peter also reminds his readers to "give . . . diligence to make your calling and election sure" (2 Pet. 1:10). So, as one can see, the fact that the Bible teaches in many places that God has called individuals cannot be denied. My intention here is not to discuss each of these verses in detail. Rather, I cite them only to show that there are numerous passages throughout the New Testament that indeed support the notion that Christians have been called by God. But before we are too quick to excuse faith healers and others who claim they have been called to do one thing or another, let us look more closely at what the Bible has to say about this calling.

Before proceeding further, I want to make what I believe is a crucial point. My intention in the following pages is not to argue with individuals who subjectively claim that they have either seen a vision or audibly heard some type of voice. I am willing to grant individuals their experience. They have seen what they have seen and heard what they have heard, and I am empirically in no position to question whether someone experienced something or not. However, was what an individual claims to have seen or heard really from God? This is the question. What I am contending is that the Bible does not support the idea that what a person may have seen or heard was actually God or even an inner impression from God, which I hope to demonstrate momentarily. If the Bible is to be the final say in matters of religion, as many Christians believe, then we need to challenge the testimonies of individuals in light of what the scriptures actually teach. It is one thing for individuals not to understand what the Bible says about the call of God, but it is another thing altogether for a person to know what the scriptures teach yet continue to argue that their personal experience was somehow quite different—even better—than what the Bible really suggests. In other words, it is quite a different matter when an individual elevates the experiential over the scriptural, which is really what faith healers and other Charismatics have done through the years.

TO WHAT HAS GOD CALLED US?

Having established the fact that, according to the scriptures, Christians have been called by God, we now turn to the very important question of what God has called us to do. This question has often been overlooked because many people have just assumed that they already knew the answer. After all, those who claim that God called them to do one thing or another—like faith healers—are in no short supply. A quick glance at the Bible will provide us with a proper understanding of the answer to the above question.

In what is perhaps one of the most often quoted verses within Christianity today, Jesus said, "Come to Me, all who are weary and heavy-laden, and I will give you rest. Take My yoke upon you and learn from Me, for I am gentle and humble in heart, and you will find rest for your souls. For My yoke is easy, and My burden is light" (Matt. 11:28–30, NASV). Here is yet another example of the call of God. This time we notice that we have been called unto a type of rest.

In speaking to his apostles in Matthew 28:18–19, Christ commanded them to "Go therefore and make disciples of all the nations, baptizing them into the name of the Father and the Son and the Holy Spirit, teaching them to observe all that I commanded you" (NASV). While one could argue that this is actually a commandment that Christ gave to his apostles, we should also classify this as a type of calling. And while the commandment was originally directed toward the apostles, it was also intended for the disciples (i.e., learners) whom the apostles were to teach, including people today. So, realistically, one can say that all disciples of Christ have been called in a general sense to share the gospel with others.

Both Romans 1:7 and 1 Corinthians 1:2 reveal that individuals in the churches at Rome and Corinth were "called to be saints." In some religions today, sainthood is something reserved for extraordinary Christians—the super holy. The thinking among these groups is that saints were people who, when they were alive, were so good that after they themselves had received credit for their own righteousness, they had a little bit left over to give to other people. The Bible, however, does not define sainthood in this manner. Nor does the Bible require a saint to have performed a miracle. "Saint" was simply another word for "Christian," and Paul twice says that those in the churches at Roman and Corinth were "called to be saints."

In 1 Corinthians 1:9, the apostle Paul suggests that the Corinthians were also "called into the fellowship of [God's] Son Jesus Christ our Lord." The point here is not how this occurred—although we will address this question momentarily—but that it did occur. Christians have been called into a type of communion. Simply put, they have a relationship with Christ.

In a concept reminiscent of what we read earlier about what Jesus said in Matthew 11:28, Paul urges the church at Colossae to "let the peace of Christ rule in your hearts, to which indeed you were called in one body" (Col. 3:15, NASV). In other words, Paul suggests that Christians have been called into the peace of God, much like when Christ said, "you will find rest for your souls."

Writing to the church at Thessalonica in 1 Thessalonians 2:12, Paul reminds them that they had been called into God's "own kingdom and glory." Sometimes in the New Testament, the word "kingdom" is used to refer to heaven itself (Matt. 25:34; 2 Peter 1:11). Other times, however, it simply refers to the church in a universal sense (Matt. 16:18–19; Acts 8:12; Col. 1:13; Rev. 1:6, 9), which is how Paul is using the word here. In his second letter to the Thessalonians, Paul suggests that they were called "to the obtaining of the glory of our Lord Jesus Christ" (2 Thess. 2:14). More will be said in the next section on how all of this occurred.

Like Paul, the apostle Peter also tells us that we have been called "out of darkness into his marvelous light" (1 Pet. 2:9) and unto suffering (1 Pet. 2: 19–21). He goes on to say that we have been called "unto his eternal glory," which suggests, in part, that heaven awaits the faithful (1 Pet. 5:10).

The final verse I wish to point out is found in the book of Revelation, where the apostle John writes, "Blessed are they that are bidden [i.e., called] to the marriage supper of the Lamb" (Rev. 19:9, KJV). Writing in the first century to comfort Christians who were undergoing heavy persecution, John is symbolically suggesting that those who have a relationship with Christ (i.e., who are in his church) are blessed because they have been called. Using the metaphor of a marriage ceremony, just as Christ did in Matthew 22: 1–14, John is suggesting that those guests who are in attendance at the marriage feast of the Lamb (i.e., who are in the body of Christ, the church) are considered "blessed." This would have been a good position for one to be in, regardless of the persecution he or she might have been undergoing in the first century.

These examples are in no way exhaustive of all the verses in the Bible that discuss the call of God. However, while each of these verses says something different, they all have one thing in common. All of them suggest that the call of God is spiritual in nature. In no way do we read about God calling us into anything physical—no job, no occupation, no profession, no convocation, other than simply being a Christian. In other words, according to what we read in the New Testament, God did not really call Omari Thompson, Todd Burpo, or Marjoe Gortner into the ministry. Nor did he tell Ray Lewis to retire from football and go into some other line of work or Oral Roberts to raise eight million dollars. According to the scriptures, God has not called any faith healer—or any other preacher, for that matter—into a specific ministry, any more than he called me to be a college professor (which he did not) or my grandfather to be a carpenter (which he did not). Moreover, if we are to believe the Bible, God has not called anyone into any profession any more than he has called them to live in a specific city, attend a particular school, declare a specific major in college, marry a given individual, or wear a certain cologne for that matter.

If God has not called us into any of these areas of life, as so many people claim, why do they continually insist that he has? One reason, I believe, is that people want to sound authoritative if not religious. For them, it is not enough to follow what the scriptures teach. They want something more. They want something above and beyond—exciting, definitive, and in some cases, even sensational. Moreover, they do not want anyone questioning their decisions. If they can say, "God called me," or, "God is leading me to do this or that," then who are we to question? That settles it. In his book *Just Do Something: A Liberating Approach to Finding God's Will*, DeYoung supports this notion when he observes, "If we say 'God told me to do this' or 'God's leading me here,' this puts our decisions out of reach from criticisms or concerns."[12]

In his book *Decision Making and the Will of God*, Friesen addresses people's tendency not to question others when they claim to have been called by God. He discloses that before he actually began studying the topic of God's will, he would often hear individuals testify about "God's specific detailed guidance of which they were 100 percent certain." Feeling inadequate because he was never sure of what God's specific will was for himself, unlike what many of those around him were articulating, Friesen felt frustrated, as though something was missing in his own experience. He confesses, "We all just nodded at the testimony and said to ourselves, 'Yes, that is the way it should be.' Mum was the word." After all, "Who were we to question speakers whom we really respected?" Friesen reveals, "We sincerely believed that our frustrations must have been the result of sin or insincerity in our hearts."[13] Moreover, to question these types of testimonies within Christianity might cause one to be labeled a heretic.

Other possible reasons some individuals claim that God called them to do what they do may be because of either their spiritual immaturity or their lack of understanding of the scriptures. Perhaps they do so in an attempt to bolster their self-doubt or possibly to camouflage a bad decision. Whatever the reasons, the reality is that the scriptures simply do not support the idea that individuals have received a personal, divine calling from God to go into one occupation or another, whether that line of work involves the ministry or some secular job.

Nate Jackson, former wide receiver for the Denver Broncos, recently wrote a book titled *Slow to Get Up*. In his book, Jackson chronicles the numerous injuries he incurred during his six-year career. When asked in an interview on National Public Radio whether it was worth it to him to play for six years in the National Football League and deal with all of his aches and pains, Jackson emphatically responded, "Absolutely!" He went on to discuss something that, I believe, applies to those who say they have been called by God into the ministry or some other specific line of work. "We do what we do," said Jackson, "because we feel compelled to."[14] Notice what Jackson did not say. He did not say, "We do what we do because God has called us." The truth is, many people do what they do simply because they want to, or feel personally compelled to because they are good at it, but not because God told them to. However, in an attempt to sound authoritative—and in some cases perhaps even pious—they attribute their personal decision to the call of God, rather than to their own personal desires. After all, attributing one's decision to God sounds faultless and conclusive.

Friesen correctly argues that God does not have a specific, individual will for different people. In other words, he has not called some individuals into one type of occupation and others into another. Rather, God has a moral will for everybody alike, and as long as individuals operate within that moral code, they are actually doing his will. Practically speaking, then, this means that God does not really care whether one is a carpenter, a plumber, or an electrician. For that matter, God does not care whether one is a minister or not.[15] What is important is that an individual is a hard-working carpenter, a conscientious plumber, an honest electrician. Furthermore, being a faithful Christian is sufficient. One does not have to be in some type of clergy to be in the will of God. One is free to choose whatever line of work one would like to go into as long as it is compatible with living a morally upright life. God does not want us to be pimps, prostitutes, drug dealers, hustlers, and the like because these "occupations" are outside of his moral will.[16] If there is no moral or civil law against it, then we are free to choose. Indeed we are even expected to make the decision for ourselves. So rather than asking, "What is the will of God for me?" we should ask ourselves, "Is what I am doing within the will of God as it is revealed in the scriptures?"

The apostle Paul underscores the above notion when he asserts that "where there is no law, neither is there transgression" (Rom. 4:15). His point is that if there is no moral law against something, then the activity cannot be legitimately criticized as being morally wrong. I may not personally like the choices that another person makes, but as long as the individual has not violated any moral code, he or she cannot be condemned. If an individual, for example, wants to wear overalls to church, who am I to say that is wrong because I myself may prefer a suit and tie? If a person chooses to be a vegetarian, why should I care? For that matter, why should vegetarians care if I eat meat, since eating meat is not a moral violation according to the Bible? (See, e.g., Gen. 1:29–30; 1 Cor. 8:8, 10: 23–26; 1 Tim. 4:4; Rom. 14: 1–3.) When it comes to occupations, the general rule should be that if a job is necessary, it is honorable. God does not care what type of occupation a person has, as long as the job does not violate morality as revealed in the scriptures.

In summary, nowhere in the Bible are we taught that God has called us into or out of a specific occupation—the testimonies of Omari Thompson, Todd Burpo, Ray Lewis, Oral Roberts, or any other faith healer or minister notwithstanding. Friesen cogently points out, "What is so striking, as one searches the pages of the New Testament, is the glaring absence of such expressions."[17]

One might raise the objection, "Was not Moses called by God from a burning bush? Did not Christ personally call his apostles? Was not Saul called on the road to Damascus? Was not Peter called by God in a vision to teach Cornelius? Why, then, can we not say that people today are called in a similar fashion?" In an attempt to address these questions, let us turn our attention to the next major section of this chapter. If, indeed, the scriptures teach that Christians have been called spiritually but not occupationally, how then are they called? Knowing the answer to this question will help us resolve our quandary.

HOW HAS GOD CALLED US?

Addressing the church at Thessalonica, the apostle Paul unambiguously reminds his readers that they were "called . . . through our gospel" (2 Thess. 2:14). What does this mean? The gospel, or "good news," came to the Thessalonians through Paul's preaching. Paul established the church at Thessalonica on his second missionary journey. Acts 17 relates how, when Paul arrived in Thessalonica, he went into a synagogue "as his custom was" and "for three Sabbath days reasoned with them from the scriptures." The Bible uses words like "opening and alleging" to describe what Paul did. He proclaimed to them. He reasoned orally with the crowd. In other words, he preached to them. What was the result? The scriptures say, "some of them were persuaded and consorted with Paul and Silas; and of the devout Greeks a great multitude, and of the chief women not a few" (Acts 17:1–4). In other words, the church had been established there. When Paul later wrote back to the brethren at Thessalonica, he reminded them how they had been called by God—through the gospel. And they had received the gospel through his preaching.

Other verses in the Bible support preaching and teaching as the method by which people are called. In Romans 10: 13–14, Paul makes the argument that "Whosoever shall call upon the name of the Lord shall be saved." As if anticipating the very question that we are addressing, Paul went on to ask rhetorically, "How then shall they call on him in whom they have not believed? And how shall they believe in him whom they have not heard? And how shall they hear without a preacher?" (Rom. 10:14). The point is, Paul inextricably connects preaching to the call of God—no preaching, no calling.

The apostle Peter reminds us that Christians have been "begotten again" "through the word of God" (1 Pet. 1:3). As we noted earlier, Paul reminded the Corinthians that they were "called into the fellowship of his Son Jesus Christ our Lord" (1 Cor. 1:9). Being "begotten again" is equivalent to being "called into the fellowship" of Christ. If we are "begotten again" "through the word of God," as Peter explains, then we have been "called into the fellowship" "through the word of God" as well.

Christ himself reveals how individuals come to God. While he does not mention the word "calling," per se, he states that "No man can come to me, except the Father that sent me draw him." But how does this drawing occur? On its face, what Christ said may sound mysterious. Does Christ audibly talk to humankind? Quoting from "the prophets," Christ revealed, "And they shall all be taught of God. Everyone that hath heard from the Father, and hath learned cometh unto me" (John 6:44–45). When Christ says that everyone who "hath heard from the Father" would be saved, he is not talking about something audible and mysterious. Rather he is speaking metaphorically. If he meant this literally, then anyone who has never heard the literal voice of God could never be saved, which would leave out most of us. Using words like "taught," "heard," and "learned," Christ is suggesting that being drawn by God is actually a rational, intelligent process, not something esoteric and mysterious that has happened only to a select group of people. When we hear the gospel taught, then and only then can we learn about God. Then, in other words, we have been called by God.

In reality, nowadays God does not call mankind to him audibly in a "still, small voice"[18] like we read about in 1 Kings 19:12 when he spoke to Elijah in a cave. Peter points out that "the word of good tidings . . . was preached unto you" (1 Pet. 1: 23–25). In effect, God delivers his word through "earthen vessels" (2 Cor. 4:7; 2 Tim. 2:20–21)—that is, through other humans. This is precisely what happened on the day of Pentecost, when Peter preached the inaugural address of Christianity and over three thousand souls answered the call of God after they had heard Peter's sermon.[19]

Acts 8 tells the story of an Ethiopian treasurer who had been to Jerusalem to worship. On his way back home he was reading from the prophet Isaiah when the scriptures say that the evangelist Phillip approached him and heard him reading. Phillip asked him, "Do you understand what you are reading?" The Ethiopian replied, "Well, how could I, unless someone guides me?" He then "invited Philip to come up and sit with him" and teach him what Isaiah meant. After Philip had taught the Ethiopian, a little while later he baptized him, and the Ethiopian "went on his way rejoicing" (Acts 8: 27–40, NASV). He had experienced the call of God through Philip's preaching.

One of the best verses, in my opinion, in the entire New Testament that shows how God speaks to people today is Hebrews 1:1–2. There the writer says, "God, having of old time spoken unto the fathers in the prophets by divers portions and in divers manners, hath at the end of these days spoken unto us in his Son." The point is, while God used to speak to individuals according to the scriptures through things like burning bushes, donkeys, "still small voices" (1 Kings 19:12), voices in the night (1 Sam. 3: 1–10)—that is, in "divers" ways—the writer says that now God speaks to us through his son. But how can this be since Jesus Christ is no longer living on the earth to speak face-to-face with people? For a long time this puzzled me, until I realized that God did not mean that Christ was speaking literally and directly to humankind. Rather, he speaks indirectly through the Bible, which his apostles wrote down. I will say more about how this process unfolded when we address the subject of the Holy Spirit later in this book, but for now the point I want to emphasize is that when one reads the Bible, in effect, one is being spoken to by Christ, albeit indirectly. DeYoung underscores this argument when he contends, "When we read the Bible, we know we are hearing from God."[20]

Nowhere in the New Testament are we told that God calls us audibly through a still small voice in the quiet of our rooms, nor by a wind that blows through our house, nor by a bright light that shines at the foot of our bed in the middle of the night.[21] Furthermore, neither are we called by an impression laid upon the heart. The prophet Jeremiah even warns that "the heart is deceitful above all things, and it is exceedingly corrupt: who can know it?" (Jer. 17:9). Jeremiah is saying, in other words, "You cannot trust inner feelings." This idea is similarly taught in Proverbs 28:26, when Solomon says, "He who trusts in his own heart is a fool" (NASV).

Friesen cogently argues that "the Bible does not invest inner impressions with authority to function as indicators of divine guidance. Impressions are real; believers experience them. But impressions are not authoritative. Impressions are impressions." Almost humorously, Friesen also points out that impressions can be brought on by a number of factors such as "hormonal imbalance, insomnia, medication, or an upset stomach," all of which lead to a "subjective quagmire of uncertainty" in the final analysis.[22] DeYoung calls relying on inner impressions "hopeless subjectivism"[23] and warns that "If a thought or impulse pops into your head, even if it happens while reading Scripture, don't assume it is a voice from heaven."[24]

In short, the Bible is really all one needs to know what God expects of him or her. After stating that "Every scripture [is] inspired by God," the apostle Paul said that it is "also profitable for teaching, for reproof, for correction, for instruction which is in righteousness; that the man of God may be complete, furnished completely unto every good work" (2 Tim. 3:16–17). There is no need for extra-biblical revelation like those that faith healers and Charismatics have testified to having received.

Underscoring the central role that the Bible plays in directing people's lives, Friesen points out that "It is the Bible that tells us to acquire wisdom and apply it to our decisions. It is the Bible that tells us where wisdom is to be found. It is the Bible that tells us of God's involvement in giving us wisdom. It is the Bible that establishes the objective standard by which we may define and recognize what is moral and wise." One can also add that it is through the Bible that God calls us.

Addressing first-century Christians at Ephesus, the apostle Paul told them that they could know God's will because Paul had written it down so that "when you read you can understand my insight into the mystery of Christ" (Eph. 3:3–4, NASV). What at one time may have been a mystery to the Ephesians and other first-century believers was now fully understandable to anyone who would take the time to read the letters that Paul had written and which were circulating among the various churches of his day. Those same letters are available for us to read now.

Before we address the question of how individuals know when they have answered the call of God, let me deal explicitly with the objection that since God called people audibly in the Bible, why does he not call people audibly today? The answer is found, in part, in what I said earlier in this book, about miracles. If God were truly to speak audibly to a human, this would obviously be a violation of natural law and would therefore qualify as a miracle. However, 1 Corinthians 13: 8–12 teaches that miracles would cease when "that which is perfect is come." I pointed out earlier that Paul was not referring to the second coming of Jesus Christ, as many people today believe. Instead, he was probably talking about the completed revelation, which we now have in book form—the Bible. Since miracles probably ended between the end of the first century and the middle of the second century, we cannot and should not expect God to communicate with us in similar "divers manners" (Heb. 1:1) that the scriptures say he once employed in times past. Furthermore, to say that God has given a direct revelation to some people and not others would make God a respecter of persons, which flies in the face of what we are taught in the scriptures (Acts 10:34; Rom. 2:11; Eph. 6:9; James 2:9).

HOW DO WE ANSWER GOD'S CALL?

If God calls humankind—not audibly, but through the Bible—to things spiritual but not things physical, how can one be sure if and when one has actually answered the call of God? The Bible provides us an answer to this question, too.

Perhaps the most explicit verse in the entire New Testament that specifically addresses this issue is found in Acts 22. This chapter narrates the conversion of Saul of Tarsus who, before his submission to the call of God, "laid waste [i.e., "made havoc," KJV] the church" (Acts 8:3). Christ had told Saul to go into Damascus, and "there you will be told of all that has been appointed for you to do." When Ananias, a "devout" man, "well spoken of by all the Jews who lived there" came to Saul, he asked him a pointed question: "Now why do you delay? Get up and be baptized, and wash away your sins, calling on His name" (Acts 22:12–16, NASV).

Although many people today believe that one answers the call of God with their voice through prayer (much like one would verbally answer the telephone), the Bible actually teaches that this call is answered, in part, through an action—baptism. This premise is also seen in Peter's sermon in Acts 2. During the course of his address, Peter, quoting from the prophet Joel, reminds those individuals who had gathered in Jerusalem to keep the Feast of Pentecost, that "whosoever shall call on the name of the Lord shall be saved." How was this "call" supposed to be accomplished, through prayer? Nowhere in his sermon does Peter tell them to "fall down on their knees and pray to God." Rather, when they cry out, "Brethren, what shall we do?" Peter tells them two things: "Repent, and each of you be baptized in the name of Jesus Christ for the forgiveness of sins" (Acts 2:38, NASV). This is what at least three thousand people did. They had called on the name of the Lord as Joel had prophesied. They had answered God's call.

Peter went on to remind his audience that God's promise was to "you," "your children, and to all that are afar off, even as many as the Lord our God shall call unto him" (Acts 2:39). This calling, as we have seen in the previous section, was to salvation and was to be accomplished through oral discourse (i.e., the preaching of good news; Rom. 1:16).

In other words, a person does not answer the call of God by praying for salvation or by falling down upon his or her knees and audibly begging for forgiveness. And while the phrase "God, be merciful to me, the sinner" *is* found in Luke 18:13 (NASV), in the story of the Pharisee and the publican who went into the temple to pray, it was never intended to be the guiding method by which individuals were to answer the call of God. Instead, it merely teaches the right attitude of heart that one should have, "for every one who exalts himself will be humbled, but he who humbles himself will be exalted" (Luke 18:14, NASV). If this were the case, then the conversion stories in the book of Acts should reveal that individuals merely prayed for salvation. Instead, the conversions in the book of Acts all involved baptism after having been preached the gospel (i.e., called by God). They did not pray for salvation.

I once saw a billboard on the side of an interstate that read, "John 3:16—Pray!" While I am in no way contesting with what John 3:16 says,

I am suggesting that "Pray!" is nowhere in the context. "Pray!" was added by someone who did not understand specifically how the New Testament teaches that we answer God's call.

Before I close this chapter, I would like to address one last question. If, as I have argued above, God calls us to salvation and other things spiritual through the preaching of the gospel, why do some people today claim that they have been called by God to certain occupations, or even to something as silly as wearing a certain shirt,[25] and on occasion, these callings have allegedly even been audible? In her book *When God Talks Back: Understanding the American Evangelical Relationship with God*, psychological anthropologist Tanya Luhrmann provides us a possible explanation.

She argues "that people learn specific ways of attending to their minds and their emotions . . . and that both what they attend to and how they attend changes their experience of their minds, and that as a result, they begin to experience a real, external, interacting presence." In other words, people "learn to identify" some of their own personal thoughts "as God's voice, some images as God's suggestions, some sensations as God's touch or the response to his nearness."[26]

Elsewhere she contends that "knowing God is something people learn to do. It takes a lot of work, and that work changes people. Evangelical prayer practice can really enable those who pray to experience God as a person who interacts with them—and sometimes even speaks audibly. That's not because they are crazy, but because the learning practice changes the way they learn to use and pay attention to their minds."[27] She goes on to say that with many evangelicals, "Hearing a voice when alone, or seeing something no one else can see, is pretty common." According to her, "At least one in 10 people will say they have had such an experience if you ask them bluntly."[28] What Luhrmann, who is not an Evangelical herself, is saying, is that certain individuals' ways of learning cause them to use their minds differently and pay attention to things that others might not, which could cause them to attribute what they think they have seen or heard to an outward, physical expression of God himself. She is not suggesting that God is actually talking to people. Rather, she is pointing out that people think that God is talking to them because of the way they use their minds.[29]

Writing in rebuttal to those who would say they have audibly heard the voice of God directing their lives, Erin Benziger correctly argues, "the only way that a Christian can truly know that they [sic] are hearing from God is to open His Word and read it. The man or woman who has been transformed . . . understands that what God has revealed in His word is sufficient and that new revelation is unnecessary (2 Tim. 3:16–17).

Scripture is the objective means by which the Christian can know, unequivocally and without confusion, what it is God would have him to know." Benziger adds that unless Christians have "a firm foundation in Scripture," they can be easily deceived, which is why "it is essential that the believer turn to God's Word to know what is true, rather than what he perceives to be true based upon emotional experience."[30]

CONCLUSION

In this chapter, I have addressed what the Bible has to say about the call of God. I have attempted to answer four questions in particular: (1) Does the Bible indeed teach us that God has called us? (2) If so, to what has he called us? (3) How has he called us? (4) How do we know when we have answered his calling? I have suggested that the Bible does indeed teach that God has called us, but that this calling is a spiritual calling. Nowhere are we taught that God has called us into anything physical—no specific occupation, profession, or job, the testimonials of faith healers or any other individuals notwithstanding. Further, I have tried to demonstrate that this calling comes through the preaching of the gospel. In other words, it comes through the Bible. It does not come through some still, small voice, a bright light in the middle of the night, an epiphany, an angel, or some impression laid upon the heart, to name a few. Finally, I have attempted to demonstrate that this call is answered, in part, through repentance and baptism—a physical action instead of an oral outcry, which is counterintuitive to what some Christians and practically all televangelists and faith healers today believe and teach.

My hope is that after reading this chapter, people of faith will have a better understanding about the call of God and will not be so easily swayed by faith healers and others who claim that God called them to do this or that. Nowhere in the scriptures can we read that God calls people today like he did with Moses, for example.

I think it is important to note, too, that not even the apostles always claimed to be directed by a miraculous voice from God. Sometimes they made decisions much like people today should—by relying on wisdom, common sense, and good judgment. For example, in dealing with the Grecian widows who had been neglected "in the daily ministration" in Acts 6:1–4 (NASV), the apostles said, "It is not desirable for us to neglect the word of God in order to serve tables." In other words, "we do not think it is a good idea to stop what we're doing to wait on people." They then told the church to "select from among you seven men of good reputation," etc. The church was not to wait on some mystical call of God to guide them but to make a reasonable decision based on their best judgment against the criteria that the apostles set forth.

The apostle Paul told the Thessalonians on one occasion, "Wherefore when we could no longer forbear, we thought it good to be left behind at Athens alone" (1 Thess. 3:1). Here Paul leaves nothing to the imagination. He simply made a decision based on his personal reasoning. He did not attribute his decision to the call of God, to the indwelling of the Holy Spirit, or to any other mystical occurrence.

Elsewhere Paul told the Philippian church, "But I thought it necessary to send to you Epaphroditus." Who told him to? Certainly it was not the voice of God. Paul simply made a unilateral decision based on what he thought was best to do at the time.

During what has sometimes been referred to as the Jerusalem conference in Acts 15, when the early church was struggling with the question of circumcision, after the matter had been laid before the feet of the apostles, the scriptures state, "Then it seemed good to the apostles and the elders, with the whole church, to choose men . . . and send them to Antioch with Paul and Barnabas." The church at Jerusalem then wrote a letter to the Gentile church in Antioch, to be delivered by the men who had been chosen from Jerusalem. In that letter, twice they used the expression "it seemed good unto us" or "it seemed good to the Holy Spirit, and to us" (Acts 15:23–28). My point here is that we should not expect a specific revelation from God on what to do. Instead we need to decide first whether an action violates God's expressed will as found in the scriptures, and then whether the decision is a wise one. To expect a direct revelation from God is to expect too much.

And so, while the scriptures do indeed teach that God calls people today, we should be careful not to assume that this calling is audible or that God calls us to do things that the scriptures simply do not teach, such as becoming a fireman, a policeman, or any other professional—including a minister in the traditional sense of the word, and certainly not a faith healer. Instead, if individuals want to know what God expects of them, they should simply read the scriptures. Then, and only then, will they discover that God is more concerned about their spiritual lives than with how they make their living, where they should live, or what college they should attend, among other life decisions. Perhaps if faith healers and others who claim to have been called by God understood this, there would be far less confusion. Certainly there would be fewer people buying their discourse, and the topic would not seem as esoteric today as some people would lead us to believe.

6

"All Things Are Possible":
When "All Things" Does
Not Mean All Things

They came to worship God, to receive a healing, or perhaps merely to catch a glimpse of Benny Hinn, one of the best-known faith healers of our time. Close to fifteen thousand people from all socioeconomic levels packed the Memorial Coliseum in Portland, Oregon. Wearing a white, double-breasted suit, white shirt, and gray-patterned tie, with his salt-and-pepper- hair combed neatly back over his ears but covering his collar, Hinn, stylishly handsome, walked slowly to the middle of the stage with microphone raised to his lips. The healing service was about to begin. The lights were dim, and the audience was quiet as the words rolled ever so slowly and deliberately off his tongue: "All — things — are — possible — to — him — that — believeth." He paused to give the audience time to contemplate what they had just heard. No one made a sound. "All things are possible to him that believeth," Hinn slowly repeated, followed by another brief moment of silence. "All things." He paused. "All [pause] things." After another brief interlude, he finished with the words, "Every need, every prayer." Then, as if the audience had not heard him the first few times, Hinn said it again: "All things are possible. All you have to do is believe because everything is possible with God." Surely the audience had never heard a more dramatic introduction, poignantly driven home by one of the most popular faith healers today.[1]

Several years ago when I visited one of Ernest Angley's Friday-evening miracle services in Akron, Ohio, when was time for him to begin the service, Angley strolled confidently onto the stage, where he quickly set his Bible and notes on the podium. He then walked briskly out of the pulpit in front of each of the five sections of pews of his old Grace Cathedral on South Canton Road. In an attempt to motivate those in attendance, Angley stood in front of each section and, like a cheerleader, began to yell to his audience, "You're a what?" "A winner!" came the reply. "With God, all things are . . . ?" "Possible!" yelled his followers in unison. The voiceover at the start of Angley's long-running television program *The Ernest Angley Hour* for many years reminded his viewers to "Let God move for you, for with God all things are possible."

On one occasion, renowned faith healer Oral Roberts, trying to convince his critics that even the dead can be raised, argued, "The Bible tells us again and again that *nothing* is impossible with God. . . . And what I have claimed is that the resurrection power of Jesus Christ has flowed through the human vessel of Oral Roberts at times in my crusade services, and at such time I have seen the dead raised in my ministry." All of this occurred, Roberts assured, because with God, all things are possible.[2]

Even today, Richard Roberts, Oral Roberts's son, who is following in his father's footsteps, uses the phrase "All things are possible" to persuade his audiences that they can receive miraculous cures. On his website, for instance, Roberts has posted page after page of "Living Proof Videos," where the reader can view the testimonials of individuals who claim to have received miraculous healings. One, in particular, directs the visitor to "Meet Mark from California, who was healed of debilitating seizures after receiving prayer at a Richard Roberts healing service. With God, nothing is impossible."[3]

Suffice it to say that the idea, if not the very expression itself, that "All things are possible" is frequently heard among faith healers and Charismatics today. In fact, it has been used for decades. This expression, taken from the words of Christ in the synoptic gospels, is often used to prove that in the present day, God can and does perform miracles among his people. What seems impossible with men is certainly possible with God, goes the thinking. As I suggested in the introduction to this book, the exclamation "All things are possible" is so commonplace among faith healers that historian David E. Harrell chose it as the title of his book on the history of healing ministries in this country in the twentieth century.[4] This expression, perhaps more than any other, seems to capture the essence of what faith healers have traditionally believed and taught.

The phrase "All things are possible" appears indisputable on its face. After all, we are reminded, it can be found in the word of God, spoken by none other than Christ himself. Therefore, surely it must support the idea that miracles exist today—or at least that they are possible. Otherwise, why would evangelists quote it? And why would Jesus have said it in the first place if it were not true? Moreover it may even be religiously chic to repeat, marking one as an insider—a person of profound faith—among those who believe in miraculous healings. But does this verse, or other verses like it, really mean what faith healers would have us to believe it means? I'm not convinced. In this chapter I would like to look at a number of verses in the New Testament that contain the words "all" or "all things," to show that these verses might not actually suggest what, upon first glance, we might think they mean. In short, I will attempt to prove that quite often "all" does not really mean all. "Every" may not always mean "every."[5] My hope is to show that, even though the expression "all things are possible" is biblically based, it really was never meant by Jesus to be used to prove that miracles would occur two thousand years later. Let us turn to the biblical context of eating meats for our first demonstration.

"ALL THINGS ARE LAWFUL"—1 COR. 10:23

The first-century church at Corinth had more than its share of internal problems. One of the issues, among many others, was that some Christians at Corinth were not convinced that it was okay for them to eat meats that had originally been offered to pagan idols and later sold at the local meat market. Others, however, could not have cared less where or how the meat was obtained; they would eat it with no qualms. Writing to the church, the apostle Paul offered them guidance.

After explaining that "we know that no idol is anything in the world"—meaning, idols are not living deities with any power—Paul concluded that "food will not commend us to God; neither, if we eat not, are we the worse; nor, if we eat, are we the better." In other words, to put it in modern vernacular, eating meats sacrificed to idols was really "no big deal" in and of itself (see 1 Cor. 8). Paul eventually followed up with the statement, "Whatsoever is sold in the shambles"—that is, the meat market—"eat, asking no question for conscience sake" (1 Cor. 10:25). However, some weaker Christians did not possess the knowledge and confidence to consume meat offered to idols without violating their conscience, effectively sinning. Paul warned those who were comfortable eating such meat not to do so in front of weaker brethren, because they might "become a stumbling block" to those brethren by causing them to eat and "wounding their conscience." Paul concluded that the right thing to do was to refrain from eating meats in the company of weaker members (see 1 Cor. 8).

In trying to show that it was okay to eat the meat if it did not violate one's conscience, Paul explained, "All things are lawful, but not all things are expedient. All things are lawful; but not all things edify" (1 Cor. 10:23). What did Paul mean by this? Was he talking about moral issues? Did he mean that lying was lawful? Did he mean that theft was lawful? Was he referring to drunkenness? After all, one could argue, semantically, these technically fall under the category of "all things." The answer to the above questions is, of course not. In other words, "all things" did not really mean *everything*. It only had to do with "eating meats." The context dictates the meaning. This is an easy example to understand. I know of no one who would disagree with this conclusion. Although this text says nothing about the miraculous, I mention it here simply to show that sometimes verses in the Bible should not be taken too literally. Verses appear in a context and must be explained within that context.

Let us proceed to other passages that are perhaps more controversial. Eventually we will return to the popular phrase "All things are possible," so frequently found in the preaching of faith healers, to determine what Christ meant when he said it and whether faith healers should be quoting it today as proof of the miraculous.

"THEY GLORIFY GOD FOR . . . THE LIBERALITY OF YOUR CONTRIBUTION UNTO THEM AND UNTO ALL"—2 COR. 9:13

In the first century, a drought struck the region of Judea, the capital of which was Jerusalem. Obviously a drought would leave many in need. Paul wrote to the Corinthians, who lived in the region of Achaia, in modern-day Greece, to instruct them as to how they could help their Christian brethren in Jerusalem: "Now concerning the collection for the saints, as I directed the churches of Galatia [roughly modern-day Albania and Bulgaria], so you also," wrote Paul. "On the first day of every week each one of you is to put aside and save, as he may prosper, so that no collections be made when I come" (1 Cor. 16:2, NASV). Make no mistake: Paul was gathering a collection from various churches to help "saints" in Jerusalem. Apparently the church at Corinth rose to the occasion—so much so that

Paul commended them for "the liberality of your contribution unto them and *unto all*" (2 Cor. 9:13, emphasis mine).

About whom was Paul speaking when he said, "unto them and unto all?" Did he mean all men, as some would have us believe? Was this a contribution intended for the general public? Or was Paul specifically referring only to saints (i.e., Christian brethren)? Allow me to suggest that "all" in this context was limited only to Christians, even though others besides Christians may have been impacted by the drought.[6] When Paul gave his original instruction in 1 Corinthians 16:2, he made it clear that this "collection [was] for the saints." Surely Paul would not have taken up a collection under false pretense. Second Corinthians 9 begins with Paul introducing the topic that he wished to discuss with the Christians at Corinth: "For as touching the ministering to the saints." "Ministering to the saints," then, was what was on Paul's mind. In 2 Corinthians 9:12, Paul reaffirmed whom this collection was for when he wrote that "the ministration of this service [i.e., the Corinthians' collection] not only filleth up the measure of the wants of the saints, but aboundeth also through many thanksgivings unto God."

"All" was limited, then, only to Christians. It did not mean everyone. It certainly would have excluded those who were not in need—perhaps the wealthy, for example. Moreover, it is doubtful that Paul had in mind the lazy, because he said on another occasion that those who refused to work should not eat (2 Thess. 3:10). Elsewhere he argued that "if any provideth not for his own, and specially his own household, he hath denied the faith, and is worse than an unbeliever" (1 Tim. 5:8). Not taking care of one's own family, in the early New Testament church, was not an option. It is difficult to imagine that Paul had such individuals in mind when he used the phrase "unto them and unto all." Finally, at the end of the chapter, Paul wrote that the individuals for whom the collection had been taken up made "supplication [i.e., prayed] on your [the Corinthians'] behalf" (2 Cor. 9:14). Would an unbeliever make supplication for a believer? In fact, would an unbeliever "make supplication," period? This is doubtful. So, based on the context, it appears that the phrase "unto all" really does not mean anyone and everyone.

"YE KNOW ALL THINGS"—1 JOHN 2:20

Writing to Christians in the first century, the apostle John made a rather curious statement in 1 John 2:20: "And you have an anointing from the Holy One, and ye know all things." What "all things" was John referring to? Was he saying that they were well-educated people who knew everything—geometry, biology, history, geography, etc.? Those topics, obviously, were not what John had in mind. The very next verse provides us the clue to what he meant. In verse 21, he reminded his readers that "I have not written unto you because you do not know the truth, but because you do know it, and because no lie is of the truth" (NASV). In other words, when John says they knew "all things," he was specifically referring to religious truth. John later exhorted his readers to "let that abide in you which you heard from the beginning" (NASV). John was referring to the truth in general and "that Jesus is the Christ" in particular (vs. 22). That is what they had learned "from the beginning." John was concerned that there were some who would try to "lead you astray" (vs. 25) with their false teaching. He was confident that his audience knew "all things" and that "you have no need for anyone to teach you" (vs. 27, NASV). So, "all things" in this context, like those discussed above, is also limited.

"ALL THINGS WORK TOGETHER FOR GOOD"—ROM. 8:28

In this verse, the apostle Paul explained to the church at Rome, "And we know that to them that love God all things work together for good, even to them that are called according to his purpose." This verse is taken by many Christians today to suggest that anything bad that happens to those "that love God" will ultimately turn out to be beneficial for those individuals. Thus, if one's house burns to the ground, one's family is tragically killed, or one becomes paralyzed for life, somehow all of these will turn out to one's good—if not in this life, certainly in the afterlife—as long as that individual loves the Lord. Popular faith healer Kathryn Kuhlman once wrote of this verse, "That text [Rom. 8:28] is not for Christians whose lives are not surrendered to Christ, but to Christians who, through the indwelling Holy Spirit, permit troubles to become God's agents that will bring forth the best in them."[7]

Patton reminds us that in the face of some tragedy today, people of faith can sometimes be heard asking, "Why is God doing this to me?" "What have I done to deserve this?" When this happens, "Under these conditions it is not uncommon to hear someone (sometimes a preacher) say in an effort to comfort, 'All things work together for good.'"[8] In their commentary on the book of Romans, for example, Lipscomb and Shepherd contend that when Paul uses the phrase "all things," "he means even things that are painful; for even if affliction, poverty, imprisonment, hunger, death, or any other thing, come upon them, God is able to turn all things to their good and fit them for his eternal home."[9]

This notion is certainly a very comforting thought. To be fair, in a general sense the Bible does teach that God has promised to take care of his followers. Hebrews 13:5, for example, suggests that Christians should be "free from the love of money, being content with what you have." The reason follows: "for He Himself [God] has said, 'I will never desert you, nor will I ever forsake you'" (NASV). First Peter 4:16 teaches that suffering is beneficial. Second Corinthians 4:17 tells us that afflictions can make us better people. James 1:3 even teaches that "the trying of your faith worketh patience" (KJV).

The apostle Paul once disclosed to the church at Corinth that he had "a thorn in the flesh." We are not told exactly what this was other than the metaphor "a messenger of Satan to buffet me." This could have been a physical malady, or it could have been some form of persecution, but whatever it was, it bothered Paul greatly, so much so that he prayed to God three times for it to be removed. Paul revealed that God's reply was simple: "My grace is sufficient for thee." Paul could have asked incredulously, "My grace is sufficient for thee? That's it? Nothing else? Is that the best I can hope for?" Yet, without complaint, he was willing to accept God's promise. Although God was not going to remove the hardship, he pledged to give Paul the strength to carry on in spite of the difficulty. Moreover, Paul was willing to turn his handicap into something positive. He confessed, "I rather glory in my weaknesses, that the power of Christ may rest upon me." He would actually "take pleasure in weaknesses, in injuries, in necessities, in persecutions, in distresses" because "when I am weak, then am I strong" (2 Cor. 12: 7–10).

But is all of this actually taught in Romans 8:28? The context leads us to believe otherwise. Patton wisely argues that the "all things" of Romans 8:23 "must be understood with limitation, otherwise we involve ourselves in serious contradictions."[10] For example, he cites the words of Jesus in Matthew 24:12: "And because iniquity shall abound, the love of many shall wax cold." "Here is one thing that happened to one who loved God which did not work together for his good," contends Patton. He also refers to the chapter about eating meats discussed earlier, where Paul said, "For if any man see thee which has knowledge sit at meat in the idol's temple, shall not the conscience of him which is weak be emboldened to eat those things which are offered to idols; And through thy knowledge shall the weak brother perish, for whom Christ died?" (1 Cor. 8: 10–11). "Here is another thing that could have happened to one 'called according to his purpose' which would not 'work together for good,'" argues Patton. He continues, "To say that "God overrules all things that we experience to our good . . . shifts the issue from the 'all things' that happens to us to the overruling power of God."[11] And this is not what Romans 8:28 actually says.

If the "all things" of Romans 8 is not referring to everything good or bad that happens to a person in this life, then what does Paul have in mind? In the entire context of Romans 8, Paul is talking about all things that God has done for humankind of a spiritual nature, not the things that happen to us in this life that bring upon us misery and heartache. For example, early in the chapter Paul reminds the Romans that they were "free from the law of sin and death" (vs. 2) because of things that God had done for them, like "sending his own Son" (vs. 3). Later he reminds them that they were "saved" (vs. 24). Shortly afterward, he tells them that "all things work together for good" (vs. 28), immediately followed by the idea that God had "foreordained" them, that God had "called" them, that God had "justified" them, and that God had "glorified" them (vss. 29–30). These were things of a spiritual nature that God had done on their behalf. Paul then concludes by asking, "What shall we say to these things?" He argues that if God "spared not his own Son . . . how shall he not also . . . freely give us all things?" (vs. 32). Three times in this context Paul uses either the phrase "all things" or "these things." What things is Paul talking about? He is talking about all things that God has done to bring about the salvation of mankind.[12] Because of "these things," Paul concludes that "we are more than conquerors through him that loved us" (vs. 37). Patton suggests that the "limited use of 'all things' comports with the theme of the whole chapter, which is God's Love For Us, or The Actions of Deity In Our Behalf (Patton's capitalization).[13]

"I CAN DO ALL THINGS THROUGH CHRIST WHICH STRENGTHENETH ME"—PHIL. 4:13

One of the most popular phrases from the Bible in our culture today is this verse from Paul's letter to the Philippian church. Not surprisingly, this verse has often been used to motivate athletes. Perhaps many a Little League baseball player—or even a big league player, for that matter—has scrawled these words under the bill of his cap to remind him that he can do great feats as long as Christ is on his side.

A few years ago I saw on the route of an iron-man triathlon, where I was cheering on a friend, a homemade poster that read, "John, you can do all things through Christ who strengthens you (Phil. 4:13)." In fact, I saw a number of similar signs directed toward other participants, for them to read as they passed by. It seemed as if this verse were now being used in ways which the apostle Paul never really envisioned, let alone intended—to motivate triathletes, or to encourage salespersons to achieve their monthly quotas. All of this made me stop to think. Was this what the apostle Paul really had in mind when he penned those words to the Philippians in the first century? Can people of faith really do "all things" of a physical or mental nature through Christ? Does this mean, for example, that I could run a four-minute mile or a 26.2-mile marathon, even if I trained hard? Could I throw a fastball ninety-five miles an hour or kick a seventy-yard field goal? If not something physical, could I do something mental, like memorize all the names and phone numbers of a city's phone directory if I were inclined to do so? Am I capable of winning a spelling bee because of what Paul said in Philippians 4:13?

A look at the context of Philippians chapter four suggests to us that "all things" here is limited, but to what? Just prior to Paul making the observation that he could do "all things," he reminds the Philippians that he had learned to be content "in whatsoever state I am [in]." He knew how to be "abased." He knew how to "abound." In fact, Paul said that "in everything and in all things have I learned the secret both to be filled and to be hungry, both to abound and to be in want." Paul is stating that because of his relationship with Christ, he could be content in whatever state he finds himself. However, performing some athletic or intellectual achievement was the furthest thing from Paul's mind. As Carson suggests,

> The "everything" cannot be completely unqualified (e.g. jump over the moon, integrate complex mathematical equations in my head, turn sand into gold), so it is commonly expounded as a text that promises Christ's strength to believers in all that they have to do or in all that God sets before them to do. That of course is a biblical thought; but as far as this verse is concerned it pays insufficient attention to the context. The "everything" in this context is contented living in the midst of food or hunger, plenty or want (Phil. 4:10–12). Whatever his circumstances, Paul can cope, with contentment, through Christ who gives him strength.[14]

When I recently pointed the above criticism out to a friend, she boldly asked, "Well, if it works, what's the harm in using this verse to motivate people to achieve secular goals?" From that standpoint, my response was "Nothing, really." Let me be the first to admit that this verse often does motivate people to do things they may not have thought possible. I am in no way denying that. If people find motivation in Philippians 4:13 to press on athletically or intellectually, that is fine. The problem, however, is that when we take verses like this one out of their context and use them any way we see fit if they serve our purpose, they lose their true intent and serve to perpetuate religious myths. People stop critically evaluating and assume that the verse can be used to prove something it was never intended to mean. Over time, individuals begin using verses in ways that they should not, as I pointed out in chapter 1 regarding faith healers' use of Hebrews 13:8 ("Jesus Christ is the same yesterday and today and forever," NASV). When a verse is quoted over and over again in connection with some external stimuli (e.g., laying hands upon a person), then the verse comes to mean what the external stimuli would suggest, taking us in a different direction from what the writer originally had in mind. This, then, brings us back around to the phrase made popular by so many faith healers to prove divine, miraculous cures.

"ALL THINGS ARE POSSIBLE"

The expression "All things are possible" is found four times in the New Testament: in Matthew 19:26, Mark 10:27, Luke 18:27, and Mark 9:23. The first three of these contexts are the synoptic gospels' account of Jesus's teaching about riches. Christ said that "It is easier for a camel to go through a needle's[15] eye, than for a rich man to enter into the kingdom of God." When his disciples heard this, realizing the impossibility of a camel going through such a tiny hole, their response was, "Who then can be saved?" Jesus's response was, "With men this [i.e., salvation] is impossible; but with God all things are possible." In this context Christ is demonstrating to his disciples that things that seem unlikely with men, even counterintuitive, like rich people going to heaven, can happen with God.

If these three verses about camels going through the eye of a needle and rich men going to heaven were the only ones in the New Testament that used the phrase "All things are possible," my task of showing why faith healers should not use it nowadays would be much simpler, because the context of the above verses deals only with salvation, not with the performing of miracles. Most people, I believe, can see this. However, there is one other context in the New Testament that is more relevant and a little more difficult to understand in light of what faith healers preach.

Mark 9:17–29 is the story of a man whose son had been possessed by a demon. The boy's father approached Christ and asked for help. With doubt in his voice, the man begged, "if You can do anything, take pity on us and help us!" (NASV). Detecting this man's uncertainty of his ability, Jesus immediately responded, "If You can?" as if to say, "What do you mean, 'If I can?' Of course I can! But do you believe that I can?" Foster points out that Jesus "threw the words back at the speaker with a ringing challenge. The idea of anyone saying 'If thou canst . . . ,' to the Son of God!"[16] Trying to persuade the man to believe in him, Jesus taught, "All things are possible to him who believes." The father then confessed, "I do believe; help my unbelief." The narrative suggests that Christ then cast out the unclean spirit.

As I pointed out in the chapter on miracles, almost always when a miraculous healing occurred in the Bible, faith was not a prerequisite, unlike what many faith healers today claim. At times Jesus rewarded faith, as he does in this context, but the reality was that faith was not necessary for one to receive a miraculous cure in most every case. Nor was it necessarily a prerequisite in this context either. When Jesus said, "All things are possible to him who believes," he was trying to convince the man of who he, Christ, was—not necessarily to persuade the man that if he had enough faith then good things would happen to him in life. Jesus was saying to the man in so many words, "I am God. There is nothing that I cannot do. Therefore, you can believe in me as the son of God." The casting out of the demon was really secondary to what Jesus was trying to get the man to believe—that is, that Christ was divinity.

In commenting on what Jesus meant when he said, "All things are possible to him who believes," McGarvey offers the following explanation:

> "All things are possible to him that believeth," does not imply inability to heal an unbeliever, for many of the miracles were wrought on persons who had no faith; but it hinted at a possible refusal, as at Nazareth, to heal those who in the face of competent evidence were still unbelievers. It also served as an incentive to the father to get rid of the doubt implied in his petition, and it was an assertion in the presence of the scribes who had exulted over the failure of the disciples, that "all things were possible" with himself.[17]

As I suggested earlier, although faith is necessary for God to answer prayer, no amount of faith today will bring about miraculous results, as faith healers would have us believe—the expression "All things are possible to him that believeth" notwithstanding. God can answer prayer without performing a miracle. Answered prayers, in other words, are not violations of natural law. The issue is not, is God capable of performing a miracle? The question is, will he? If "All things are possible to him that believeth" truly means *all things*, then it stands to reason that if a person were to believe, he or she could have a missing appendage restored or a glass eye instantaneously changed to a functioning eye of flesh and blood. Better still, he or she could have a dead relative raised from the grave—that is, if one takes the phrase "All things are possible" literally. As I argued before, a person of faith can pray until he or she is blue in the face that such events would occur, but they will never happen because miracles were never intended to last forever.

Some would accuse me of putting limitations on God. The truth is, I could not do that even if I wanted to. God could do whatever God wants to do. However, as I suggested in the chapter on miracles, the scriptures instruct us that miracles would cease "when that which is perfect is come," which probably refers to God's revelation of the scriptures (1 Cor. 13:8). Since that has already happened, individuals today will never witness a miraculous healing (i.e., a violation or interruption of natural law) according to what the Bible teaches. God will not go back on his word because, as Hebrews 6:18 instructs, "it is impossible for God to lie."

CONCLUSION

In this chapter, I have tried to take some of the rhetorical force out of the often-heard preaching of faith healers that with God "All things are possible to him who believes" (NASV). For people of faith, God can do great things. God continues to do great things. But God is no longer in the miracle business.

Several years ago when I was trying to explain this point to a friend, in trying to refute what I was saying, his response to me was, "Well, the greatest miracle I ever experienced was my own personal salvation"—as if to say, "There's one miracle you haven't accounted for: the saving of souls." What my friend failed to understand is that even spiritual matters like salvation are not miraculous. While those of the Christian faith would argue that Christianity and what it teaches about salvation were founded upon the resurrection of Jesus Christ,[18] which would indeed constitute an interruption of natural law—what C. S. Lewis partly referred to as "the grand miracle"[19]—salvation itself is not miraculous. People of faith believe that God has put certain spiritual laws in place regarding salvation. When one obeys these laws, just as when one follows the laws of nature, no miracle occurs. One has only done what God has asked him or her to do.

To say that God is no longer in the miracle business may sound like heresy to people of faith. However, this is the reality of the scriptures. Mark 9:23 was never intended to serve as proof that God would work miracles for all people of all times. So, just as many other verses in the New Testament that contain the words "all things" do not really mean all things, the phrase "All things are possible" really does not mean all things are possible in our day and age. My intent is not to be disrespectful to anyone nor to the Bible. Nor am I trying to put people off. I am simply trying to show the reality of the verse in light of its context and in light of several other verses throughout the New Testament that contain the phrase "all things." To say "all things" is to use hyperbole, an exaggeration to prove a point. To push the hyperbole to its logical conclusion would mean that all types of things would and should occur today, like people regrowing appendages or returning from the dead. This would fly in the face of what the scriptures otherwise teach. Moreover it flies in the face of reality.

People today often have unrealistic expectations based upon a misunderstanding of Mark 9:23. This is very unfortunate. To raise the hopes of individuals who are organically afflicted, that they can be healed if they only have enough faith—because, after all, Jesus himself said, "All things are possible to him who believes"—is not only biblically unsound but cruel.

In closing this chapter, there are at least two lessons that I believe we can draw from a study of the above verses. First, and the most obvious, is that sometimes what we think the Bible means is really not what it means at all. Therefore, we need to be careful to interpret a verse in its context. Just because someone quotes a verse from the Bible does not mean that the verse is being applied correctly. The Bible was meant to be understood correctly, even though some verses may be difficult to grasp. Although the Bible contains some difficult things to comprehend, if studied in their proper context, most verses become clearer.

A second lesson that I believe can be learned is that human tradition does not determine truth. No matter how often faith healers quote a passage from the Bible to prove some point—such as Hebrews 13:8 or Mark 9:23—merely citing it over and over again proves nothing, except that neither faith healers nor their followers understand its meaning. On one occasion Jesus himself criticized individuals who taught "as their doctrines the precepts of men" (Matt. 15:9). Just because individuals have heard something taught a certain way all of their life does not make it right.

In this chapter I have tried to demonstrate through analogy that Mark 9:23 ("All things are possible to him who believes") does not legitimately prove that miracles occur today. Just as the phrase "all things" (or "all") does not mean literally all things in verses like 1 Corinthians 10:23, 2 Corinthians 9:13; 1 John 2:20, Romans 8:28, Philippians 4:13, or Matthew 19:26, "all things" of Mark 9:23 is also hyperbole. Unless individuals realize this, they may find themselves very disappointed not to experience something that they believe the Bible teaches. And as I have argued earlier, this could possibly lead one into confusion and despair.

So whenever faith healers like Benny Hinn, Ernest Angley, or Richard Roberts, to name a few, stand before thousands of people and boldly proclaim that all things are possible in an attempt to sell the idea of divine, miraculous cures, listeners should understand that while they may be quoting from the Bible, these men really do not understand whereof they speak.

7

---◆◆◆---

"Led By the Spirit of God"[1]: The Baptism, Indwelling, and Gift of the Holy Spirit

For most of his adult life, until his death in 2003 at the age of eighty-six, Kenneth E. Hagin was a popular faith healer. He has often been referred to as the father of the "Word of Faith" movement. In fact, he was so popular and beloved that many referred to him simply as "Dad Hagin."[2] His teachings and influence were far reaching, affecting individuals such as Paul and Jan Crouch, founders of the Trinity Broadcast Network, and Kenneth and Gloria Copeland of the *Believer's Voice of Victory* television program, to name a few. In one of his many books, *The Healing Anointing*, Hagin relates a story that occurred early in his ministry in December 1950, after Jesus had supposedly appeared to him in a vision to tell him that he had been given "a special anointing to minister to the sick."[3]

After preaching one night in Jacksboro, Texas, Hagin claims that a man came into the healing line. When Hagin reached out to touch him, before he could lay his hands on the man's head, "fire jumped out of my hand and hit that young man right in the forehead." One of the fourteen ministers sitting on the platform remarked to Hagin afterwards, "'I never would have believed it if I hadn't seen it for myself." Hagin recounts how everyone in the building not only saw it but heard the "popping sound."[4]

Rather than attribute what happened to static electricity, Hagin claims it was the power of the Holy Spirit. "You see," said Hagin, "when I reached out to lay my hand on that young man, he 'jerked' that Holy Ghost power out of me with his faith. It almost felt like electricity in the natural realm. I mean, I saw stars!" "I almost fell off the platform!"[5]

According to Hagin, this was only one of many instances when something like this had occurred. "Many times when I've laid hands on people," he reveals, "it felt like I'd gotten hold of a live wire!" Describing what would often happen to people in his healing lines who "responded in faith," Hagin says, "They shook, I shook, and they fell over backward under the mighty power of God! Many times the anointing was so strong that I'd fall over too."[6] Hagin believes that all of this happened because he was "freighted with the Holy Ghost, impregnated with the power of God."[7]

Kathryn Kuhlman, who was a popular faith healer before her death in February 1976, and who, according to Benny Hinn, had a profound influence upon him when she was alive, recounts her conversion as a teenager: "Not once did I doubt that wonderful spiritual transaction that took place in a little Methodist church in Concordia, Missouri, when I was fourteen years old," writes Kuhlman. "It was real. It was wonderful. It was my first contact with the Holy Spirit."[8]

Kuhlman tells of how, while "sitting next to Mama, sharing the same Methodist hymnal and singing the closing hymn, I began to tremble. I began to shake so hard that I could no longer hold the hymnal in my hand. Little did I know that it was the mighty power of the Holy Spirit— the same power that I have experienced scores of times since but in a greater measure."[9]

Years later, after she had gone into the ministry, Kuhlman claims that as she was preaching one evening on the power of the Holy Spirit in Franklin, Pennsylvania, a woman stood up and testified that she had received a miraculous healing in the service the night before. According to Kuhlman, this was the first miraculous healing that ever occurred in her ministry. "Since that time there have been thousands and thousands of healings," reveals Kuhlman. She asks, "What is the secret to the power in this ministry? The secret is found in the Person of the Holy Spirit. I have chosen to accept the gift that Jesus left for me, and you will never regret it if you accept His gift, too."[10]

Well-known contemporary faith healer Ernest Angley has preached on the Holy Spirit for years. This topic is, without doubt, one of the main themes of his ministry. In his "giant little book" titled *The Greatness of the Fire of the Holy Spirit*, for example, Angley claims that "Just as the greatness of the fire of the Holy Spirit was necessary for the early church, it is necessary for us today. I have seen the fire of the Spirit again and again." "Miracle power" according to Angley, "will move greater and greater as the fire of the Holy Spirit burns out of us that which is unlike our Master."[11] For Angley and others like him, "Salvation is vital—it comes first—and then the baptism in the Holy Spirit, that fire of the Spirit which gives great power for service to all who will yield totally."[12] Citing verses such as Matthew 3:11 ("He will baptize you with the Holy Spirit and fire"), Matthew 28:19 ("baptizing them in the name of the Father and the Son and the Holy Spirit"), Mark 16:17 ("These signs will accompany those who have believed") and Acts 1:5 ("but you will be baptized with the Holy Spirit" [NASV])—passages that, on their face, might look as if they teach the baptism of the Holy Spirit for believers today—Angley, like other Pentecostals and Charismatics, believes that power to Christians comes "through the baptism in the Holy Ghost with its initial evidence of speaking in tongues as the Spirit gave utterance."[13]

In one of the many visions he claims to have had throughout his lifetime, Angley reveals that the Lord took him "into the miracle greatness of God" to a place he had never been before. "I thought I had seen the power of the Holy Ghost; but I had never seen it like this." According to Angley, God told him that this was "the fire of the Holy Ghost," which is still "operating today" through "signs and wonders."[14]

As an example of these "signs and wonders," Angley discloses that, early in his life, he "went to a great Healing Campaign [*sic*] to receive my healing" of an "ulcerated stomach." There, an unnamed "man of God" laid his hands on him. When this happened, recounts Angley, "The power of God shot through my body like a bolt of lightning, and I became helpless under the power of the Holy Ghost. As I had lost control of myself, four men helped me off the platform." Angley confesses, "I was healed that night, and I have never been the same person since."[15]

Not to be outdone, Benny Hinn likewise believes in the miraculous power of the Holy Spirit. With a story equally sensational as those above, Hinn tells of how while preaching in a crusade in the nation of Colombia, Hinn "felt the power of the Holy Spirit move over the service." "People stood to their feet in a spontaneous outburst of praise. But they didn't stand long," he recounts. "All over, people began to collapse and fall to the floor under the power of the Holy Ghost. They were 'slain' in the Spirit."[16] In fact, it is not uncommon to see Hinn, while on stage in his crusades, run toward entire sections of seats and wave his hands in the air while yelling, "Touch!" "Substance!" or "Fire!" as hundreds of people fall backward on top of each other, claiming to be "slain in the Spirit."

These are only a few of the thousands of testimonials that one can hear today, attesting to the mysterious power of the Holy Spirit in the lives of Christians. But is all of this actually taught in the Bible? Is the Holy Spirit really this mysterious? Or have these events been incorrectly attributed to the Holy Spirit's power? In this chapter I would like to address five separate but related questions about the Holy Spirit, again in an attempt to demystify the subject and neutralize some of the sensationalism of a topic that I'm convinced has often been misunderstood among faith healers and other religious groups: (1) According to the Bible, who is the Holy Spirit, and how is the Holy Spirit described? (2) What does the Bible say about the baptism of the Holy Spirit? Is it for people today, and does it cause people to shake, rattle, and roll, cry or laugh uncontrollably, fall backward to the ground, or see visions that other individuals do not? (3) Does the Holy Spirit literally, physically dwell within Christians today in some miraculous, esoteric, "better felt than told" way? (4) If as Romans 8:14 teaches, "For as many as are led by the Spirit of God, these are the sons of God," how does this happen? In other words, how does the Holy Spirit lead? (5) What is the gift of the Holy Spirit discussed in Acts 2:38? A proper understanding of these questions will help us to better evaluate the claims made by faith healers and others on this often misunderstood topic. Let us turn our attention to the first question.

CHARACTERISTICS OF THE HOLY SPIRIT

The first thing one should realize is that the Bible refers to the Holy Spirit not as an "it," but as "He" (see John 14:16–17; 26; John 15:26; and John 16: 7–8; 13–15). He is depicted as a personality of the Godhead (i.e., "that which is divine").[17] The word "Godhead," a term commonly used among Christians today, is found only three times in the King James Version of the New Testament, in Acts 17:29, Romans 1:20, and Colossians 2:9. The Holy Spirit, along with God the Father and God the Son, is a part of that Godhead.[18] In Acts 5:3–4, for instance, the apostle Peter asked Ananias, "why has Satan filled your heart to lie to the Holy Spirit?" Later he affirmed to Ananias, "you have not lied to men, but to God" (NASV), implying in the context that the Holy Spirit is deity.

Among many other characteristics, the scriptures reveal that the Holy Spirit is a personality that can be tempted, grieved, quenched, provoked, blasphemed, resisted, despised, or lied to (see Acts 5:9; Eph. 4:30; 1 Thess. 5:19; Ps. 106:33; Luke 12:10; Acts 7:51; Heb. 10:29; and Acts 5:3). Sometimes the scriptures depict him as a being who has a mind and who, consequently, thinks, knows, and loves, among other attributes (see Rom.

8:27; Acts 15:28; 1 Cor. 2:11; and Rom. 15:30). He is considered eternal, omnipresent, and all knowing (Gen. 1:1; Ps. 139:7; 1 Cor. 2:11). This list is not intended to be exhaustive.[19] Clearly there are many more things that the Bible reveals about the Holy Spirit, but these, I believe, give us a good understanding of the fact that, like God the Father and Christ the son, he is a living being, not just an impersonal, ephemeral force. However, despite these traits, does he operate in our day and age through the miraculous, as the aforementioned faith healers would have us believe? This is the issue at hand.

THE BAPTISM OF THE HOLY SPIRIT

As I discussed in the introduction to this chapter, belief in the baptism of the Holy Spirit is commonplace among faith healers and others. However, a closer look at the scriptures suggests that baptism in the Holy Spirit was really never meant for people in our day and age. In fact it was a promise, not a command, that Jesus personally gave only to his disciples, not to anyone else, as we shall see momentarily.

The first mention of the baptism of the Holy Spirit in the New Testament can be found in Matthew 3:11, one of the verses used by Angley, as mentioned above, as a proof text for why we should expect it in our day and age. In the context of the verse, John the Baptist was prophesying that one greater than he would soon appear on the scene. He was obviously referring to Christ. John points out, "I indeed baptize you in water unto repentance; but he that cometh after me is mightier than I, whose shoes I am not worthy to bear: he shall baptize you in the Holy Spirit and in fire." John was speaking to two classes of people in this context: (1) those who were willing to repent of their sins and receive his baptism in water, and (2) those Pharisees and Sadducees who were not. Calling the latter group "offspring of vipers" (vs. 7), John rebuked them to "Bring forth . . . fruit worthy of repentance" (vs. 8) These were the wicked whom John compared to "chaff" that would be burned up "with unquenchable fire" (vs. 12). These were the ones who were to receive the baptism by fire if they did not change.

But who were the people to receive Holy Spirit baptism? We can answer this question only by looking at passages in the New Testament where Holy Spirit baptism actually occurred. I argue that in reality John was not promising Holy Spirit baptism even to all of the good people in his immediate audience, let alone to people today, as we will see momentarily.

In Luke 24:49, Jesus told his disciples to "stay in the city [of Jerusalem], until you are clothed with power from on high" (NASV). What was this power to be? A look at Acts 1 provides the answer. In Acts 1:4–5, Christ commanded his disciples again "not to leave Jerusalem, but to wait for what the father had promised, 'Which,' He said, 'you heard of from Me; for John baptized with water; but you will be baptized with the Holy Spirit not many days from now" (NASV). In Acts 1:8 , Christ told his apostles, "but you will receive power, when the Holy Spirit has come upon you; and you shall be My witnesses both in Jerusalem, and in all Judaea and Samaria and even to the remotest part of the earth" (NASV). In this context, power is equated to the baptism of the Holy Spirit.

On the day of Pentecost, a Jewish feast day that came fifty days after the feast of Passover, the apostles were in Jerusalem, where Christ had commanded them to remain. The scriptures say they were "abiding" in "an upper chamber" when, after casting lots and choosing Matthias to replace Judas, who had committed suicide earlier, the baptism of the Holy Spirit occurred.

Acts 2:1–4 says that "when the day of Pentecost was now come, they [the apostles] were all together in one place" when "there appeared unto them tongues . . . like as of fire," which "sat upon each one of them." Then "they were all filled with the Holy Spirit, and began to speak with other tongues, as the Spirit gave them utterance."

The question in Acts 2 is not whether the baptism of the Holy Spirit occurred; everyone I have ever talked with agrees on this. What is in dispute is who the recipients of this baptism were. Who are "they" and "them" in this context? The closest antecedents to these pronouns of Acts 2:1–4 are found in the last verse of chapter 1: Matthias and "the eleven apostles." According to scripture, the baptism of the Holy Spirit fell only on them, not on everyone who was in the upper room (i.e., the one hundred and twenty). Moreover, the three thousand on the day of Pentecost who were later baptized in water by Peter and the other apostles "for the remission of sins" did not receive the baptism of the Holy Spirit, because they were not yet "come together" (Acts 2:6) when the Holy Spirit had fallen.

What occurred on the day of Pentecost squares with what Jesus taught his twelve disciples when he lived among them. During his three-year ministry with them, he repeatedly promised them, "But the Helper, the Holy Spirit, whom the Father will send in My name, He will teach you all things, and bring to your remembrance all that I said to you" (John 14:26).[20] This promise was given only to the apostles, not to anyone else; certainly not to people in the twenty-first century.

Brents concludes that when we connect John's prophecy in Matthew 3:11 to Acts 1 and 2, "we see not how it is possible to look beyond the day of Pentecost for the complete fulfillment of the promise of the Father made through John [the Baptist] concerning the baptism of the Holy Spirit."[21] When John said in Matthew 3:11 that "he shall baptize you in the Holy Spirit," he was specifically referring to the apostles, not to anyone else.

But what was the Holy Spirit supposed to do for the apostles, according to Christ? Six things can be found in the scriptures. He was supposed to (1) "teach you [the apostles] all things" (2) "bring to your [the apostles'] remembrance all that I said unto you"; (3) "bear witness of me [Christ]"; (4) "guide you [the apostles] into all the truth"; (5) "declare unto you [the apostles] the things that are to come"; (6) give the apostles "power" (John 14:26; John 15:26–27; John 16:13; and Acts 1:8, respectively). Certainly, all of this was accomplished during the lifetime of the apostles.

But this was not the only case in the New Testament where individuals received the baptism of the Holy Spirit. In Acts 10:44 we read that it fell upon Cornelius and his household, the first Gentile converts to Christianity, those individuals who were not already of the Jewish faith. What are we to make of this?

After Cornelius's conversion, Peter, who had taught Cornelius what to do to be saved, went back to Jerusalem from Caesarea, where Cornelius lived. The scriptures say that in the church at Jerusalem "those who were circumcised" (i.e., Christians who had converted from Judaism) questioned Peter on why he had gone into the home of "uncircumcised men and ate with them." For whatever reason, early Christians who had converted from Judaism did not realize that non-Jews were being accepted by God into the church. Apparently, for that matter, not even the apostles did. Peter then explained how it was that he had ended up at the home of Cornelius. He then relayed how "as I began to speak, the Holy Spirit fell upon them [Cornelius and his household], just as He did upon us [the apostles] at the beginning." He disclosed, "And I remembered the word of the Lord, how he used to say, 'John baptized with water, but you will be baptized with the Holy Spirit.' Therefore, if God gave to them [Cornelius and his household] the same gift [baptism in the Holy Spirit] as He gave to us [the apostles] also after believing in the Lord Jesus Christ, who was I that I could stand in God's way?" The scriptures say that when the "apostles and the brethren" in Jerusalem heard this, "they quieted down and glorified God, saying, 'Well then, God has granted to the Gentiles also the repentance that leads to life'" (Acts 11:1–18, NASV; compare also to ASV).

Between the establishment of the church on the day of Pentecost, around 30 to 33 A.D. (Acts 2) and the conversion of Cornelius (Acts 10) several years later, no one else had received the baptism of the Holy Spirit, even though thousands had been converted. We know this because Peter claimed that what happened to Cornelius had happened to the apostles "at the beginning" (Acts 11:16). Brents cogently asks,

> But if the baptism of the Holy Spirit was then bestowed upon all converts, as we are told it now is, why did Peter associate it with the beginning? Why not have said: "As I began to speak the Holy Spirit fell on them as on all others converted?" Surely some such style would have been appropriate. Many thousands had been converted from the day of Pentecost to that time, yet the language employed is calculated to make the impression that such an event had not come under their notice from the beginning until that time.[22]

The baptism of the Holy Spirit was given to Cornelius and his household for a different reason than it had been given to the apostles at Pentecost. But this was a special case that had not occurred since the time the apostles had received it, nor did it ever occur again in the New Testament. Even though it was the baptism of the Holy Spirit, Jesus had not made the same promises to Cornelius that he had made to his apostles. In fact, it is more than likely that Cornelius had never even met Jesus. Holy Spirit baptism occurred to Cornelius merely to prove to Peter and the other apostles in Jerusalem that God was now accepting Gentiles into the church. It was not given to do the same thing that it was promised to do for the apostles. Cornelius's case should in no way suggest to us today that we, too, can receive Holy Spirit baptism, because the reasons for which both the apostles and Cornelius and his household received it no longer exist.

In summary, we can conclude that the baptism of the Holy Spirit was a promise given by Christ to his apostles, not a command. There is absolutely nothing that we can do today to bring it upon ourselves even if we wanted to. While one can obey a command, one cannot obey a promise. As Brents rightly points out, "promises may be enjoyed but cannot be obeyed."[23] One has no control over a promise, as one does a command. With promises, humans have to wait on God. With commands, God has to wait on humans. Because the baptism of the Holy Spirit was a promise, I have no idea how people today would be expected to comply with it, since they would have absolutely no control over it, just as neither the apostles nor Cornelius and his household had control over it. In the two examples of Holy Spirit baptism in the New Testament, individuals neither asked for it nor sought it out. Other than going to Jerusalem and waiting, there was really nothing the apostles could do to bring it about. It just happened. Secondly, this promise was administered by God, not by man (like water baptism, as we shall see in a moment). Thirdly, the baptism in the Holy Spirit was given for reasons that no longer exist (i.e., to guide the apostles into all the truth and to show the apostles that God was accepting Gentiles into the church).

As I pointed out in chapter 5, all we have to do today to know God's will is read the Bible. There is no need for a latter-day revelation from an angel of God or a vision brought upon us by the baptism of the Holy Spirit, as Ernest Angley and others would have us believe. In other words, there is no need to be guided into all truth—or any truth for that matter—like the apostles were. This had already occurred. First Peter 1:3 tells us that God has already "granted unto us all things that pertain unto life and godliness." How has he accomplished this? Second Timothy 3:16 tells us that all scripture is "profitable for teaching, for reproof, for correction, for instruction . . . in righteousness; that the man of God may be complete, furnished completely unto every good work." The apostles, who were guided into all the truth, wrote down God's will once for all time and "delivered" it "unto the saints" (Jude 3; see also Eph. 3:3–5). We have it now in book form; it is called the Bible. Hence, there is no further need for what the baptism of the Holy Spirit was designed to accomplish in the first place: guidance of the apostles into all truth. It was the apostle Paul who wrote in Ephesians 3:3–4, that "by revelation there was made known to me the mystery, as I wrote before in brief. By referring to this, when you read you can understand my insight into the mystery of Christ" (NASV).

But some are quick to remind us of what the apostle Paul also says in 1 Corinthians 12:13, that "by one Spirit are we all baptized into one body . . . and have been all made to drink into one Spirit" (KJV).[24] Does this not teach that people today are baptized in the Holy Spirit? Were not the Corinthians in the first-century church also baptized in the Holy Spirit? Brents points out that "Although this passage was written in close proximity to Paul's explanation of the miraculous gifts of the Spirit . . . it falls very far short of proving that they [the Corinthians], or any of them, are baptized with the Holy Spirit."[25] Here's why.

In Ephesians 4:5, the apostle Paul reminds us that there is "one baptism" for which we should be accountable. What baptism did Paul have in mind? After all, the scriptures mention several baptisms: the baptism of John (Matt. 3:6; Matt. 21:25), the baptism in water for the remission of sins (Acts 2:38; Mark 16:15–16; Matt. 28:19–20), the baptism of the Holy Spirit (Matt. 3:11; Acts 1:4), the baptism of suffering (Matt. 20:22–23, KJV),[26] the baptism by fire (Matt. 3:11),[27] and the baptism "unto Moses in the cloud" (1 Cor. 10:2).[28] Was it Holy Spirit baptism, as faith healers and others would have us believe? I believe the apostle Paul was referring to water baptism for the remission of sins (i.e., the great commission baptism).

If we look at the cases of conversion in the book of Acts,[29] we will see that every one of them involved water baptism for the remission of sins, the great commission baptism that Christ mentioned in Mark 16:15–16 and Matthew 28:19–20 when he sent his apostles out to preach the gospel. None of the conversions in Acts, with the exception of Cornelius in Acts 10, involved the baptism of the Holy Spirit. Even in the case of Cornelius, who received Holy Spirit baptism, Acts 10:48 tells us that Peter still "commanded" Cornelius and his household to be "baptized [in water] in the name of the Lord," just as he had commanded those on the day of Pentecost when he told them to "repent and be baptized for the remission of sins" in Acts 2:38. Why would Peter command something if he did not feel it absolutely necessary? This is the same baptism that Paul mentions in Romans 6:3–4 and Galatians 3:27. In Romans 6:17, Paul told the Romans that "though you were slaves of sin, you became obedient from the heart to that form of teaching to which you were committed" (NASV). They had become obedient, in part, through water baptism. The apostle Peter explicitly says that it is this type of baptism that "now saves you" (1 Pet. 3:21, NASV).[30]

Brents suggests that 1 Corinthians 12:13 means, "By (the teaching of) one Spirit (the Holy Spirit) we are all baptized (in water) into one body (the church). This seems to be the obvious import of the passage, and it is in harmony with the whole tenor" of what the New Testament has to say about baptism. Brents argues that if we insist that 1 Corinthians 12:13 means that we are baptized by the Holy Spirit, "then we make Paul contradict himself" when he says in Ephesians 4:5 that there is "one baptism."[31] Moreover, the baptism that Paul had in mind in Ephesians 4:5 was water baptism, because he says in Ephesians 5:26 that Christ "cleansed" the church "by the washing of water with the word." Just as Christians understand that there is "one Spirit" (i.e., the Holy Spirit) and "one Lord" whom we should worship (Eph. 4:4–5), there is only one baptism that Christians should adhere to—water baptism, not the baptism of the Holy Spirit, or any other type of baptism, for that matter. Since the baptism of the Holy Spirit was never meant for people today, we should neither pursue it nor expect to receive it.

THE INDWELLING OF THE HOLY SPIRIT

One of the mistakes people today make is confusing passages that talk about the indwelling of the Holy Spirit with passages that deal with the baptism of the Holy Spirit. These are not the same. Just as all verses that talk about baptism are not referring to the baptism of the Holy Spirit, not all passages that refer to the indwelling of the Holy Spirit are talking about the baptism of the Holy Spirit. But what about all of those passages that tell us that the Holy Spirit dwells in us? Even if they do not refer to Holy Spirit baptism in the sense that the apostles and Cornelius experienced, does the Bible still not teach that the Holy Spirit nonetheless dwells within us? If so, what does this mean? This is an important question that needs to be addressed.

Numerous verses peppered throughout the New Testament emphatically teach that the Holy Spirit does indeed dwell within Christians. First Corinthians 3:16, for example, says, "Do you not know that you are a temple of God and that the Spirit of God dwells in you?" (NASV). In 1 Corinthians 6:19, the apostle Paul asks rhetorically, "Or do you not know that your body is a temple of the Holy Spirit who is in you?" (NASV). Romans 8:9 reminds us, "you are not in the flesh but in the Spirit, if indeed the Spirit of God dwells in you. But if anyone does not have the Spirit of Christ, he does not belong to Him" (NASV). Ephesians 5:18 even commands us to be "filled with the Spirit." Writing to his young friend Timothy, the apostle Paul exhorted, "Guard, through the Holy Spirit who dwells in us, the treasure which has been entrusted to you" (2 Tim. 1:14, NASV).[32] How much clearer could the New Testament be that the Holy Spirit dwells within Christians?

These are only a few of the many verses in the New Testament that tell us that the Holy Spirit dwells in Christians. The question, though, is not whether the Holy Spirit dwells in Christians, but how? In other words, what does it mean to say that the Holy Spirit dwells in Christians? In what sense does he dwell in us? To answer this question, we must look at other verses in the New Testament that talk about (1) God the Father dwelling in Christians, (2) God the Son dwelling in Christians, (3) God the Father dwelling in God the Son and God the Son dwelling in God the Father, (3) Christians dwelling in God the Father and God the Son, and (4) Christians dwelling in other Christians.

First John 4:12–16 states that God "dwells" in Christians "if we love one another" and "[dwell] in love" (KJV). Christians are said to be "a temple of the living God." Because of this, God said, "I will dwell in them and walk in them" (2 Cor. 6:16). Does this mean that God literally dwells and walks in us?[33]

In addition to God the father dwelling in Christians, God the Son also dwells in Christians, according to the scriptures. Romans 8:10 reminds the reader, "And if Christ is in you, the body is dead because of sin." Ephesians 3:17 teaches that Christ dwells in Christians' hearts "through faith." The apostle Paul reminded the Christians at Colossae that God was "pleased to make known what is the riches of the glory of this mystery among the Gentiles, which is Christ in you" (Col. 1:27).

Not only do the scriptures teach that God the Father and Christ the Son dwell in Christians, but the Bible also says that God the Father dwells in Christ the Son and that Christ the Son dwells in God the Father. On one occasion Jesus said that God the father was in him and he was "in the Father" (John 10:38). Speaking to his disciples, Jesus once asked, "Do you not believe that I am in the Father, and the Father in me? . . . Believe me that I am in the Father, and the Father is in me" (Jn. 14:10–11, NASV). Later, in the same context, Jesus revealed, "In that day you will know that I am in my Father, and you in Me, and I in you" (John 14:20, NASV).

First John 2:5 tells us that "we [Christians] know that we are in him [Christ]" if we keep his word. Later, John writes, that "If what you heard from the beginning abides in you, you also will abide in the Son, and in the Father" (vs. 24, NASV). First John 4:15–16 points out that "Whosoever shall confess that Jesus is the Son of God, God dwelleth in him and he in God . . . God is love; and he that dwelleth in love dwelleth in God, and God in him" (KJV).

These verses remind us that Christians dwell in both God the Father and Christ the Son as long as certain conditions are met. Moreover, 2 Corinthians 5:17 points out, "wherefore if any man is in Christ, he is a new creature." Romans 8:1 tells us that there is "no condemnation to them that are in Christ Jesus." Jesus once said—speaking figuratively, of course—"He who eats My flesh and drinks My blood abides in Me, and I in him" (John 6:56, NASV). Using the metaphor of a vine and its branches, Jesus told his disciples, "Abide in Me, and I in you. As the branch cannot bear fruit of itself unless it abides in the vine, so neither can you unless you abide in me. I am the vine, you are the branches; he who abides in Me, and I in him, he bears much fruit" (John 15:4–5, NASV). In the salutations of both letters that he wrote to the church at Thessalonica, the apostle Paul mentioned that Christians there were "in God the Father and the Lord Jesus Christ" (1 Thess. 1:1; 2 Thess. 1:1).

As if all of these dwellings were not enough, the Bible also says that Christians dwell in other Christians. In 2 Corinthians 7:3, for instance, the apostle Paul reminded the Corinthians that "you are in our hearts to die together and live together" (NASV). Paul also told the Philippian church something similar when he said, "I have you in my heart" (Phil. 1:7). Obviously, he did not mean this in a literal sense.

By now our heads may be spinning. Everyone seems to be dwelling in everyone. But the scriptures do not stop here. The Bible reveals that sin dwells in us, the word of God dwells in us, faith dwells in us, love dwells in us, truth dwells in us, and humans dwell in the teaching of Christ (see Rom. 7:17, Col. 3:16, 2 Tim. 1:5, 1 John 3:17, 2 John 2, and 2 John 9, respectively). The Bible even suggests that Satan dwelled in the church of Pergamum (Rev. 2:13). At this point, you may be saying, "Stop the merry-go-round and let me off!"

What do all of these dwellings mean? In his book *The God of the Bible*, Pratte asks, "If we can believe without confusion that the Father and Son dwell in us, why are we so confused by the fact the Holy Spirit dwells in us? If we can understand how the Father and Son dwell in us and we in them, then we can understand how the Spirit dwells in us, *since the same language is used for all these cases*" (emphasis mine).[34]

One of the first things that we should note is that unlike Holy Spirit baptism, the indwelling of the Holy Spirit was intended for all Christians of all ages, and began at the point of their conversion. Acts 5:32, for example, tells us that God has given the Holy Spirit "to them that obey him." The apostle Paul reminded the Romans that those who had a hope of salvation had the "love of God . . . shed abroad in our hearts through the Holy Spirit which was given unto us" (Rom. 5:5). Realistically, one cannot have a hope of salvation unless one is converted. When hope comes at the point of conversion, so does the indwelling of the Holy Spirit.

However, this does not mean that everyone who receives the Holy Spirit has miraculous powers, as faith healers would have us believe. In fact, in his book *The Holy Spirit and the Christian*, Jenkins goes so far as to say that "we do not believe that there is, or has to be, any sensible evidence of the Spirit's presence."[35] He further points out, "The New Testament never tells how anyone felt when he received the Holy Spirit."[36] Thus, "feelings, emotionalism, and non-rational behaviour"[37] should never be used to conclude that one has the Spirit of God in his or her life. Unlike what faith healers today teach, nowhere in the Bible are we told that Christian converts who had the indwelling of the Holy Spirit (and this included everyone) ever shook, laughed or cried uncontrollably, trembled, collapsed on the floor, or fell backward to the ground as if they had been "slain in the Spirit" as faith healers and others would have us believe. In fact, 1 Corinthians 14:32 teaches just the opposite—that "the spirits of the prophets are subject to the prophets; for God is not a God of confusion, but of peace." Furthermore, the Bible never even uses the expression "slain in the Spirit." As MacArthur rightly points out in his book *Strange Fire*, "being 'slain in the Spirit' is a modern charismatic invention. The practice is mentioned nowhere in the Bible; it is completely without scriptural warrant. The modern phenomenon has become such a common and popular spectacle that the average charismatic today takes it for granted, assuming it must have some kind of clear biblical or historical pedigree."[38] MacArthur further reveals that "even the pro-charismatic *Dictionary of Pentecostal and Charismatic Movements*" does not uphold the idea. Rather, it notes, "An entire battalion of Scripture proof texts is enlisted to support the legitimacy of the phenomenon, although Scripture plainly offers no support for the phenomenon as something to be expected in the normal Christian life."[39]

Just as nowhere in the scriptures are we told that one's inward feelings were ever a sign of the presence of the Holy Spirit, nowhere are we ever told that feelings were ever a sign of salvation either. As Jenkins further reminds us, it would be "illogical and unscriptural" to "assume . . . that feelings were an evidence of salvation" either in the New Testament or in our day and age.[40] Certainly, the Bible never likened the indwelling of the Holy Spirit to electricity or lightning, as some faith healers suggest. All of these points run counter to what faith healers teach and practice.

While those few who received Holy Spirit baptism (i.e., the apostles and Cornelius and his household) spoke in tongues, not all Christians in the first-century church who were filled with the Holy Spirit were able to speak in tongues or do any of the other spiritual gifts mentioned in 1 Corinthians 12 (vss. 1–11, 29–30). In this chapter Paul said that different people had different kinds of gifts. And what is more, speaking in tongues was the least valuable gift to possess (1 Cor. 12:28). Perhaps more important to understand, some people—in reality, most people in the early church—did not have any spiritual gift whatsoever. If we listen to faith healers, they would leave us with the impression that more people today possess miraculous, spiritual gifts than people in the first-century church had.

Furthermore, the Bible tells us that those in the early church that did have miraculous gifts received them only by the laying on of the apostles' hands, not merely by receiving the Holy Spirit (i.e., coming into fellowship with him) at conversion. For instance, the seven men who were chosen to serve tables in Acts 6 had the apostles' hands laid upon them. Afterward, the Bible says that Stephen, one of the men on whom the apostles laid their hands, was "full of grace and power [and] wrought great wonders and signs among the people" (vs. 8). Although some people argue that the apostles laid their hands on these men merely as an act of acceptance or approval, the context suggests otherwise. How could Stephen have done what the scriptures say he did, had the apostles not laid their hands upon him—even though the Bible says that Stephen was "full of faith and of the Holy Spirit" before the apostles ever touched him (vs. 5)? But being filled with the Holy Spirit did not necessarily mean that Stephen already had miraculous abilities any more than any other convert who received the Holy Spirit at conversion (Acts 5:32). If that were the case, why did not everyone who received the Holy Spirit at conversion have miraculous abilities? The same could be said about people today: there are plenty of people nowadays who are filled with the Spirit but have no miraculous powers whatsoever, through no fault of their own.

In Acts 8:14–24, after Philip the Evangelist baptized the Samaritans, the brethren in Jerusalem sent the apostles Peter and John to the city of Samaria to lay hands on them so that the Samaritans could perform miracles. In fact, this was so impressive to a man named Simon, who "saw that through the laying on of the apostles' hands the Holy Spirit was given, he offered them [Peter and John] money, saying Give me also this power, that on whomsoever I lay my hands, he may receive the Holy Spirit" (vss. 18–19). Note that Simon did not offer money to Philip, even though Philip was capable of performing miracles himself because he, too, had had the apostles' hands laid upon him in the same context that Stephen did (Acts 21:8; Acts 6:6). Rather, Simon offered money only to the apostles Peter and John, because he knew that they were the only ones who could impart miraculous gifts, not Phillip. Moreover, if Philip could have imparted the ability to perform miracles, why did the church at Jerusalem send Peter and John to Samaria?

In Acts 19, when the apostle Paul found twelve men at Ephesus who knew only the baptism of John, he baptized them "into the name of the Lord Jesus" and then "laid his hands upon them," after which "the Holy Spirit came on them and they spake with tongues and prophesied" (vss. 5–6). Had Paul not laid his hands upon them, they would not have been able to perform these miraculous gifts, even though they, like all other converts, in one sense had already received the Holy Spirit at conversion (Acts 5:32). When Acts 19:6 states that the Holy Spirit came upon the Ephesians only after Paul had laid his hands upon them, Luke is suggesting a different measure of the Holy Spirit than what they received at conversion (Acts 5:32)—one that now enabled them to perform miracles.

The apostle Paul reminded his young friend Timothy to "stir up the gift of God, which is in thee through the laying on of my hands" (2 Tim. 1:6). That was the only way Timothy would have been able to perform a miracle even though, like other Christians, he, too, had already received the indwelling of the Holy Spirit at conversion (2 Tim. 1:14).

Writing to the church at Rome, in a similar fashion, the apostle Paul confessed, "For I long to see you so that I may impart some spiritual gift to you, that you may be established" (Rom. 1:11, NASV). Why did not Paul impart this gift from a distance? Better still, why did he not just pray that this gift come upon them? Paul understood that he needed to be there physically for this miraculous ability to be imparted. Moreover, his reason for imparting it was so that they could be grounded in the faith. That was the point of miraculous gifts in the early church in the first place, as I pointed out in chapters 2 and 3.

The conclusion that we should draw from the New Testament is that once the apostles and those on whom the apostles imparted miraculous gifts died, miracles no longer existed. Once the apostles died, the ability to impart or receive spiritual gifts died with them. In his book *How Does the Holy Spirit Work in a Christian?* Pope rightly argues the following:

> The special role of the apostles was unique. They did not establish a chain of *apostolic succession* (as our Roman Catholic friends try to affirm). There is no Scriptural evidence that their authority as "ambassadors of Christ" (2 Corinthians 5:20) passed to others beyond their death. In the same way, the special ability bestowed upon them to lay hands upon others and distribute spiritual gifts, was not passed on to others upon their death. There is no Scriptural evidence that one who received a miraculous spiritual gift had the ability to "lay hands on" others in order to distribute such gifts. As a result, upon the death of the apostles the Scriptural means to distribute spiritual gifts came to an end. Upon the death of those who had received the "laying of the hands of the apostles" all miraculous spiritual gifts came to an end.[41]

So if the indwelling of the Holy Spirit does not mean that people today can perform miracles, what does it mean? In whatever way God the Father and God the Son dwell in Christians, or in whatever way Christians dwell in God the Father and God the Son or each other, so does the Holy Spirit. Pratte rightly argues that "Many people become completely flustered trying to grasp the idea that the Holy Spirit dwells in them, yet they seem to have no problem whatsoever with the fact the Father and Son also dwell in them!" He goes on to say that of all the passages in the Bible that talk about God and Christ dwelling in Christians and Christians dwelling in God and Christ or each other, "no one finds them particularly difficult or confusing. And no one assumes that these passages refer to some kind of direct, personal inhabiting of our bodies."[42]

When the scriptures say that deity is dwelling in humans and other deity (i.e., God and Christ in Christians, Christians in God and Christ and each other, and the Holy Spirit in Christians), they are merely suggesting that we have a relationship with deity and with each other. In other words,

Christians have fellowship with deity and with other Christians. The apostle John reminds us that if we "walk in the light . . . we have fellowship one with another" (1 Jn. 1:7)—that is, God with Christians and Christians with Christians. In fact we have fellowship not only with God but with Christ, the Holy Spirit, and with fellow Christians. In other words, we have fellowship both vertically and horizontally. There is nothing mysterious about any of these indwellings. While our personal spirits may dwell directly and literally in our bodies those of the Godhead do not any more literally dwell in our physical bodies than our personal spirit literally dwells within the Godhead. In fact Ephesians 3:17 tells us specifically that Christ dwells in Christians "through faith." Why should God the Father and God the Holy Spirit not also dwell in us in a similar manner? Along these lines, reasoning by analogy, Pratte raises some persuasive questions:

> Some people will argue at length that the Holy Spirit "personally" indwells Christians, yet they almost never argue that the Father and Son "personally" dwell in us or we in them. Why not? Why do we not see just as much effort to prove a personal indwelling of the Father and Son as for the Holy Spirit? Why not argue that we personally dwell in the Father and Son? Evidently we all know the Father and Son do not personally dwell in us, we in them, etc. So why conclude that the parallel language for the Spirit means a personal indwelling?[43]

When the apostle John wrote about the church at Pergamum, Revelation 2:13 records the words of Christ: "I know where you dwell, where Satan's throne is" (NASV). Did Christ mean that they had literally moved into Satan's palace? Was Satan's house literally at Pergamum? Or, when Christ said that "Satan dwells" "among you," did he mean that Satan had moved to Pergamum? Was he suggesting that Satan literally lived there? The answer to all of these questions is no. Christ neither meant that those at Pergamum lived under the same roof where Satan's throne was nor that Satan had moved in with them. In fact, John did not mean that Satan literally sat upon a throne at all. However, he did mean that Satan had a strong influence on the church at Pergamum. They were not the kinds of people they should have been, because they allowed evil to influence them. In short, they had a relationship with the devil that they should not have had. Just as those of Pergamum had a relationship with Satan who "dwells" there, Christians have a relationship with God the Father, God the Son, God the Holy Spirit, and other Christians when they dwell with each other.

LED BY THE SPIRIT OF GOD

If the Holy Spirit does not literally and personally indwell the Christian, but Romans 8:14 tells us, "For as many as are led by the Spirit of God, these are the sons of God," then how does this work? How does he lead? Does he lead in some miraculous, mysterious, "better felt than told" manner? A closer look at the scriptures will reveal that the Holy Spirit leads individuals through the Word—the Bible.

A number of verses in the Bible tell us what the Holy Spirit does. In fact, we would not even know how the Holy Spirit operates unless we had the Bible to tell us. Among other things, for example, the Bible reveals that the Holy Spirit teaches, begets, convicts the world of sin, bears witness, has power, sanctifies and justifies, gives life, has fellowship, speaks, saves and renews, testifies, and calls (see Neh. 9:30; John 3:5–8; John 16:8; Rom. 8:16; 1 John 5:7; Rom. 15:13; 1 Cor. 6:11; 2 Cor. 3:6; John 6:63; Phil. 2:1; 1 Tim. 4:1; Titus 3:5; 1 Pet. 1:10–12; Rev. 22:17, respectively). These are only a handful of the many things the Bible has to say about the work of the Holy Spirit. But how does he do these things? The very same ideas can also be said about scriptures.[44] For example, scriptures also teach, beget, convict the world of sin, bear witness, have power, sanctify and justify, give life, provide for fellowship, speak, save and renew, testify, and call (2 Tim. 3:16–17; James 1:18; 1 Cor. 4:15; Titus 1:9; Heb. 4:12; John 5:39; Rom. 1:16; Heb. 4:12; John 17:17; Gal. 2:16; Rom. 10:17; Phil 2:16; 1 John 1:1–7; 1 Tim. 4:6; James 1:21; John 5:39 [KJV]; 2 Thess. 2:14). Furthermore, just as the Bible commands to "be filled with the Spirit" (Eph. 5:18, NASV), it also commands to "Let the word of Christ dwell in you richly" (Col. 3:16). MacArthur explains the connection between these two commands:

> Thus, we can see that obeying the command to be filled with the Spirit does not involve emotional hype or mystical encounters. It comes from reading, meditating on, and submitting to the Word of Christ, allowing the Scriptures to permeate our hearts and minds. Said another way, we are filled with the Holy Spirit when we are filled with the Word . . . As we align our thinking with biblical teaching, applying its truth to our daily lives, we come increasingly under the Spirit's control.
>
> To be filled with the Spirit, then, is to yield our hearts to the authority of Christ, allowing His Word to dominate our attitudes and actions. His thoughts become the object of our meditation, His standards become our highest pursuit, and His will becomes our greatest desires.[45]

The Holy Spirit is not the Bible, and neither is the Bible the Holy Spirit. The Bible is the instrument or agent through which the Holy Spirit leads, though not through some inward impression laid upon the heart or in some other mysterious manner that I mentioned in chapter 5. The scriptures teach that it was the Holy Spirit who revealed the mind of God to the apostles, who wrote it down for people to read and follow (1 Cor. 2:10; Eph. 3:3–5). In Ephesians 6:17, as part of putting on "the whole armor of God" (vs. 13) the apostle Paul urged the Ephesian Christians to "take . . . the sword of the Spirit, which is the word of God." Why did Paul not say, "seek the baptism of the Holy Spirit to guide you into all truth" or some other similar expression? He did not tell them this because the word is the mechanism through which the Holy Spirit leads. Moreover, it was through the preaching of the gospel and the obedience to the gospel on the part of the listener that the Holy Spirit indwelled individuals in the first place (Gal. 3:2).

In an article titled "How the Spirit Indwells," Puckett rightly points out that it is "through the medium and power of the gospel [as revealed in the Bible] that the Holy Spirit affects the conviction and conversion of the alien sinner." After citing 1 Thessalonians 4:1–7, which teaches Christians things they should do "to walk and to please God" and to be sanctified, Puckett continues:

> The word of God . . . has called upon us to live lives of purity and holiness and sanctification, telling us how to live those lives. We don't need some additional influence. Spirituality is not developed within us by some mysterious, separate and apart indwelling of the Holy Spirit, but is developed within us through the power of the teaching of the word of the Lord. That word of God is sufficient to instruct us in everything that is needed to make our lives and our characters exactly what we ought to be.[46]

Second Thessalonians 2:13–14 remind us that "God hath . . . chosen you to salvation through sanctification of the Spirit and belief of the truth; whereunto he called you by our gospel, to the obtaining of the glory of our Lord Jesus Christ" (KJV). This verse mentions "sanctification of the Spirit" and the "gospel" in the same breath, implying that the Spirit works through the word in making us holy. Puckett rightly concludes that "the power and the conviction and conversion of the alien sinner is in the gospel," just as "the power for the development of the saved, the development of spirituality is in the same gospel."[47] No doubt this is why the apostle Paul urged Timothy to "give heed to reading, to exhortation, to teaching"—"doctrine," in the KJV—of the scriptures (1 Tim. 4:13).

The apostle Paul reminded the Romans that "I am not ashamed of the gospel: for it is the power of God unto salvation to every one that believeth; to the Jew first, and also to the Greek" (Rom. 1:17). We can see this power unfurled, for example, on the day of Pentecost, when the apostle Peter preached the first sermon of Christianity. After Peter had concluded the preaching of the gospel, Luke records, "Now when they [Peter's audience] heard this, they were pricked in their heart, and said unto Peter and the rest of the apostles, Brethren, what shall we do?" Thus, the Holy Spirit, through the preaching of the gospel, had "convict[ed] the world in respect of sin, and of righteousness, and of judgment" (John 16:8)—but not in a miraculous, mysterious manner. The writer of Hebrews echoes a similar sentiment about the power of the gospel when he asserts that "the word of God is living, and active, and sharper than any two-edged sword, and piercing even to the dividing of soul and spirit, of both joints and marrow, and quick to discern the thoughts and intents of the heart" (Heb. 4:12).

But one may be quick to point out that Romans 8:26–27 tell us that the Holy Spirit "maketh intercession for us [i.e., the saints]." Surely this means that the Holy Spirit miraculously and personally dwells within us? Kenneth Hagin, for example, suggests, "This [intercession] isn't something the Holy Ghost does apart from us. Those groanings come from inside us and escape our lips . . . He is sent to dwell in us as a Helper and an Intercessor."[48] Although scriptures teach us that the Holy Spirit makes intercession for us, we really are not told how he does this. We are merely told that he does. Furthermore, this passage does not require a direct, literal indwelling. The Holy Spirit could intercede on our behalf outside of our bodies. He does not have to physically dwell within us to accomplish this feat. Additionally, the scriptures tell us that Christ also makes intercession for us (Rom. 8:34; Heb. 7:25), yet why do we not hear people today argue that he too must physically dwell within us to accomplish this task?

Again, some may be quick to point out Romans 8:16, which states that "The Spirit himself beareth witness with our spirit, that we are children of God." Surely this must require a literal, miraculous indwelling. Actually, as I just pointed out, it is the Spirit who, through the Bible, tells us how to be "children of God." Our spirits tell us whether we have obeyed the commands of God, after we have read the Bible. Thus, the Holy Spirit, through the Bible and our spirit (by reading and following the Bible), bear witness with each other "that we are children of God." There is nothing mysterious about this process, and it certainly does not require some kind of literal, miraculous indwelling.

The last verse that I wish to deal with, which people sometimes use to prove that the Holy Spirit literally dwells within us and gives us miraculous abilities, is Mark 16:17–18, cited by Ernest Angley in the introduction of this chapter. There, speaking to his apostles, Christ affirmed, "And these signs shall accompany them that believe: in my name shall they cast out demons; they shall speak with new tongues; they shall take up serpents, and if they drink any deadly thing, it shall in no wise hurt them; they shall lay hands on the sick, and they shall recover." These prophecies were fulfilled on a number of occasions in the New Testament (see Acts 8:6–8; Acts 28:3–5; Acts 28:8–9, among others). Just as Joel did not have in mind birds, fish, animals, or even all humans when he said that God would "pour forth of my Spirit upon all flesh" (Acts 2:17), Christ did not mean that everyone who believed would be able to do all of these miraculous works mentioned in Mark 16:17–18. He was specifically referring to the apostles to whom he was speaking, because verse twenty suggests that they "went forth, and preached everywhere, the Lord working with them [the apostles], and confirming the word by the signs that followed." Even those in the first century who believed but who did not have the apostles' hands laid on them were not able to perform miracles. As I pointed out above, only the apostles and those on whom the apostles laid their hands were able to do these things. What both Christ and Joel (through Peter's preaching in Acts 2) were saying, in their respective contexts, was that miraculous abilities in a general sense would take place. The gifts of the Spirit would begin to be poured forth. Even so, we know that these miraculous abilities would happen only to a limited number of people for a limited amount of time, as I pointed out in chapters 2 and 3. So, Mark 16:17–18 does not prove that anyone today has miraculous abilities brought on either by an indwelling of the Holy Spirit or simply by believing and being baptized.

THE GIFT OF THE HOLY SPIRIT

In Acts 2:38, Peter commanded, "Repent, and each of you be baptized in the name of Jesus Christ for the forgiveness of your sins; and you will receive the gift of the Holy Spirit" (NASV). What is this gift of the Holy Spirit? After all, it was promised to all who would repent and be baptized. And people today are still repenting and being baptized. So, people today should still be receiving the gift of the Holy Spirit. But does this verse imply the ability to perform miracles like the apostles did after they received Holy Spirit baptism? Even if it does not, might it suggest an indwelling of the Holy Spirit, as discussed above, or does it mean something else?

The expression "gift of the Holy Spirit" is a rather nebulous phrase. Does it mean that the Holy Spirit is the gift, or does it mean that the Holy

Spirit is the giver of some gift, which is not actually named in the verse? Looking at the phrase by itself, one could conclude either interpretation. But which one is correct?

There are many who believe that the gift of the Holy Spirit is salvation that the Holy Spirit made possible by revealing the mind of God to the apostles (1 Cor. 2:10–13), who then preached and wrote down God's will. When we read and understand that will and follow it, then we can be saved. Thus, we have received a gift that the Holy Spirit gave. Drawing on Acts 2:39, which says, "For to you is the promise, and to your children, and to all that are afar off, even as many as the Lord our God shall call unto him," Puckett, for example, suggests that this "promise" and the "gift of the Holy Spirit" are the same thing. "Whatever the promise is, it extends to the Jews and their posterity, and to all Gentiles," he concludes. Therefore, whatever the "gift of the Holy Spirit" is, it too, "extends to the Jews and their posterity, and to all Gentiles."[49]

But what is "the gift of the Holy Spirit" that is involved in this promise? Puckett asks, "Is it the gift of 'Holy Ghost baptism?' . . . Do all who are 'called of God' receive Holy Ghost baptism? No! Such was never promised." Continuing his query, Puckett asks, "Is it the gift of 'miraculous powers?' Certainly not! Such were imparted [only] through the laying on of apostolic hands." He raises a third question: "Is the gift, then, the third Person of the godhead, the divine Being Himself, to dwell—actually and literally, directly, immediately, and without medium, completely separate and apart *as a person* in the physical bodies of all who repent and are baptized in the name of Jesus Christ for the remission of sins? If so where is that promise found?" Finally, Puckett asks, "Is the gift a blessing given by the Holy Spirit, and bestowed in keeping with a definite promise upon those who meet the conditions stipulated?" Whatever this blessing is, it "extends" to "as many as the Lord our God shall call."[50]

Citing Acts 2:17, where Peter, quoting the prophet Joel, says that God would "pour forth of my Spirit upon all flesh," Puckett argues that God pours forth from the Holy Spirit, not the Holy Spirit himself, "but the blessings and effects which proceed from the Spirit." These blessings are the "prophetic revelation" of Joel, which Peter reminded his audiences of on the day of Pentecost; "miraculous demonstration," which was also manifested on the day of Pentecost; and "spiritual salvation," which likewise came on the day of Pentecost. These, suggests Puckett, are "correctly called gifts of the Spirit." He concludes that, "salvation is a gift of (or from) the Holy Spirit, poured out along with and at the same time when divine revelation and miraculous demonstrations of the Spirit were given to usher in the gospel dispensation." He contends that even though supernatural gifts "were poured out for a limited time upon a select few for the purpose of inspiration, revelation, and confirmation," "salvation is a spiritual gift poured out for all time upon all who obey the gospel. This then is the gift [of the Holy Spirit] contained in 'the promise' of Acts 2:39," which extends to everyone, "to all that are afar off, even as many as the Lord our God shall call."[51]

Anticipating that some would charge Peter with redundancy if Acts 2:38 means what he says it means, Puckett argues, "'Remission of sins' and 'salvation' are not equivalents. Remission of sins is a condition of and precedent to salvation. Salvation is a consequent result of remission of sins. Hence, there is no repetition or redundancy in saying that in this passage salvation is 'the gift of the Holy Spirit.'" So, according to Puckett, the "gift of the Holy Spirit" in Acts 2:38 "is justification by faith or spiritual salvation."[52]

Others, however, take a different view. Jenkins, for example, points out that the Greek word for "gift" in Acts 2:38 is *dorea*, which is always singular when used in the New Testament. Whenever the Bible refers to "spiritual gifts," like those mentioned in 1 Corinthians 12, 13, and 14, the Greek word is *charisma*, which is plural. These terms, he suggests, should never be confused. Although Jenkins admits that when the Bible refers to the "gift of God" (John 4:10) or "the gift of Christ" (Eph. 4:7), it is referring to something that both God and Christ gave (hence, a gift), the meaning is different in Acts 2:38. Just as the "gift [*dorea*] of the Holy Spirit" that was given to Cornelius in Acts 10:45 was the Holy Spirit himself, the "gift [*dorea*[of the Holy Spirit" in Acts 2:38 was the Holy Spirit as well—even though it was not the baptism of the Holy Spirit like what Cornelius received. It was a different operation of the Holy Spirit—the indwelling of the Holy Spirit—but the Holy Spirit, nonetheless. While Jenkins readily admits that Acts 2:38 "is a difficult passage," he believes that "the Holy Spirit is the *gift* to those who repent and are baptized."[53]

Jenkins suggests that there are several benefits that a Christian enjoys as a result of having the indwelling of the Holy Spirit: (1) Christians are sealed—a sign of ownership—by the Holy Spirit (2 Cor. 1:21–22; Eph. 1:13–14); (2) Christians have the Holy Spirit as an "earnest" or down payment on salvation (2 Cor. 1:21–22; Eph. 1:13–14); (3) The Holy Spirit helps the Christian with his or her infirmities (Rom. 8: 26–27); (4) Christians have been promised "life . . . to your mortal bodies through his Spirit that dwelleth in you" (Rom. 8:11). In spite of this, none of these constitute a miraculous indwelling in Jenkins' thinking.[54]

We can also add that having the Holy Spirit dwell within a person (i.e., being in a proper relationship with the Holy Spirit) will produce the "fruit of the Spirit," which is "love, joy, peace, longsuffering, kindness, goodness, faithfulness, meekness, [and] self-control" (Gal. 5:22–23). MacArthur suggests, "When we consider the New Testament epistles, where believers are given prescriptive instruction for church life, we find that being filled with the Spirit is demonstrated not through ecstatic experiences but through the manifestation of spiritual fruit. In other words, Spirit-filled Christians exhibit the fruit of the Spirit . . . [T]hose who are Spirit-filled seek to please God by pursuing practical holiness."[55]

Pratte helps to bridge the two positions above—that the gift of the Holy Spirit is salvation, versus the gift of the Holy Spirit being the Holy Spirit himself. Although he believes that the "gift of the Holy Spirit" in Acts 2:38 "best fits the description of the *indwelling* of the Spirit," as opposed to salvation that the Holy Spirit makes possible (and certainly not Holy Spirit baptism), Pratte suggests that "since the indwelling is just fellowship with the Holy Spirit, this has the same effect [as salvation], since only those who have salvation have fellowship with the Spirit."[56] In any event, the gift of the Holy Spirit is not a literal, physical indwelling that causes one to be able to perform miracles such as speaking in tongues, healing people by laying on of hands, etc.

CONCLUSION

In this chapter I have tried to demystify a topic that heretofore has been not only enigmatic to people today but controversial as well. Perhaps it has been so controversial because people have sensationalized it. I have attempted to explain who the Holy Spirit is, what the baptism of the Holy Spirit is, what the indwelling of the Holy Spirit is, how one is led by the Spirit of God, and what the gift of the Holy Spirit is in Acts 2:38.

I have argued in this chapter that the Bible reveals the Holy Spirit to be a member of the godhead who is a living deity with emotions and cognitions, not a cold, impersonal force. I have attempted to show that the baptism of the Holy Spirit should not be confused with the indwelling of the Holy Spirit, and that it was given only to the apostles and Cornelius and his household for reasons that no longer exist. Thus, we should never pursue the baptism of the Holy Spirit nor expect to receive it. I have tried to show that even though Christians today do not receive the baptism of the Holy Spirit, the Bible assures us that Christians do indeed have the indwelling of the Holy Spirit, just as Christians have God the father, Christ the son, and other Christians dwelling in them. This dwelling is really a metaphor for an intimate relationship. I have also suggested that the Bible is the "sword of the spirit," and that it is through the Bible that the Spirit leads us today, not through some direct, miraculous, personal indwelling.

Finally, I have tried to offer two possible explanations for the gift of the Holy Spirit, which the apostle Peter promised to all who repent and are baptized. Along the way, I have attempted to show that whenever individuals in the early New Testament church were depicted as being able to perform a miracle, it was either through a direct baptism of the Holy Spirit (and that happened only to the apostles and to Cornelius and his household) or by the apostles laying their hands directly upon an individual to impart some miraculous gift. I suggested that often—indeed more often than not—people in the early church who had the indwelling of the Holy Spirit still did not possess any type of miraculous, spiritual gift.

While I have not systematically addressed in this chapter all of the issues surrounding spiritual gifts given to some in the first century by the Holy Spirit as mentioned in 1 Corinthians 12–14, I have suggested that spiritual gifts were given only to a limited number of people in the infant church, for the purpose of edification in the absence of written scripture and for a limited period of time. Certainly, the spiritual gifts mentioned in 1 Corinthians 12–14 should not be expected to occur in our day and age, because their purpose has ceased.

So, when one hears a faith healer like Kenneth Hagin, Kathryn Kuhlman, Ernest Angley, Benny Hinn, or anyone else make some sensational, outrageous claim about the Holy Spirit, prudence demands that we listen closely to what they are teaching so as not to be persuaded by something that the Bible really does not say. Just because they have national and international reputations and credibility with certain followers, this does not mean the rest of us who hear them ought to buy into what they are espousing. One should not throw open the doors of one's mind and yell, "Come on in; no one's at home!" If anything, we need to test what is being said against what the Bible actually teaches. Or as the apostle John writes, "believe not every spirit, but prove the spirits whether they are of God" (1 John 4:1). When we do so, I believe we will see that—just as in the claims about miraculous healings, demon possession, and the call of God—statements faith healers often make about the Holy Spirit do not always line up with what the scriptures really have to say.

8

Name It and Claim It: The Gospel of Health and Wealth

One Saturday morning a few months ago, I awoke unusually early and turned on the television. In the predawn darkness of my room, as I was surfing through the channels, I landed on a station that was airing a sermon being preached by forty-four-year-old Todd Coontz, founder and president of RockWealth Ministries, in Aiken, South Carolina. According to his website, Coontz is a "businessman, entrepreneur, television host, financial teacher, philanthropist, and best-selling author." Moreover, he is the "owner and president of *Coontz Investments & Insurance, Inc.*, billed as a "financial services firm" that has been "helping people make wise money decisions since 1992."[1] This morning, however, Coontz was preaching in a prerecorded program originally taped as part of *Inspiration Camp Meeting* at the Evangel World Center in Louisville, Kentucky.

While the title of his sermon was not immediately discernable, his message was loud and clear. "Three things happened at Calvary," boasted Coontz. "Jesus Christ died on the cross and resurrected to redeem us from sin." Jesus also "purchased our divine healing. I do not have to be sick any longer." Thirdly, "He purchased and bought your divine prosperity," which, according to Coontz, is something "almost nobody wants to talk about." Coontz promised those in attendance that "your best days are getting ready to happen." "I believe God is going to unlock a [financial] harvest that's never happened to you before," whether it be a business deal, a real estate transaction, or some other monetary investment. "You are going to defeat Satan." According to Coontz, God was going to give those within earshot of his voice an economic "breakthrough." In fact, he was so confident that he promised, "When others are being laid off, you'll get that promotion."[2]

But how was all of this supposed to happen? Because "God connects me to people who need a financial miracle," guaranteed Coontz, "I have an anointing on my life for increase." "Whoever I come into contact with is blessed," he assured his listeners. "When others are losing money in the stock market, you can be making money." And what is more, an individual's "financial miracle" could occur in as soon as twenty-four or seventy-two hours, but certainly within ninety days of sowing a seed if he or she would follow Coontz's advice.[3]

In an attempt to convince his followers of his message, Coontz focused on ten principles "that God promises you and I [sic]," which he extrapolated from Deuteronomy 28: "Geographical Blessings," "Family Heritage & Health," "Occupational Blessing," "Multiplication of Possessions," "Supernatural Increase," "Territorial Dominion," "Victory in [Every] Battle," "Godly Favor," "Financial Prosperity," and "Divine Promotion."[4] Forget the fact that Deuteronomy 28 is a record of a conversation between Moses and the ancient Israelites who were trudging their way to the Promised Land. Coontz was applying that message to people today with rhetorical verve and fluency.

Perhaps his most persuasive tactic was when he gave his personal testimony about his "FedEx/UPS" "miracles." Years ago, according to Coontz, he planted a seed of $1,000 on his credit card for "a triple favor" when he donated money to a ministry. He disclosed that "month after month after month after month" thereafter, he received a check in the mail from the FedEx delivery driver. On another occasion, twenty-four hours after sowing a financial seed, he received a check from a business man for $30,000, hand-delivered by none other than the people in brown—UPS.[5]

After telling these stories, Coontz called for 1,189 individuals (this number is apparently the number of chapters in the Bible, according to Coontz) to call in and pledge $1,000.[6] "You're going to have miracle after miracle after miracle," he promised, "if you plant this . . . seed." Not only would "Satan give back to you what you've lost," but "God will give you seven-fold what Satan has stolen from you." "Favor will explode in your life," Coontz promised. He even guaranteed some of his listeners "a real estate miracle" if they were to plant a seed of $1,000. He urged individuals to call in "quickly" in "swift obedience" and tell the operators standing by that "I am one of the 1,189 people" whom he was imploring to donate.

Sounding more like the emcee of a phone-a-thon than a preacher, Coontz urged "thirty or forty of you who are hesitating" to sow the seed any way "even though your account is down." God would bless them. Even though "I can't explain it," disclosed Coontz, "when you connect with me, your financial life will change."[7] While he was imploring his listeners to call in with their pledges, the names of individuals who apparently had already donated began to scroll across the bottom of the screen for viewers to see. No doubt, this was another one of his techniques to persuade people to contribute money to his ministry.

Coontz is only one of many in a long line of preachers, several of whom were faith healers, to teach what he and others refer to merely as "Seed-Faith." The idea is, plant a seed (usually making a financial contribution to some ministry); reap a financial harvest. Others have sometimes referred to this notion as the health and wealth gospel or the abundant life theory. Bowman, for example, writes that "The Abundant Life theory, briefly stated, says that when God promised to atone for man he promised to save him from his sins, to cure the physical diseases of his body, and to make financial prosperity a reality in his life."[8]

One of the most famous faith healers of the entire twentieth century to espouse this doctrine was Oral Roberts. In fact, it was Oral Roberts who had the greatest influence on Todd Coontz. In their coauthored book, *The Miracle of Seed-Faith*, published in 2009, the same year Roberts died, Coontz discloses how, sitting in Roberts' home one evening in 2008, "I could feel something dynamic was happening. I knew that God had joined our hearts and lives together, that this was a once-in-a-lifetime opportunity—a friendship that would begin to nurture and grow, even to the writing of this book." It was that night that the two of them discussed "Roberts' 31 Secrets of Seed-Faith and how they have forever changed my [Coontz's] life."[9]

Coontz discloses that when he asked Roberts how he handled individuals who criticized him for his believe in "Seed-Faith," Roberts turned the question back on him and asked, "What are you doing now?" "Well, Dr. Roberts," he responded, "I am persuaded about Seed-Faith. Nobody can talk me out of it." Roberts then looked at Coontz and replied, "No one has been able to talk me out of it for 61 years either."[10]

Roberts claims that he first discovered the principles of Seed-Faith in 1947, when he was only twenty-nine years old and pastoring a church in Enid, Oklahoma, while attending the now-defunct Phillips University. He discloses that he was "living on the edge of poverty" with his wife and the first two of his four children in a two-bedroom house with another couple and their children, when he sowed his "$55 a week" check toward the "down payment on a parsonage." After his congregants saw him "lay it on the altar," he writes, "nearly everyone present rushed forward and placed their gifts alongside mine." Roberts admits, "Seed-Faith was a term I had never known before. I had no idea I was sowing a seed out of my need (and those with me) for a desired result." He reveals that seven hours later, an Oklahoma farmer named Art Newfield knocked on his door at 4:00 in the morning, "getting me out of bed and placing four $100 bills in my hand" toward the purchase of a new home. The farmer, who was sowing a seed of faith himself, said, "This is not just money; it is a seed for a harvest for me to save my farm." A year later, according to Roberts, Newfield "was once again a prosperous farmer and was very successful materially and spiritually.[11]

Although not a faith healer in the traditional sense as discussed in chapter 1, one of the best-known preachers today to teach the gospel of prosperity is the Texas-born Joel Osteen. Osteen, who once attended Oral Roberts University, where he studied television and radio, began his ascent to prominence among contemporary televangelists shortly after the death of his father John Osteen, who passed away from a heart attack on January 23, 1999, at the age of seventy-seven. Two weeks later, Joel Osteen was thrust into the pulpit of the 7,500-seat Houston-based Lakewood Church, which his father had begun, even though he had only preached for the first time on January 17, 1999. Later that year he was named Senior Pastor.

With Joel Osteen at the helm, in time, the Lakewood Church would grow to 16,000 members. On July 16, 2005, after a $95 million renovation, the church moved into the Compaq Center, the old home of the NBA's Houston Rockets. According to the Lakewood Church's website, today Osteen preaches live each week to over 38,000 attendees. His weekly television program is seen by over 20 million individuals a month and is carried in over 100 countries in the world. According to this website, no other "inspirational figure" in the United States is watched more often than he is. Osteen is also author of several best-selling books. In 2006, Barbara Walters named him as one of the "10 Most Fascinating People" of that year, and *Church Report Magazine* selected him as the "Most Influential Christian in 2006."[12]

Osteen is probably best known for his positive, upbeat messages, among which is the idea that God wants his people to prosper financially. For example, in his best-selling book *Your Best Life Now: Seven Steps to Living at Your Full Potential*, Osteen writes, "God wants to increase you financially, by giving you promotions, fresh ideas, and creativity."[13] He believes that there "is a seed within you trying to take root. That's God trying to get you to conceive. He's trying to fill you with so much hope and expectancy that the seed will grow and bring forth a tremendous harvest." Osteen teaches that an individual can be "set free" from sicknesses, "all kinds of addictions," and "all kinds of bad habits." "You may be struggling financially, in all kinds of debt, but this is the time for promotion. This is your time for increase. Friend, if you will get in agreement with God, this can be the greatest time of your life," he assures his readers.[14]

In his book *Bad Religion, How We Became a Nation of Heretics*, *New York Times* columnist Ross Douthat points out that Osteen and others are "heirs to a particular strain of prosperity preaching, which has its origin in the late-nineteenth-century movement known as New Thought." Douthat defines the New Thought Movement as "a loosely affiliated collection of ministers, authors, activists, and organizations, united by their belief in the extraordinary potential of the human mind." According to Douthat, these "practitioners argued that mental and spiritual realities shaped material events, that God (or 'Infinite Intelligence,' to the more secular-minded) pervaded the universe, and that the physical realities that human beings experienced—good health and bad, bankruptcy and success—had their origins in the mental and metaphysical spheres." This meant that good health could be accomplished through prayer and that financial wealth could be attained through thinking positively, if a person were to line up the "divinity" in one's self with the "divinity" of the universe.[15]

The many individuals who were part of this movement included L. Ron Hubbard, founder of the Church of Scientology, who died in 1986; Mary Baker Eddy, founder of the Church of Christ, Scientist (commonly referred to simply as Christian Science), who died in 1910; and a little-known New England preacher by the name of E. W. Kenyon, who died in 1948. According to Douthat, Kenyon had a profound effect upon Kenneth Hagin, another adherent of the health and wealth gospel. In fact, Douthat suggests that Hagin plagiarized "huge chunks" of what he taught from Kenyon. Likewise, McConnell contends that "Hagin plagiarized in word and content the bulk of his theology from E. W. Kenyon. All of the Faith teachers, including Kenneth Hagin and Kenneth Copeland, whether they admit it or not, are the spiritual sons and grandsons of E. W. Kenyon," who "formulated every major doctrine of the modern Faith Movement."[16] Moreover, Hagin influenced millions with his preaching, including John Osteen, father of Joel Osteen, and contemporary televangelist Kenneth Copeland.

It was not uncommon to hear Hagin, the father of the contemporary faith movement, say things like, "Christians should have super-prosperity and super-success!" In fact, Hagin was so bold as to command it from God, not merely to pray for it.[17]

Kenneth Copeland, who was greatly influenced by both Kenneth Hagin and Oral Roberts (Copeland was once Roberts's airplane pilot and chauffer, which gave him "constant exposure" to Roberts's teachings [18]), also taught the doctrine of abundant life through "positive confession," the idea that God will grant affluence and health to those who verbalize their faith.[19]

Perhaps the results of "positive confession" are best articulated in Copeland's magazine *Believer's Voice of Victory*. Each issue is saturated with the idea of Christian prosperity. For instance, Copeland says, "Jesus will teach you how to prosper. I don't care who you are. . . . Jesus will teach you how to be well, spirit, soul, and body, regardless of your circumstances."[20] Moreover, he writes, "God has provided a success principle in His Word whereby you may prosper spiritually, mentally, emotionally, physically, financially, and socially."[21] He suggests, "The body of Christ should be the wealthiest . . . people in all of the world, including and most especially in the area of finances."[22] Copeland teaches that Christians should be free of diseases and financial woes when he asks, "Is there a mountain in your life that needs to be moved? Is it a mountain of sickness, disease, financial lack or family trouble? The Word has the answers and all we must do is learn how to receive from God."[23] He urges his followers not to grow discouraged: "Don't give up if your seeds are still in the beginning stages. Just keep watering and nurturing the seeds and eventually they will grow and produce results."[24]

The above figures are only a handful of preachers who believe that God has promised his people health and wealth. And for every faith healer or televangelist espousing this doctrine, there are thousands lined up behind them, willing to follow blindly along. Citing Allen's book *The Future Church*, MacArthur points out, for instance, that "prosperity theology is 'a defining feature of all Pentecostalism' such that 'majorities of Pentecostals exceeding 90 percent in most countries hold to these beliefs.'"[25] He further reveals that even though "almost nine of every ten Pentecostals live in poverty, the prosperity gospel continues to lure people into the movement."[26] Perhaps it is *because* there is so much poverty among Pentecostals that this doctrine is so appealing. In other words, planting a seed of faith is like playing a spiritual lottery. Adherents to the theory give money often in hopes of reaping a tenfold return.

The idea of God promising an abundant life to those who have enough faith—like other theological concepts taught by faith healers—raises the question, has God really promised his followers health and wealth? What do the scriptures really have to say about this doctrine? Moreover, if the Bible does not guarantee physical well-being and financial prosperity, what—if anything—does it promise that Christians can expect to receive from God? These are the questions I will attempt to answer in this chapter.

WHAT THE BIBLE TEACHES ABOUT HEALTH

When we take a look at what the scriptures really have to say about a Christian's health, we are met with a number of examples that scream just the opposite of what the above faith healers and televangelists espouse. In 2 Timothy 4:20, for example, the apostle Paul reminds us that "Trophimus I left at Miletus sick." In Philippians 2, Paul explains to the Philippians how he wanted "to send to you Epaphroditus, my brother and fellow-worker and fellow-soldier" but that "he was sick nigh unto death." In fact, Epaphroditus was in such bad shape physically that Paul used the phrased "nigh unto death" twice to explain his pitiful condition (Phil. 2:25–30). Additionally, Paul once directed his young Christian brother Timothy to "use a little wine for the sake of your stomach and your frequent aliments" (2 Tim. 5:23, NASV). It appears, then, that even Timothy, who possessed the ability to perform miracles (2 Tim. 1: 6), on more than one occasion did not enjoy the greatest of health. Sickness appeared to afflict the faithful in the early New Testament church just as it affects Christians nowadays. Eventually, everyone dies.

Even the apostle Paul himself may not have enjoyed the greatest of health. As I pointed out in chapter 6, Paul revealed that "there was given to me a thorn in the flesh, a messenger of Satan to buffet me" so that he "should not be exalted overmuch." Three times he prayed to God to remove it from him, but it was not to be. Paul had to live with whatever this thorn in the flesh was (2 Cor. 12:7–9). This "thorn in the flesh" could have been a physical ailment, or it could have been persecution. The word for "infirmities" (KJV) or "weaknesses" (ASV) in this context is from the Greek *astheneia*. Strong suggests that this could be translated "malady," "frailty," "disease," "infirmity," "sickness," or "weakness." But whatever it was, it hardly qualifies as the abundant life that so many people today are preaching. In fact, the notion of an abundant life, as defined by contemporary faith healers, was the furthest thing from Paul's mind.

On one occasion, Paul explained to the readers of his first epistle to the Corinthians, "we are pressed on every side, yet not straitened, perplexed, yet not unto despair; pursued, yet not forsaken; smitten down, yet not destroyed; always bearing about in the body the dying of Jesus, that the life also of Jesus may be manifested in our body." Paul went on to say that "we who live are always delivered unto death for Jesus' sake, that the life also of Jesus may be manifested in our mortal flesh." Once Paul even said that his "outward man [i.e., his body]" was "decaying," not improving (2 Cor. 4:8–16). For Paul, the body this side of heaven was corrupt, dishonorable, and weak. In other words, our physical bodies are prone to sicknesses, ailments, and maladies. Elsewhere, Paul wrote to the Galatian churches that "I bear branded on my body the marks of Jesus" (Gal. 6:17). Admittedly, while all of these bodily hardships that Paul discusses might be a result of beatings or other forms of persecutions, rather than sicknesses and diseases, these verses hardly sound like the abundant life that faith healers and other Charismatics are talking about. If there was a gospel of health and wealth in the first century, the apostle Paul, by his own admissions, certainly did not enjoy it.

Regarding the above examples, Bowman rightly contends:

> It should be easy to see that good health is not a part of the plan of redemption by looking at the maladies of the special servants of the Lord. . . . These were men of God; redeemed men; men who were teaching others about the atonement and who were possessed in many instances with the power to heal people from sickness and diseases, and yet they themselves did not enjoy perfect health.[27]

He goes on to argue that "If freedom from sickness and disease is part of the atonement then all men who receive the benefits of Christ's provision should receive it. Forgiveness of sin is universal, so should be the healing of the body. But it is not so. Why are there daily hospital admissions by thousands who claim to have accepted the salvation that is in Christ? Is healing on demand a part of the atonement? Experience alone would seem to deny it."[28]

One is therefore forced to ask, if life is supposed to be so abundant for people of faith, why do so many suffer hardships? Why does everyone eventually die? How long is the abundant life supposed to be in effect—six months, one year, twenty years, eighty years? Why should it be longer for some and not for others? The scriptures reveal a different picture than what faith healers would have us believe. Job, for example, once said, "Man, that is born of a woman, Is of few days, and full of trouble" (Job 14:1). In other words life is short and difficult, even for people of faith. In conclusion, in his article "The Work of the Spirit: A Health and Wealth Gospel?" Hilliard argues, "Even a casual perusal of the Scriptures shows that good health is not a part of God's plan for redemption."[29]

WHAT THE BIBLE TEACHES ABOUT WEALTH

If the Bible is clear about the fact that people of faith should not expect to always possess great health, it is even clearer about what to expect when it comes to material possessions. To be fair, the Bible does tell us that God will provide the physical needs of his people. One need look no further than Jesus's Sermon on the Mount to establish this. There he told his listeners not to be "anxious, saying, What shall we eat? or, What shall we drink? or, Wherewithal shall we be clothed?" After reminding his audience that God knows their needs, he exhorted them to "seek first His kingdom and His righteousness, and all these things [i.e., food, clothing, shelter] will be added to you" (Matt. 6:31–33, ASV & NASV). Similarly, the apostle Paul told the Philippians that "my God shall supply every need of yours according to his riches in glory in Christ Jesus" (Phil. 4:19).

But having one's basic needs met is a far cry from the gospel of health and wealth, whereby individuals are led to believe that they will essentially be wealthy if they plant the right seeds in the right places and stay patient. On the contrary, Jesus—the very founder of Christianity and the man who the scriptures say, "has nowhere to lay his head" (Matt. 8: 20, NASV)—cautioned that "You cannot serve God and wealth" (Matt. 6:24, NASV). And while the Bible does not necessarily condemn possessing money per se, it never promises us that we will have an overabundance of it either. To the contrary, the Bible warns against the "love of money." The apostle Paul had the following to say, for example:

> But godliness with contentment is great gain; for we brought nothing into the world, for neither can we carry anything out; but having food and covering we shall be therewith content. But they that are minded to be rich fall into a temptation and a snare and many foolish and hurtful lusts, such as drown men in destruction and perdition. For the love of money is a root of all kinds of evil; which some reaching after have been led astray from the faith, and have pierced themselves through with many sorrows. (1 Tim. 6:6–10)

Paul concluded this chapter with these words: "Charge them what are rich in this present world, that they be not highminded, nor have their hope set on the uncertainty of riches, but on God, who giveth us richly all things to enjoy; that they do good, that they be rich in good works, that they be ready to distribute, willing to communicate [i.e., share]" (1 Tim. 6:17–18).

Likewise, James warns against the corrupting influence of riches:

> Come now, you rich, weep and howl for your miseries which are coming upon you. Your riches have rotted and your garments have become moth-eaten. Your gold and your silver have rusted; and their rust will be a witness against you and you will consume your flesh like fire. It is in the last days that you have stored up your treasure! Behold, the pay of the laborers who mowed your fields, and which has been withheld by you, cries out against you; and the outcry of those who did the harvesting has reached the ears of the Lord of Sabaoth. Ye have lived luxuriously on the earth and led a life of wanton pleasure; you have fattened your hearts in a day of slaughter. (James 5:1–5, NASV)

James is not necessarily describing the Christians to whom he is writing. Instead, he is probably writing about worldly people for the benefit of his Christian audience. Like the apostle Paul, he is describing the dangers of putting one's faith in riches, in the hope that his Christian readers might avoid the same pitfall. The bottom line is that scriptures warn us against setting out to become wealthy.[30] Hebrews 13:5 teaches us, "Make sure that your character is free from the love of money, being content with what you have; for He Himself has said, 'I will never desert you, nor will I ever forsake you'" (NASV).

But how does one reconcile the above verses with what he or she actually sees in the scriptures? To be sure, many people of faith throughout the Bible possessed much of this world's goods. Abram (whose name was later changed to Abraham) and Lot, his nephew, for instance, had so much that, while they were traveling together, "the land was not able to bear them . . . for their substance was great so that they could not dwell together." The scriptures say that "Abram was very rich in cattle, in silver, and in gold." "Lot also . . . had flocks, and herds, and tents" (Gen. 13:1–6). In spite of this, they were both still very godly men. In fact, Abraham is even referred to as the "father" of the faithful and "the friend of God" (James 2:21–23).

There were other godly individuals besides Abraham and Lot who also possessed great wealth: Isaac, Jacob, Joseph, Job, David, and Hezekiah, for instance. The Bible says that Isaac "waxed great, and grew more and more . . . and he had possessions of flocks, . . . herds, and a great household; and the Philistines envied him" (Gen. 26:13–14). Jacob, too, "increased exceedingly, and had large flocks, and maid-servants and men-servants, and camels and asses" (Gen. 30:43). Jacob's son Joseph eventually rose to second in command of Egypt. Even before this occurred, the Bible says that "Jehovah was with Joseph, and he was a prosperous man" (Gen. 39:2). God described Job, who had great wealth, as "a perfect and an upright man, one that feareth God, and turneth away from evil." He said of him, "for there is none like him in the earth" (Job 1:1–8). God called David, the second king of Israel, who had everything at his beck and call, "a man after mine own heart" (Acts 13:22, KJV; 1 Sam. 13:14). The scriptures say of Hezekiah, a king of Judah during the divided kingdom, that "he clave to Jehovah; he departed not from following him, but kept his commandments," so much so "that after him was none like him, among all the kings of Judah, nor among them that were before him" (2 Kings 18:6). So, in spite of their great wealth, these individuals remained loyal to God.

Possessing material wealth is not necessarily a problem, depending on how one handles it. The trouble comes, however, when one is "minded to be rich." When one's focus in life is on making money purely for the sake of making money to become wealthier, one's priorities are misplaced, which is why Christ said "You cannot serve God and wealth." Such a person "will hate the one, and love the other; or else he will hold to one, and despise the other" (Matt. 7:24).

In Matthew 19:23–26, Jesus warned that it "is hard for a rich man to enter into the kingdom of heaven." In fact, he said that "it is easier for a camel to go through a needle's eye, than for a rich man to enter into the kingdom of God." As I pointed out in chapter 6, the "needle" under consideration is a sewing needle, not a large gate as some have suggested (*needle* is translated from *raphis*, meaning "to sew").[31] In reality, it is impossible for a camel to go through the eye of a needle, yet Jesus said that this was more likely to occur than for a rich man to make it to heaven.

When Jesus's disciples heard this, they were perplexed, asking, "Who then can be saved?" He replied, "With men this is impossible; but with God all things are possible." This was because Jesus did not have in mind the quantity of one's possessions, but one's attitude toward those possessions, relative to one's attitude toward God. If one has the right attitude toward his or her belongings, there is nothing wrong with owning things, including money. In fact, the apostle Paul once commanded, "Let him that stole steal no more; but rather let him labor, working with his hands the thing that is good, that he may have whereof to give to him that hath need" (Eph. 4:28). This is the attitude that one should have, in spite of the fact that one might possess many material things. Not to possess a certain amount of money would not allow an individual to do what the apostle Paul commanded—to have so that we might be able to help those who have not.

In realty the Bible never condemns riches from the standpoint of how much one owns. If that were the case, then how could Abraham, Lot, Isaac, Jacob, Joseph, Job, David, Hezekiah, and others be considered faithful servants of God, since they possessed so much of this world's goods? If possessing things, in and of itself, were sinful, these individuals would all have been condemned merely on the basis of what they owned.

In the Bible, being "rich" is a qualitative notion. It is a matter of the heart, not the wallet. What is important is not how much money one has (if so, what is that amount?), but what one does with the money that one does have. From a Christian perspective, one can be condemned with only five dollars in one's pocket just as easily as one can be condemned with five thousand or five hundred thousand dollars, if one is not willing to share it with others who may be in need. That person has become covetous when he or she selfishly hoards the money to him- or herself. Money—in this case only five dollars—has become one's idol. This is the type of "riches" the Bible condemns. It is a direct affront to what Jesus taught in his Sermon on the Mount when he said, "Give to him who asks of you, and do not turn away from him who wants to borrow from you" (Matt. 5: 42, NASV). Christians should be some of the most benevolent individuals in the world, regardless of whether they have much or little. In fact, Jesus commended the woman who had only "two mites" to her name, but was willing to give it back to the Lord (Luke 21:1–4). She was applauded for her unselfish sacrifice.

On one occasion, when a wealthy "young man" came to Jesus, asking him what he should do that he "may have eternal life," Jesus told him to "keep the commandments." "Which?" the young man asked. Jesus then listed a number of them: "Thou shalt not kill, Thou shalt not commit adultery, Thou shalt not steal, Thou shalt not bear false witness, Honor thy father and thy mother; and, Thou shalt love thy neighbor as thyself." "All of these have I observed from my youth," assured the young man. Jesus responded, "If you wish to be complete, go and sell your possessions and give to the poor, and you will have treasure in heaven; and come, follow Me" (NASV). The scriptures say that "when the young man heard the saying, he went away sorrowful; for he was one that had great possessions" (Matt. 19:16–22; see also Mark 10:17–22).

Jesus never said that the rich man's problem was how much money he had. His problem was his attitude toward his money. His money had become his world. Jesus wanted the young man to put him first in his life, not his money. The point of this story is that Jesus wants whatever is in the way of serving him to be removed from one's life. This underscores the point that the gospel can sometimes be very demanding. On one occasion,

Jesus said, "If any man would come after me, let him deny himself, and take up his cross daily, and follow me" (Luke 9:23).

In spite of the above discussion on what the Bible says about the quantity of one's possessions, contrary to what some faith teachers espouse, it still never promises that the faithful will be financially wealthy in this life. The reality is that most people will not be, especially if they live in a country where the economy is weak. In fact, some individuals—even faithful servants of God—may be poor. This was certainly the case with one of the greatest apostles of the New Testament.

In 1 Corinthians 4:10–12, the apostle Paul writes, "Even unto this present hour we both hunger, and thirst and are naked, and are buffeted and have no certain dwelling place." One is tempted to ask, "What's wrong with you, Paul? Have you not heard about the doctrine of abundant life? Why haven't you taken advantage of it?" In his second letter to the Corinthians, Paul writes about how poor the brethren in Macedonia were, yet even in their "deep poverty" they gave liberally for the poor saints at Jerusalem (2 Cor. 8:1–4; see Acts 11:27–29 on the famine that affected Christians in Judaea). Apparently neither the Macedonian Christians nor the poor saints at Jerusalem had ever heard of the abundant life theory espoused by faith healers today, or else why would they—along with the apostle Paul—have been so financially destitute?

In the same context where he reminded the Corinthians about the Macedonian brethren's poverty, Paul went on to say, "For you know the grace of our Lord Jesus Christ, that though he was rich, yet for your sake he became poor, so that you through his poverty might become rich" (2 Cor. 8:9, NASV). The idea here is not—as Abundant Life teachers would have us believe—that through the poverty of Christ, Christians would be wealthy financially. Rather, Paul was suggesting that Christians would be spiritually rich because Christ "counted not the being on an equality with God a thing to be grasped"—that is, held on to—but "emptied himself, taking the form of a servant, being made in the likeness of men" (Phil. 2:6–7).[32] This is the same person, by the way, who, as I noted earlier, when he was on earth, said that he "has nowhere to lay His head" (Luke 9:58, NASV). Apparently, Jesus himself had never heard of the gospel of health and wealth either.

Instead of Christians trying to amass more of this world's goods, they should have the attitude expressed in Proverbs 30:8–9: "Give me neither poverty nor riches; Feed me with the food that is my portion ["needful for me" in the ASV]: That I not be full and deny You, and say, 'Who is the Lord?' Or that I not be in want and steal, And profane the name of my God" (NASV). For one to possess this attitude, he or she should "Set your mind on the things that are above, not on the things that are upon the earth" (Col. 3:2). Similarly, Jesus taught, "Do not store up for yourselves treasures on the earth, where moth and rust destroy, and where thieves break in and steal. But store up for yourselves treasures in heaven, where neither moth nor rust destroys, and where thieves do not break in or steal; for where your treasure is, there your heart will be also" (Matt. 6:19–20, NASV). The truth is, Jesus taught just the opposite of the Abundant Life theory.

Let me say, before moving to the next section, that in spite of what the scriptures say regarding "the love of money" being the "root of all kinds of evil" (1 Tim. 6:10), I am not suggesting that there is necessarily any virtue in being poor either. Just because one is poor does not make a person attractive to God. Some of the meanest, most corrupt people on earth are poor. Let the point be clear: one's status before God simply is not determined on the basis of how much money one possesses—whether little or great—but whether one has obeyed the gospel and has the right attitude toward both God and money.

PROOF TEXTS EXAMINED

One of the rhetorical strategies that faith healers employ, as I observed in chapter 1, is to cite verses from the Bible in support of their position. They attempt to do this with regard to the Abundant Life theory as well. Moreover, this strategy works on many people because it is sometimes confusing to keep straight what the Bible actually teaches on this topic, especially since faith healers can be so adamant. The truth is, there is really nothing wrong with this strategy as long as the verses being used actually say what faith healers claim they say. However, as we shall see, none of these verses actually teaches what faith healers say they teach. It looks as if faith healers have concocted an idea and then gone searching for scriptures that, on their face, appear to support the principle being taught. John 10:10 is one of them.

In John 10:10, Jesus said, "I am come that they might have life, and that they might have it more abundantly" (KJV). Citing this verse, Kenneth Hagin argues, "For too long the Church has been weakness-minded, sickness-minded, inferiority-minded, trouble-minded, and poverty-minded . . . The Church has operated more or less on a psychology of unbelief, which has robbed believers of vibrant Christian faith and living. It has robbed us of the abundant life Jesus intended us to have."[33] But did Jesus really mean, as Hagin suggests, that he came so that individuals might have an abundant life of health and prosperity in the here and now?

Bowman correctly points out that the "context in which this passage is set shows that the abundant life to which he refers is not physical at all, but eternal life." In John 10:28, for example, Jesus promised, "I give unto them [his followers] eternal life." Bowman explains that Jesus is "using the same figure of the shepherd and the sheep" in verses 27–28 that he used in verses 10–11. "The abundant life he here explains . . . is eternal life and does not refer to man's physical well-being," Bowman argues; "I do not deny that God provides for his own, but I do vehemently deny that the abundant life he provides is one free from disease or devoid of financial distress."[34]

A second popular group of verses among faith healers used to prove the gospel of health and wealth is Galatians 6:7–9. In fact these verses can be found multiple times throughout Oral Roberts' book *The Miracle of Seed-Faith*. They state, "Be not deceived; God is not mocked: for whatsoever a man soweth, that shall he also reap. For he that soweth unto his own flesh shall of the flesh reap corruption; but he that soweth unto the Spirit shall of the Spirit reap eternal life. And let us not be weary in well-doing: for in due season we shall reap, if we faint not." Roberts argues that this verse means, "Sow a financial seed into good soil—for a good purpose—and it will return back to you multiplied. Likewise, do a good deed for a good purpose and it will come back to you in due season, also multiplied." Neither of these ideas could be further from the truth.

In this context, Paul is specifically talking about how the things that one does in this life will have a bearing on one's afterlife. The principle is simple. If one sows to the flesh, one will reap corruption (i.e., condemnation). If one sows with the Spirit of God in mind (i.e., the things of the Spirit) he or she "shall reap eternal life." How much clearer can Paul be? So, while Paul is indeed talking about sowing and reaping, he is not talking about sowing financial seeds or other deeds that might benefit someone socially down the road in this life. He is talking about deeds that we commit that will have a bearing on our "eternal life," not on our present situation.

Furthermore, when Paul says that we will reap if we faint not, he is suggesting something similar to what Christ said, as recorded by the apostle John in Revelation: "Be faithful until death, and I will give you the crown of life" (Rev. 2:10, NASV). After discussing the miserable hardships that many people of faith had undergone in this life, yet remained faithful to God, the writer of Hebrews concludes, "Therefore let us also, seeing we are compassed about with so great a cloud of witnesses, lay aside every weight, and the sin which doth so easily best us, and let us run with patience the race that is set before us" (Heb. 12:1).

One might argue, if Galatians 6:7–9 does not support the doctrine of abundant life, surely 2 Corinthians 9:6–7 does. There the apostle Paul makes a similar argument when he says, "he who sows sparingly will reap also sparingly, and he who sows bountifully will also reap bountifully. Each one must do just as he has purposed in his heart, not grudgingly or under compulsion, for God loves a cheerful giver" (NASV). In this context, Paul is talking about the contributions that the Corinthians had taken up for the poor saints at Jerusalem. The key to what these verses mean can be found in verses 8–12:

> And God is able to make all grace abound to you, so that always having all sufficiency in everything, you may have an abundance for every good deed; as it is written, "He scattered abroad, He gave to the poor, His righteousness endures forever." Now he who supplies seed to the sower and bread for food will supply and multiply your seed for sowing and increase the harvest of your righteousness; you will be enriched in everything for all liberality, which through us is producing thanksgiving to God. For the ministry of this service is not only fully supplying the needs of the saints, but is also overflowing through many thanksgivings to God. (NASV)

In what way had the Corinthians reaped bountifully? The Corinthians, through their liberal giving, had helped to meet the needs of the poor saints in Jerusalem, even though they themselves did not have much to give. Moreover, in meeting the physical need of other brethren, they had also received a spiritual blessing for their efforts. They had done a mighty work. Were they now financially better off? Were they now enjoying the abundant life? No. In fact, they were still as poor financially as they ever were—perhaps even more so. However, they were rich spiritually. Through their liberal financial contribution, they had met a physical need of brethren in another country. Consequently, Paul says, they had done a "good work" and had been "enriched." God had been glorified because of their liberality. Sowing bountifully, then, does not necessarily mean that one will become wealthy in this life. In this context, it means the Corinthians had reaped spiritually. In his commentary on 2 Corinthians, Barclay makes a similar point:

> Paul insists that no man was ever the loser because he was generous. Giving is like sowing seed. The man who sows with a sparing hand cannot hope for anything but a meagre harvest, but the man who sows with a generous hand will in due time reap a generous return.

> The New Testament is an extremely practical book and one of its great features is that it is never afraid of the reward motive. It never says that goodness is all to no purpose, that life is exactly the same for the man who obeys God and the man who does not. It never forgets that something new and precious and wonderful does enter into the life of the man who accepts God's commands as his law. *But the rewards that the New Testament envisages are never material rewards. It does not promise the wealth of things; but it does promise the wealth of the heart and of the spirit.* [Emphasis mine.][35]

Among the things that a "generous man [can] expect," according to Barclay, are to be "rich in love," "rich in friends," "rich in help [from others]," and "rich towards God." These are all spiritual blessings that one harvests from sowing good deeds.[36] But a person should never expect to become wealthy financially because he or she has made some type of liberal financial contribution.

A third popular verse among faith healers to support the idea of the health and wealth gospel is 3 John 2. In the salutation to this little book near the end of the New Testament, the apostle John writes, "Beloved, I pray that in all respects you may prosper and be in good health, just as your soul prospers." One might think, if any verse in the New Testament supports the abundant life theory, surely it is this one. Of this verse, Kenneth Copeland, for example, asserts, "He [God] blesses you materially as your soul prospers on His Word. Then, as the seeds of prosperity are planted in your mind, in your will, and in your emotions, and as you allow those seeds to grow, they eventually produce a great financial harvest—no matter how bad the conditions around you may be."[37] But is this really what John is talking about?

The word "prosper" in this verse is translated from the Greek *euodoo*, meaning "to succeed in reaching; to succeed in business affairs; to have a prosperous journey."[38] Vine suggests that it has to do with both physical and spiritual health.[39] In his commentary on 3 John, Barnes says that to prosper "would include success in business, happiness in domestic relations, or prosperity in any of the engagements and transactions in which a Christian might lawfully engage."[40] While this verse does indeed carry with it the idea of doing well physically, spiritually, and even economically, it is merely a statement of endearment on the apostle John's part. John is not guaranteeing anything. Instead, he is simply wishing his readers well. It is no different than telling someone who is about to undergo medical tests, "I hope everything turns out okay and that you receive a good report." But just because one person wishes another one well does not guarantee positive results. There is absolutely nothing in this verse that promises the reader anything related to an abundant life as faith healers today teach. There is a huge difference between promising and well-wishing.

The next verse to consider is Isaiah 53:5–6. The same principle is repeated in 1 Peter 2:24. Isaiah 53 is a prophecy about the coming of Jesus Christ as the Messiah. Verses 5–6 read, "But He was pierced through for our transgressions, He was crushed for our iniquities; The chastening for our well-being fell upon Him, And by His scourging we are healed. All of us like sheep have gone astray, Each of us has turned to his own way; But the Lord has caused the iniquity of us all To fall on Him" (NASV). The belief is that, as Coontz and others suggest, because of the death of Jesus on the cross, Christian atonement involves not only forgiveness of sins but physical and financial healing as well. I am not contesting the idea that because of Christ's sacrifice on the cross individuals can receive forgiveness of sins. Every Christian I have ever talked with agrees on this point. The controversy surrounds whether Jesus's death assured physical and economic well-being. Again, I assert that nothing could be further from the truth.

All one needs to do, to understand what Isaiah is talking about, is listen to the apostle Peter. In 1 Peter 2:24, he writes, "and He Himself [Christ] bore our sins in His body on the cross, so that we might die to sin and live to righteousness; for by His wounds you were healed" (NASV). Using similar terminology that Isaiah uses, Peter suggests that the healing that Christ provided was spiritual when he says that Christ "bore our sins in His body on the cross." In fact, Peter went on to say that "you were continually straying like sheep, but now you have returned to the Shepherd and Guardian of your souls." In this context, Peter says nothing about Christ bearing our physical ailments or our financial problems. To infer these ideas is to read too much into what these verses teach. Instead, Peter is talking about things of a spiritual nature.

In his book *Christianity in Crisis*, Hanegraff observes—as I pointed out earlier in this book—"If healing is in the atonement and is accessed by faith, then those who die due to lack of faith must remain in their sins. They die without hope. Why? Because if both healing and salvation are included in this passage, they must be accessed in the same way. And if one does not have enough faith to make oneself well, it follows that he cannot have enough faith to be saved."[41] But what about Isaiah 53:4? Does this verse not clearly connect physical healing to Christ? After all, Matthew alluded to this verse when he said that when Jesus cast out demons and healed sick people, this was a fulfillment of what the prophet Isaiah said in chapter 53 (Matt. 8:16–17).

Hanegraff agrees that "Physical healing here [Isaiah 53:4] is not only crystal clear in context, but it is also affirmed by the Gospels, where it is given an important qualification." Citing Matthew 8:16–17, Hanegraff points out, "This [Christ's healings] was to *fulfill what was spoken through the prophet Isaiah. . . .* Thus the healing mentioned in Isaiah 53:4 was fulfilled *during the healing ministry of Christ*—before His atonement on the cross!—and consequently does not guarantee our healing today."[42]

Another verse that faith healers have employed to sell the idea of health and wealth for people of faith is 1 Timothy 4:8. There the apostle Paul writes, "for bodily exercise is profitable for a little; but godliness is profitable for all things, having promise of the life which now is, and of that which is to come." Regarding this verse, faith healer Kenneth Hagin, for example, says, "'Having promise'—that's present tense. The life that now is means right now *in this present world*." Hagin argues, "There is a life that *now is*, and there is a life that *is to come*. I'm more concerned about the life that now is than I am about the life that is to come. Because the life that 'now is' is the life I'm living right now."[43] According to Hagin, this godliness that Paul speaks of, among other things, "ensures promotion" and "ensures prosperity." "When I talk about prosperity, I'm talking about enjoying an *abundant supply* and *good success* in every area of life," explains Hagin.[44]

The question in regard to this passage is not whether "godliness is profitable for all things" or that it is profitable "of the life which now is" and of "that which is to come." The question is, what are the "all things" for which "godliness is profitable" "of the life which now is"? Does Paul have in mind here that godliness is profitable for health and wealth, as Hagin and others would have us believe—or for something else, perhaps something more spiritual in nature? Bowman argues, "The Pentecostal theory puts undue stress on 'the life that now is' and gives it a meaning not intended by God. One must not read into it any reference to the provisions for health and wealth. I aver that the promises referred to here concern the godliness which furnishes us here in life whatever is necessary to insure for us those things we need in order to procure the life that is to come."[45] The apostle Peter, for example, exclaims that God "hath granted unto us all things that pertain unto life and godliness" (1 Pet. 1:3).

But what are some of these things that God has provided, according to Bowman? Among these are "the gospel to save (Rom. 1:16–17); the peace of knowing you are right with God (Phil. 4:7); the way of escape from temptation (1 Cor. 10:13); the encouragement to help overcome trials (2 Cor. 1:7); the avenue of prayer (Heb. 4:16); and the church for our mutual provocation (Heb. 10:24)."[46]

In commenting on the meaning of 1 Timothy 4:8, Bowman points out that in verses 9 and 10, Paul explains: "This is a faithful saying and worthy of all acceptation. For therefore we both labour and suffer reproach because we trust in the living God" (KJV). Bowman asks, "Does that sound like he is speaking of the relief of difficulties and the provisions of riches? I think not. He says we labor and suffer reproach, a clear reference to being uncomfortable because of living a life for God." So, while 1 Timothy 4:8 teaches that "godliness is profitable for all things" in both this life and in the life to come, once again, the phrase "all things" is limited, in context, to things spiritual. It does not include promotions and prosperity, as Hagin suggests. Further, "all things" here does not include everything like "peace," because elsewhere Paul writes that "all that would live godly in Christ Jesus shall suffer persecutions" (2 Tim. 3:12). This hardly sounds like the abundant life.

In addition to the above verses, Luke 6:38 is sometimes used to prove the gospel of health and wealth. There, in speaking to his disciples, Jesus said, "Give, and it will be given to you; They will pour into your lap a good measure—pressed down, shaken together, and running over. For by your standard of measure it will be measured to you in return" (NASV). Kenneth Hagin argues that this passage, among others, proves that not only will God grant one's needs, he will likewise grant an individual's wants. In recalling a conversation that he claims to have had with God, Hagin writes, "Now, Lord, I can believe that You want to meet our needs—but our wants?" According to Hagin, God replied, "You claim to be a stickler for the Word. In the 23rd *Psalm* that you quote so many times, it says, 'The Lord is my shepherd; I shall not WANT' [v. 1] . . . Claim whatever you need or want. Say, 'Satan, take your hands off my finances . . .' Turn your order in!"[47] Make no mistake: Hagin is teaching here that God will grant individuals not just what they need but what they desire. But did Jesus really intend to teach this in Luke 6:38?

Jesus is merely making a general statement that when a person gives to others, others will give back to him or her. This is not always the case, but often—perhaps even usually—it is. Of this verse, Barnes suggests "that the man who is liberal shall find others liberal to him in dealing with them, and when he is also in circumstances of want. A man who is himself kind to the poor—who has that character established—shall find many who are ready to help him abundantly when he is in want. He that is parsimonious, close, niggardly, shall find few, or none, who will aid him."[48]

Not only does Hagin overstate the meaning of Luke 6:38, but he misses the Psalmists' point when he quotes Psalm 23:1, "The Lord is my shepherd; I shall not want." The idea here is simple. God supplies the needs of the faithful. The word "want" here is translated from the Hebrew *chacer*, meaning "to lack." So when the writer affirms that because the Lord is his shepherd he shall not want, he is suggesting only that his needs will be met. He will not lack for the necessities of life. The Psalmist is not, however, saying that God will necessarily supply what he desires. Psalm 23:1 is not talking about this type of want. Again, Hagin has read too much into the verse.

WHAT THE BIBLE REALLY PROMISES

If the Bible does not promise individuals health and wealth, as faith healers throughout the twentieth and into the twenty-first century suggest, what does it promise? Ephesians 1:3 teaches, "Blessed be the God and Father of our Lord Jesus Christ, who hath blessed us with every spiritual blessing in the heavenly places in Christ." This verse emphasizes the spiritual, not the physical as faith healers do. Just as I explored in chapter 5 that we are called to things spiritual, not to things physical, the scriptures emphasize the spiritual over the physical when it comes to blessings in Christ. But what are some of these?

Bowman has already listed a number of these above: salvation (Rom. 1:16–17); peace that comes from understanding that one is in a right relation with God (Phil. 4:7); being able to escape temptation (1 Cor. 10:13); encouragement to overcome trials of life (1 Cor. 1:7); prayer (Heb. 4:16); and provocation to good works through the church (Heb. 10:24).[49]

In addition to and similar to those above, one can add justification through forgiveness of sins (1 Cor. 6:11; Eph. 2:1–5; Col. 1:14), fellowship with God and his people (1 John 1:7), a hope of heaven (Col. 1:5), and the promise of never being failed or forsaken by God (Heb. 13:5). Others that I pointed out in chapter 7 are the gift of the Holy Spirit (Acts 2:38), being led by the Holy Spirit (Rom. 8:14), being sealed with the Holy Spirit (Eph. 1:13), and having the Holy Spirit as an earnest, guarantee, or down payment of "our inheritance" (Eph. 1:14). But while the scriptures tell us that God will provide us with these spiritual blessings as well as meet our physical needs, they in no way suggest that we will enjoy a life free of sickness, persecution, or financial hardship.

Make no mistake: the scriptures do indeed teach that "Every good gift and every perfect gift is from above, coming down from the Father of lights, with whom can be no variation, neither shadow that is cast by turning" (James 1:17). This involves everything—physical as well as spiritual. But this is not what is under dispute. I am not arguing that God does not supply our needs, or that our physical blessings in this life do not come from God. Instead, I am trying to keep people from believing and teaching that somehow they are going to become wealthy because they have made a financial contribution to the Lord. Giving was never designed to make one wealthier. God is not a spiritual stock market in whom individuals can invest their money and wait for a high rate of financial return. This simply is not the reality of the scriptures. Even when Jesus said in Luke 18:29–30, "There is no man that hath left house, or wife, or brethren, or parents, or children, for the kingdom of God's sake, who shall not receive manifold more in this time, and in the world to come eternal life," he was merely assuring that his disciples would be surrounded by those who would love them and who would not allow them to go without their necessities being met.

CONCLUSION

In this chapter, I have tried to explain why, contrary to what faith healers and other Charismatics teach, the Bible does not support the abundant life theory, sometimes known as the gospel of health and wealth. Not only have people of faith suffered poor health for as long as they have been on the earth, but the majority that we read about in the scriptures have also suffered other hardships, including poverty and persecutions.

When discussing this topic, it is important to keep the issues straight. While the Bible does indeed teach that God will grant one's needs, and that he provides his people even with physical as well as spiritual blessings, nowhere do the scriptures teach that an individual will necessarily be wealthy or enjoy good health because he or she is a person of faith. To explicitly state, or even to leave an audience with the impression, that one can become wealthy or enjoy good health is to go too far. As I pointed out earlier, having one's needs met is a far cry from having much money or other possessions. Regardless of how much one has, an individual should be willing to share with those who are less fortunate. This is the simple truth that is taught in the scriptures.

In criticizing the gospel of health and wealth preached by faith healers and other Charismatics, MacArthur writes in his book *Strange Fire*,

> Rather than denouncing wrong desires, it glorifies worldly lifestyles, feeds on sinful greed, and makes poppycock promises to desperate people: 'Get right with the Lord and he will give you a well-paid job, a nice house and a new car.' The prosperity gospel is more morally reprehensible than a Las Vegas casino because it masquerades as religion and comes in the name of Christ. But like the casinos, it

attracts its victims with glitzy showmanship and the allure of instant riches. After devouring their last cent, like a spiritual slot machine, it sends them home worse off than when they came.[50]

Similarly, in his commentary on Proverbs, Ortlund contends, "The prosperity gospel is coldhearted materialism in religious disguise. It chooses Bible verses selectively to fit a name-it-and-claim-it theory, but it does not love God. It wants to use God for selfish, infantile purposes."[51] Prosperity theology is false doctrine, plain and simple. To borrow MacArthur's words, it "replaces true worship with a wish list" and "substitutes a genuine love for others with a selfish desire for material gain."[52] Suffice it to say that the gospel of health and wealth, or the abundant life theory, as portrayed by Coontz, Roberts, Osteen, Hagin, and Copeland, is nowhere taught in the scriptures.

9

In the Final Analysis, Why Care?

On July 11, 1984, faith healer Ernest Angley was arrested in Munich, West Germany. Among other things, he was charged with practicing medicine without a license and claiming to be a faith healer, both of which were against the law. Angley had gone to Munich to hold a healing revival. After an intense five-and-a-half-hour, perspiration-soaked service in which he laid hands on over 130 people, German authorities placed Angley under house arrest in his hotel room before ultimately moving him to a jail cell. There he remained for the next eight hours. Eventually he was released after reportedly posting a $14,000 bond. During his ordeal, Angley claims to have been roughed up by police officers. Looking back on his experience, he recounts, "It's hard to tell how long they held me; the brutality was unreal . . . I wasn't struggling; I had nothing to hide. The violence they used was really unnecessary."[1]

But Angley was not the first faith healer ever to be arrested for practicing medicine without a license. In 1956, popular faith healer Jack Coe attempted to heal of polio George Clark Jr., the three-year-old son of George and Ann Clark. After anointing the boy with oil and laying hands on him, Coe told the child's mother to take off his braces. When she did so, he crumpled to the ground. Coe then told her to take her son home and allow him to regain strength. The boy's mother confessed, "We decided maybe God couldn't heal George right away, so we took the minister's advice. But the day after we took off the braces, George's legs puffed up and his ankles turned sideways."[2] Shortly thereafter, the Clarks took the matter to the authorities. On February 6, 1956, while holding a revival in Miami, Florida, Jack Coe was arrested and charged with practicing medicine without a license. After being jailed, where he proudly posed for a picture behind bars, he was released on a $5,000 bond. His trial lasted for two days before Justice of the Peace Hugh Duval Jr. dismissed his case, claiming that he could not "condemn the defendant or anyone who in good faith advocates and practices Divine Healing."[3]

These are extreme cases of how we have looked at faith healing through the years, at least from a legal perspective. While obviously some agreed with the arrests, others would argue that such approaches were uncalled for—overreactions to individuals who did not deserve the attention they were given. Whether one agrees or disagrees with how the cases were handled, both of these examples cause us to reflect on how much we ought to care about what faith healers and others who hold similar beliefs teach and practice. Whether we are talking about attempting to miraculously cure someone with an infirmity, exorcise an evil spirit, claim a special calling from God, or suggest that, in some way, the Holy Spirit miraculously endows us with special gifts, should these and similar topics espoused by faith healers really matter to us? And, if so, why should they matter? In other words, are the issues that I have addressed in this book really important for us to consider, or are they merely a waste of our time? These are the questions that I wish to address in this chapter. I will argue that, while I believe that arresting someone for practicing medicine without a license is an overreaction—even quite radical—we should not ignore what faith healers are teaching and practicing, for several reasons.

First, as I articulated earlier in this book, innocent, unsuspecting individuals could lose their lives if they, like thousands before them, thinking they were healed when they were not, were to throw away their medicines. Even worse, children of parents who are true believers are particularly vulnerable. I'll offer just one example to illustrate this point.

In February of 2014, Herbert and Catherine Schaible were sentenced to three and a half to seven years in prison for failing to seek medical treatment for two of their children, who were suffering from pneumonia, because the couple believed in faith healing. While they had not actually taken their children into the healing line of a faith healer to have hands laid on them, nonetheless they articulated what many faith healers preach: "We believe in divine healing, the [sic] Jesus shed blood for our healing and that he died on the cross to break the devil's power," said Herbert Schaible, who professed being Pentecostal. Unfortunately, not seeking medical attention in 2009 for their two-year-old cost the child's life. In that case, the parents were sentenced to ten years' probation. Four years later, the same thing happened to their eight-month-old son, who also died of pneumonia.[4] So, to say that people might lose their lives if they do not understand what the scriptures really have to say about divine, miraculous cures is in no way outside the realm of reality.

Even if no deaths occur, but a person's condition does not improve, that individual could become severely disillusioned. Individuals who are made to think that they will be miraculously healed when they will not be, might very well believe that they are to blame, that it is their fault, not the fault of the preacher.

A second reason why we should pay close attention to the themes articulated in this book is because faith healers who misinterpret the scriptures could easily lead unsuspecting individuals away from the truth contained therein. After listening to the preaching of faith healers, for example, individuals might think that God expects them to be able to speak in a foreign tongue when, in reality, speaking in tongues was never intended for people today. Faith healers may urge individuals to keep praying for God to help them, yet they are never able to speak in a language other than their own native tongue. This can be very frustrating. Individuals may feel that they are missing out on something that others reportedly have experienced. "What's wrong with me?" they might ask themselves. "Why doesn't God help me like he has helped others?"

Even if individuals believe that they are in a saved condition, the fact that they have never experienced the baptism of the Holy Spirit, that God has never spoken to them, or that their finances are no better off after having planted a financial seed of faith, might lead these individuals to conclude that they are a failure. Unfortunately, they could easily feel like second-class citizens in the kingdom of God, when the reality is that God never promised these things in the first place. The fact is, they have not missed out on anything, but they do not know any better.

A third reason to be concerned with the topics in this book is because, from a Christian perspective, the scriptures teach us to "not believe every spirit, but test the spirits to see whether they are from God, because many false prophets have gone out into the world" (1 John 4:1, NASV). Faith healers and faith teachers, in spite of their claims to the contrary, are really not following the scriptures. They simply do not understand what the Bible teaches. The problem is that they are not interpreting the scriptures that they are using, within their proper contexts against the broader picture of truth revealed in the Word. Instead they are often involved in *eisegesis*—reading into the verse what they would like for the verse to mean. Sometimes they are taking scriptures literally when they ought to be interpreting them figuratively.

A fourth problem is that faith healers and other Charismatics have often divorced themselves from the idea of *sola Scriptura*, that the scriptures alone are to be our guide in matters of theology. Potentially, this can lead to contradictions. If people believe, for example, that God is still speaking to them today in some manner other than the scriptures (e.g., a still, small voice, an impression laid upon the heart, a vision, or a dream), they are quite likely to do something that runs contrary to what the Bible really says. I have known of individuals, for instance, who threw away personal property (e.g., music albums and sports equipment) because they believed that God was personally leading them to do so. Throwing away property is not only wasteful, but these individuals may change their mind later on, regretting their actions, which actually occurred in both examples. When people throw out their belongings, they may be quitting a perfectly legitimate activity, thereby giving up on a long-term dream. This is sad. If individuals claim extra-biblical "revelations," then surely these must be just as authoritative as the Bible. After all, if God is speaking audibly or through an impression laid upon the heart, surely he must mean it as much as when he speaks it through the scriptures. What is a person to believe if another individual says that God spoke to him or her, but the message that supposedly was spoken is foreign to the Word? Knowing what the Bible really says when hearing claims about extra-biblical revelations can provide one with the confidence to reject such discrepancies.

A fifth reason for understanding the arguments I have made in this book is that faith healers cannot be taken seriously when they actually preach the truth because they have undermined their credibility by teaching doctrine that cannot be supported by the Word. My contention has never been that faith healers and faith teachers have not taught *some* truth. However, much of what they teach is so sensational and so foreign to the scriptures that it is hard for the average individual—even the average churchgoer—to know what is and what is not actually supported by the Bible.

A sixth reason to understand the material in this book has more to do with modern-day media than with faith healers per se. Movies about demon possession and the occult are constantly debuting. Although it can be argued that these are produced merely for entertainment, their potential negative effects upon viewers are astounding. Often media such as movies leave an indelible mark on the consciousness of viewers. Though the movie may portray events that are the furthest thing from reality imaginable, unsuspecting viewers who are ignorant of the truth might come away from the theater with a blurred, if not totally warped, reality.

Let me illustrate this principle with an example from one of my classes. Occasionally, in attempting to complete a course requirement, a student will choose to write a rhetorical analysis on a movie with a religious theme, in which he or she attempts to explain what reality the director was trying to convey and how he or she was attempting to sell it. Once, one of my students analyzed a movie on demon possession and concluded that, after having seen the movie, she definitely believed that demons possess people today. Needless to say, I was dismayed at her conclusion. I had incorrectly assumed that she did not believe in demon possessions and exorcisms before she saw the movie and wrote her analysis, as she had led me to believe. Although I cannot say with absolute certainty, I suspect that had she known what the scriptures really have to say about this subject, her conclusion might have been different. At least it might have been more difficult for her to believe the movie. When individuals have a better understanding of subjects like demon possession, exorcisms, and the occult, they are less likely to become caught up in them in the first place. In fact, when one understands what the Bible says about any number of theological subjects, one does not have to rely on movies to provide religious reality. For example, in the movie *Heaven Is for Real*, based upon Todd Burpo's book about his four-year-old son's near-death experience, some viewers will no doubt come away with the idea that heaven exists, simply because they saw the movie. People of faith, however, who read and understand the Bible, might say, "I don't need a four-year-old to tell me that heaven exists. I already believe it because I can read about it in the scriptures." At this point, one may be wondering, "What's the harm in believing a movie that supports what the Bible teaches—that heaven really exists?" For some people of faith, the problem is not in the conclusion that heaven is real; they already believe this. The problem is in how the conclusion was reached. If the movie leads people to believe that they can learn religious truth experientially—apart from scriptures—what is to stop them from seeking and claiming they know the truth in some other area because they believe that God has led them on some type of miraculous excursion or given them a supernatural vision?

A final reason why the material in this book is important—especially from chapter 1—is that we can develop a better understanding of how faith healers have been able to persuade individuals to join them and support them financially. This is no small matter. When one is aware of the rhetorical strategies that faith healers employ, and why some of them are not biblically based (e.g., "God called me"), one is in a better position to evaluate and, if need be, withstand their persuasive efforts. When we understand that the Bible does not support the gospel of health and wealth, for instance, then we may be more inclined to hang on to our money rather than cough it up when faith healers teach, "Name it and claim it."

I have often said to my students, "If you can see the dragon, then you can slay the dragon." This is the underlying principle behind inoculation theory, which says that if individuals are told ahead of time what they are likely to hear and how they should respond, they will become inoculated against a persuasive effort. However, if one is not aware beforehand, that person might be persuaded by what a speaker is advocating.

So there are any number of reasons why we should care about what faith healers are teaching and practicing. While it would be too radical to arrest them for their beliefs and behaviors, turning a blind eye to them would be unwise because of various potential harms, some greater than others. Faith healers have been with us for centuries. Although names and faces will change, their doctrines and practices will, in all likelihood, continue to be popular for generations to come. I am quite certain of this. To blindly accept what they preach would be naïve at best and irresponsible at worst. For individuals who profess confidence in the scriptures as a theological guide, it is important to understand what the Word really has to say about the things that faith healers champion. Perhaps then faith healing as a religious practice will be far less mystifying and attractive.

Notes

INTRODUCTION

1. John Ankerberg and John Weldon, *The Facts on The Faith Movement: Where It Came From, What It Teaches, Who It Hurts* (Eugene, OR: Ankerberg Theological Research Institute, 1993), 6. For more information on the Faith Movement, see Hank Hanegraff, *Christianity in Crisis* (Eugene, OR: Harvest House Publishers, 1993); and Hank Hanegraff, *Counterfeit Revival: Looking for God in All the Wrong Places* (Dallas, TX: Word Publishing Co., 1997).
2. Stephen J. Pullum, *"Foul Demons, Come Out!": The Rhetoric of Twentieth-Century American Faith Healing* (Westport, CT: Praeger, 1999).
3. Sociologists Neil Gross and Solon Simmons recently conducted a study involving a sample of 1,417 college professors in the United States; approximately 52% said that they believe in God. Gross and Simmons suggest, "Our findings call into question the long-standing idea among theorists and sociologists of knowledge that intellectuals, broadly construed, comprise an ideologically cohesive group in society and tend naturally to be antagonistic toward religion." Furthermore, they argue that the idea that "the worldview of the intelligentsia is necessarily in tension with a religious worldview, is plainly wrong." Cited in Amarnath Amarasingam, "Are College Professors Religious?" *The Huffington Post*, April 7, 2014, http://www.huffingtonpost.com/amarnath-amarasingam/how-religious-are-america_b_7496.
4. *Oxford English Dictionary Online*, s.v. "Metaphysics," http://oxforddictionaries.com; *American Heritage Dictionary of the English Language*, s.v. "Metaphysics."
5. Stephen J. Pullum, *"Hallelujah! Thank You, Jesus!": Selling the Miraculous in the Preaching of Faith Healers*, ed. J. Harold Ellens (Westport, CT: Praeger, 2008), 3: 139–61.

6. Stephen J. Pullum, *"That They May Believe": Distinguishing the Miraculous from the Providential*, ed. J. Harold Ellens (Westport, CT: Praeger, 2008), 1: 135–58.

7. Stephen J. Pullum, *Exorcising Evil: The Bible and Psychology on Demon Possession*, ed. J. Harold Ellens (Santa Barbara, CA: ABC-CLIO, 2011), 3: 144–63.

8. David Edwin Harrell, *All Things Are Possible: The Healing & Charismatic Revivals in Modern America* (Bloomington, IN: Indiana Univ. Press, 1975).

9. Hank Hanegraff, *Christianity in Crisis* (Eugene, OR: Harvest House Publishers, 1993), 62.

10. Ankerberg and Weldon, *The Faith Movement*, 41.

11. John Bacon, "Reality Show Snake Handler Dies from Snakebite," *USA Today*, Feb. 16, 2014, http://www.usatoday.com/story/life/tv/2014/02/16/snake-salvation-pastor-dead.

12. William A. Nolen, *Healing: A Doctor in Search of a Miracle* (New York: Random House, 1974), 65.

13. Em Griffin, *A First Look at Communication Theory*, 2nd ed. (New York: McGraw-Hill, 1994), 137–45.

14. Otis M. Walter, "On the Varieties of Rhetorical Criticism," in *Essays on Rhetorical Criticism*, ed. Thomas R. Nilsen (New York: Random House, 1968), 158–60.

15. For a thorough discussion of the three stages of rhetorical criticism—description, analysis, and judgment—see Sonja K. Foss, *Rhetorical Criticism: Exploration and Practice*, 3rd ed. (Long Grove, IL: Waveland Press, 2004); Bernard L. Brock, Robert L. Scott, and James W. Chesebro, *Methods of Rhetorical Criticism: A Twentieth-Century Perspective*, 3rd ed. (Detroit, MI: Wayne State Univ. Press, 1989).

16. Quoted in J. Jeffrey Auer, *What Does a Rhetorical Critic Do?* Unpublished manuscript in author's possession, 1981, 4.

17. Quoted ibid., 10.

18. Quoted ibid., 1.

CHAPTER 1

1. *Mrs. Doubtfire*, directed by Chris Columbus (1993; Twentieth Century Fox Productions); *Borat: Cultural Learnings of America for Make Benefit Glorious Nation of Kazakhstan*, directed by Larry Charles (2007; Twentieth Century Fox Productions); Laura Haferd, " The 'Faith-Healing' Arrest That Did Wonders," *Beacon Journal* (Akron, OH), April 3, 1987, B4.

2. "Faith Healer," *The Simpsons*, WSFX, Fox Network, Wilmington, NC, Jan. 16, 2000.

3. David Edwin Harrell, *All Things Are Possible: The Healing and Charismatic Revivals in Modern America* (Bloomington: Indiana Univ. Press, 1975); Edith L. Blumhofer, *Aimee Semple McPherson: Everybody's Sister* (Grand Rapids, MI: William B. Eerdmans Publishing Co., 1993).

4. Harrell, *All Things Are Possible*, 1975.

5. Randy Frame, "Same Old Benny Hinn, Critics Say," *Christianity Today*, Oct. 5, 1997, 52–54.

6. Sonja K. Foss, *Rhetorical Criticism: Exploration and Practice*, 2nd ed. (Prospect Heights, IL: Waveland, 1996), 229–31.

7. Dennis D. Cali, *Generic Criticism of American Public Address* (Dubuque, IA: Kendall/Hunt, 1996), 12.

8. Ibid., 12.

9. Ernest Angley, personal observation of author, Akron, OH, Feb. 19, 1988.

10. Asa Alonzo Allen, "Allen Exhorting," *Miracles Today* (Videotaped television program in author's possession), n.d.

11. Oral Roberts, "Demon Possession," in *The 4th Man and Other Famous Sermons*, 3rd ed. (Tulsa, OK: Oral Roberts, 1954), 113.

12. Jack Coe, "Big Family: The Jack Coe Story," *Jack Coe Jr. Presents Jack Coe Sr.* (videotape; Dallas: Christian Challenge, 1989).

13. Oral Roberts, "Demon Possession," 113.

14. Asa Alonzo Allen, "It Is Finished," *Miracles Today* (videotaped television program in author's possession) n.d.

15. Benny Hinn, personal observation of author, Nashville, TN, Oct. 23–24, 1997.

16. Ernest Angley, personal observation of author, Akron, OH, Feb. 19, 1988.

17. Richard Swinburne, *The Concept of a Miracle* (New York: Macmillan, 1970), 70.

18. C. S. Lewis, *Miracles* (New York: Macmillan, 1947), 59.

19. Ernest Angley, personal observation of author, Akron, OH, Feb. 19, 1988; Gloria Copeland, personal observation of author, Nashville, TN, Oct. 17, 1992; Benny Hinn, personal observation of author, Nashville, TN, Oct. 23–24, 1997.

20. William Nolen, *Healing: A Doctor in Search of a Miracle* (New York: Random House, 1974).

21. William Clements, "Ritual Expectation in Pentecostal Healing Experience," *Western Folklore* 40, no. 2 (April, 1981): 139.

22. Ibid., 148.

23. William Branham, "Deep Calleth Unto the Deep," *ABC's of God* (videotape; Baltimore: Faith Outreach Archives, n.d.).

24. Stephen J. Pullum, *"Foul Demons, Come Out!": The Rhetoric of Twentieth-Century American Faith Healing* (Westport, CT: Praeger).

25. Jack Coe, "Be of Good Cheer," *Jack Coe Jr. Presents Jack Coe Sr.* (videotape; Dallas: Christian Challenge, 1989).

26. Benny Hinn, personal observation of author, Nashville, TN, Oct. 23–24, 1997.

27. Ernest Angley, personal observation of author, Akron, OH, Feb. 19, 1988.

28. William Branham, *Elijah and Elisha* (audiotape, Phoenix, AZ, 1957); audiotapes of Branham's sermons can be found on his Voice of God Recordings website.

29. Oral Roberts, *Right Believing: The Master Key to Healing* (videotape, recorded in Portland, OR, 1954; produced in Tulsa, OK: ORUP).

30. Oral Roberts, *The Power of Positive Faith* (videotape, recorded in Phoenix, AZ, 1954, produced in Tulsa, OK: ORUP).

31. David Edwin Harrell, *Oral Roberts: An American Life* (Bloomington: Indiana University Press), 90.

32. Ibid., 110.

33. Ibid., 256.

34. Asa Alonzo Allen, "Exhorting," *Miracles Today* (videotaped television program in author's possession), n.d.

35. Asa Alonzo Allen, "It is Finished," *Miracles Today* (videotaped television program in author's possession), n.d.

36. William Hedgepeth, *Look*, Oct. 7, 1969, 29.

37. Ibid., 24, 28.

38. Jack Coe, "For I Believe in God," *Jack Coe Jr. Presents Jack Coe Sr.* (videotape, Dallas: Christian Challenge, 1989).

39. Jack Coe Jr., "Jack Coe Sr.'s Personal Testimony," *Jack Coe Jr. Presents Jack Coe Sr.* (videotape, Dallas: Christian Challenge, 1989).

40. Ernest Angley, personal observation of author, Akron, OH, Feb. 19, 1988; Gloria Copeland, personal observation of author, Nashville, TN, Oct. 17, 1992; Benny Hinn, personal observation of author, Nashville, TN, Oct. 23–24, 1997.

41. Eric Hoffer, *The True Believer* (New York: Harper and Row, 1965).

42. Todd V. Lewis, "Charisma and Media Evangelists: An Explication and Model of Communication Influence," *The Southern Communication Journal* 54 (Fall 1988): 97.

43. William Nolen, *Healing: A Doctor in Search of a Miracle*, 7, 53–55.

44. Oral Roberts, *Healing is Not a Luxury* (videotape, recorded in Anaheim, CA, 1955, produced in Tulsa, OK: ORUP).

45. Oral Roberts, *Twelve Greatest Miracles of My Ministry* (Tulsa, OK: Pinoak Publication, 1974), 7.

46. Ernest Angley, *The Ernest Angley Hour*, WHMB Television, Indianapolis, IN, Aug. 23, 1987.

47. Gloria Copeland, personal observation of author, Nashville, TN, Oct. 17, 1992.

48. Jack Coe, "Practicing Medicine Without a License," *ABC's of God* (videotape, Baltimore, MD: Faith Outreach Archives, n.d.).

49. Asa Alonso Allen and Walter Wagner, *Born to Lose, Bound to Win: An Autobiography* (Garden City, NY: Doubleday), 118.

50. William Branham, *Footprints of the Sands of Time: The Autobiography of William Marrion Branham* (Jeffersonville, IN: Spoken Word Publications, 1976), 96.

51. Benny Hinn, *Good Morning, Holy Spirit* (Nashville, TN: Thomas Nelson, 1990), 45.

52. Benny Hinn, personal observation of author, Nashville, TN, Oct. 23–24, 1997.

53. Ibid.

54. Todd V. Lewis, "Charisma and Media Evangelists," 103.

55. Ernest G. Bormann, "Fantasy and Rhetorical Vision: The Rhetorical Criticism of Social Reality," *The Quarterly Journal of Speech* 58 (1972): 401.

56. William Branham, *Footprints of the Sands of Time,* 60; William Branham, *Obey the Voice of the Angel* (audiotape), Minneapolis, MN, July 13, 1949; William Branham, *Branham's Life Story* (audiotape), Phoenix, AZ, April 15, 1952.

57. William Branham, *Footprints of the Sands of Time,* 74; Gordon Lindsey, *William Branham: A Man Sent from God,* 3rd ed. (Jeffersonville, IN: Spoken Word Publications, 1950), 77.

58. Oral Roberts, *Healing is Not a Luxury* (videotape, recorded in Anaheim, CA, 1955, produced in Tulsa, OK: ORUP).

59. Oral Roberts, *Demons and Deliverance* (videotape, recorded in Florence, SC, 1955, produced in Tulsa, OK: ORUP).

60. Asa Alonso Allen and Walter Wagner, *Born to Lose, Bound to Win,* 96.

61. Ernest Angley, *Untying God's Hands* (Akron, OH: Winston Press, 1977), 129–30.

62. John De Groot, "In Rev. Angley's Gloryland: Miracles 4 Times a Week," *Beacon Journal* (Akron, OH), June 5, 1966, G-4.

63. Benny Hinn, *Good Morning, Holy Spirit* (Nashville, TN: Thomas Nelson, 1990), 43.

64. Todd V. Lewis, "Charisma and Media Evangelists," 103.

65. Jack Coe, "Jack Coe Sr.'s Personal Testimony," *Jack Coe Jr. Presents Jack Coe Sr.* (videotape, Dallas: Christian Challenge, 1989).

66. Jack Coe, "Practicing Medicine Without a License," *ABC's of God* (videotape, Baltimore, MD: Faith Outreach Archives, n.d.).

67. William Branham, *I Was Not Disobedient to Vision* (audiotape), Zion, IL, 1949.

68. William Branham, *Unpardonable Sin* (audiotape), Jeffersonville, IN, Oct. 24, 1954.

69. Asa Alonzo Allen, "Two Services Under the Tent," *The Allen Revival Hour* (videotaped television program in author's possession), n.d.

70. Asa Alonzo Allen, "This Gospel of the Kingdom," *The Allen Revival Hour* (videotaped television program in author's possession), n.d.

71. Asa Alonzo Allen, "Skepticism," *Miracles Today* (videotaped television program in author's possession), n.d.

72. Asa Alonso Allen and Walter Wagner, *Born to Lose, Bound to Win,* 9.

73. Oral Roberts, *Right Believing: The Master Key to Healing* (videotape, recorded in Portland, OR, 1954, produced in Tulsa, OK: ORUP).

74. Gloria Copeland, *Healing School* (videotape, Kenneth Copeland Video Ministries: Fort Worth, TX, 1990).

75. Ernest Angley, personal observation of author, Akron, OH, Feb. 19, 1988.

76. Ernest Angley, interview with Fred Griffith, *The Morning Exchange*, WEWS Television, Cleveland, OH, Mar. 1, 1988.

77. *Impact*, television program narrated by John Camp, CNN, Nov. 23, 1997.

78. Jack Coe, "Jack Coe Sr.'s Personal Testimony," *Jack Coe Jr. Presents Jack Coe Sr.* (videotape, Dallas: Christian Challenge, 1989).

79. Jack Coe, "Be of Good Cheer," *Jack Coe Jr. Presents Jack Coe Sr.* (videotape, Dallas: Christian Challenge, 1989).

80. Asa Alonzo Allen, "Skepticism," *Miracles Today* (videotaped television program in author's possession), n.d.

81. Asa Alonzo Allen, *Miracles Today* (videotaped television program in author's possession), n.d.

82. Asa Alonzo Allen, "Allen Exhorting," *Miracles Today* (videotaped television program in author's possession), n.d.

83. Ibid.

84. Asa Alonzo Allen, "This Gospel of the Kingdom," *The Allen Revival Hour* (videotaped television program in author's possession), n.d.

85. Asa Alonzo Allen, "Monkey Boy," *Miracles Today* (videotaped television program in author's possession), n.d.

86. Asa Alonzo Allen, *Miracles Today* (videotaped television program in author's possession), n.d.

87. Oral Roberts, *Healing is Not a Luxury* (videotape, recorded in Anaheim, CA, 1955; produced in Tulsa, OK: ORUP); see also Oral Roberts, *The Power of Positive Faith* (videotape, recorded in Phoenix, AZ, 1954; produced in Tulsa, OK: ORUP).

88. Oral Roberts, *Venture Into Faith*, produced and directed by Herb A. Lightman (Tulsa, OK: Archangel Motion Pictures, 1952).

89. Gloria Copeland, personal observation of author, Nashville, TN, Oct. 17, 1992.

90. Gloria Copeland, *Healing School* (videotape, Kenneth Copeland Video Ministries: Fort Worth, TX, 1990).

91. Jack Coe, "Practicing Medicine Without a License," *ABC's of God* (videotape, Faith Outreach Archives: Baltimore, MD, n.d.).

92. William Branham, *Explaining the Ministry and Healing* (audiotape, Louisville, KY, 1950).

93. Oral Roberts, *Demons and Deliverance* (videotape, recorded in Florence, SC, 1955; produced in Tulsa, OK: ORUP).

94. Asa Alonzo Allen, "Two Services Under the Tent," *The Allen Revival Hour* (videotaped television program in author's possession), n.d.

95. Ernest Angley, interview with Fred Griffith, *The Morning Exchange*, WEWS Television, Cleveland, OH, Mar. 1, 1988.

96. Oral Roberts, *Making Your Believing a Definite Act of Faith* (videotape, recorded in Austin, TX, 1957; produced in Tulsa, OK: ORUP).

97. *Miracle Magazine*, Jan. 1960, 1, 7.

98. *Miracle Magazine*, Oct. 1959; Dec. 1959; Jan. 1960.

99. *Miracle Magazine*, Oct. 1961.

100. Stephen J. Pullum, *"Foul Demons, Come Out!"*.

101. For example, see Jack Coe, "That You Might Be Healed," *Jack Coe Jr. Presents Jack Coe Sr.* (videotape, Dallas: Christian Challenge, 1989).

102. Asa Alonzo Allen, "It Is Finished," *Miracles Today* (videotaped television program in author's possession), n.d.

103. Asa Alonzo Allen, *Miracles Today* (videotaped television program in author's possession), n.d.

104. Jack Coe, "Practicing Medicine Without a License," *ABC's of God* (videotape, Baltimore, MD: Faith Outreach Archives, n.d.); Jack Coe, "Message to the Modern Church," *Jack Coe Jr. Presents Jack Coe Sr.* (videotape, Dallas: Christian Challenge, 1989); Jack Coe, "For I Believe in God," *Jack Coe Jr. Presents Jack Coe Sr.* (videotape, Dallas: Christian Challenge, 1989).

105. Oral Roberts, *Your Guardian Angel* (videotape, recorded in Winston-Salem, NC, n.d.; produced in Tulsa, OK: ORUP).

106. Oral Roberts, *Demons and Deliverance* (videotape, recorded in Florence, SC; produced in Tulsa, OK: ORUP).

107. Asa Alonzo Allen, "Skepticism," *Miracles Today* (videotaped television program in author's possession), n.d.

108. Jack Coe, "Practicing Medicine Without a License," *ABC's of God* (videotape, Baltimore, MD: Faith Outreach Archives, n.d.)

109. Ibid.

110. Benny Hinn, personal observation of author, Nashville, TN, Oct. 23–24, 1997.

111. Todd V. Lewis, "Charisma and Media Evangelists," 106.

112. Jack Coe, "Practicing Medicine Without a License," *ABC's of God* (videotape, Baltimore, MD: Faith Outreach Archives, n.d.)

113. James D. Davis, "Benny Hinn," *The Phoenix Gazette*, Sept. 11, 1993, D6–D7.

114. *Impact*, television program narrated by John Camp, CNN, Nov. 23, 1997.

115. Gloria Copeland, personal observation of author, Nashville, TN, Oct. 17, 1992.

CHAPTER 2

1. Acts 8:30 (NASV); this is what Philip the Evangelist said to the Ethiopian treasurer as he was reading from the Book of Isaiah in his chariot when Philip approached him.

2. Jeffrey M. Jones, "In U.S., 3 in 10 Say They Take the Bible Literally," July 8, 2011, 1–4, http:// www.gallup.com/poll/148427/say-bible-literally.aspx.

3. Ibid.

4. "Religion Among the Millennials," Pew Research: Religion & Public Life Project, Feb. 17, 2010, http://www.pewforum.org/2010/02/17/religion-among-the-millenials/.

5. Caleb K. Bell, "Poll: Americans Love the Bible but Don't Read It Much," Religion News Service, April 4, 2013, 1–2, http://religionnews.com/2013/04/04/poll-americans-love-the-bible-but-dont-read-it-much.

6. "Few U.S. Protestant Teens Regularly Read the Bible," National Study of Youth and Religion, 2004, 1, http://www.youthandreligion.org/news/2004-0623.html.

7. Ibid., 4.

8. See, for example, D. A. Carson, *Exegetical Fallacies*, 2nd ed. (Grand Rapids, MI: Baker Books, 1996); Walter C. Kaiser Jr., *Toward an Exegetical Theology: Biblical Exegesis for Preaching and Teaching* (Grand Rapids, MI: Baker Books, 1981); or Gordon D. Fee, *New Testament Exegesis: A Handbook for Students and Pastors*, 3rd ed. (Louisville, KY: Westminster John Knox Press, 2002). Fee in particular provides a number of excellent sources on exegesis in his book. For other sources on hermeneutics, see James E. Rosscup, "Hermeneutics and Expository Preaching," in *Rediscovering Expository Preaching*, ed. John MacArthur Jr. and the Master's Seminary Faculty (Dallas, TX: Word Publishing, 1992), 119–36.

9. *The Cambridge Dictionary of Christianity*, ed. Daniel Patte (Cambridge: Cambridge Univ. Press, 2010), 508.

10. *The American Heritage Dictionary of the English Language*, ed. William Morris (New York: Houghton Mifflin, 1973), 617.

11. *Oxford English Dictionary* online.

12. *The American Heritage Dictionary*, 459.

13. *Oxford English Dictionary* online.

14. *The Cambridge Dictionary of Christianity*, 402.

15. Kaiser, *Toward an Exegetical Theology*, 47.

16. Carson, *Exegetical Fallacies*, 25.

17. Kaiser, *Toward an Exegetical Theology*, 71.

18. Ibid., 71.

19. John A. Broadus, *On Preparation and Delivery of Sermons* (New York: Harper and Row, 1944), 45.

20. Haddon W. Robinson, *Biblical Preaching: The Development and Delivery of Expository Messages* (Grand Rapids, MI: Baker Book House, 1980), 23–24.

21. Michael J. Schmidt, *How To Study the Bible*, no. pub., no date, 13. Manuscript in author's possession.

22. Fee, *New Testament Exegesis*, 182.

23. See Carson, *Exegetical Fallacies*, 115.

24. Kaiser, *Toward an Exegetical Theology*, 70.

25. Hank Hanegraaff, *Counterfeit Revival: Looking for God in All the Wrong Places* (Dallas: Word Publishing, 1997), 183. These verses and others that Hanegraaff does not mention can also be found in Stanley M. Burgess, Gary B. McGee, and Patrick H. Alexander, eds., *Dictionary of Pentecostal and Charismatic Movements* (Grand Rapids, MI: Regency Reference Library, 1988), 790–91.

26. Hanegraaff, *Counterfeit Revival*, 185–87.

27. Hanegraaff, *Counterfeit Revival*, 188–89.

28. Arthur M. Ogden, *The Avenging of the Apostles and Prophets* (Pinson, AL: Ogden Publications, 1985), 116.

29. John MacArthur, *The MacArthur New Testament Commentary: Revelation 1–11* (Chicago, IL: Moody Publishers, 1999), 47.

30. Cited in Hanegraaff, *Counterfeit Revival*, 190.

31. *Dictionary of Pentecostal and Charismatic Movements*, 790.

32. Ibid, 790.

33. Hanegraaff, *Counterfeit Revival*, 195.

34. *Dictionary of Pentecostal and Charismatic Movements*, 790–91.

35. W. E. Vine. *An Expository Dictionary of New Testament Words* (Nashville, TN: Royal Publishers, Inc.), 845–46.

36. For other possibilities, see John MacArthur's *Strange Fire: The Danger of Offending the Holy Spirit with Counterfeit Worship* (Nashville, TN: Nelson Books, 2013), 148–49.

37. MacArthur, *Strange Fire*, 148–49.

38. S. Leonard Tyler, "The Battle of Armageddon," *Guardian of Truth*, 26, no. 4, (Jan. 28, 1982): 3.

39. Franklin T. Puckett, "How the Spirit Indwells," *Searching the Scriptures*, XXIII, no. 9 (Sept., 1982): 5.

40. Carson, *Exegetical Fallacies*, 130.

41. Fee, *New Testament Exegesis*, 183.

42. Broadus, *On the Preparation and Delivery of Sermons*, 47.

43. David E. Pratte, *The God of the Bible: A Study of the Father, Son, and Holy Spirit* (www.lighttomypath.net/sales, 2013), 136.

44. Ernest Angley, "Why I Lay Hands on People," *The Power of the Holy Ghost Magazine*, Dec. 2007, p. 3; retrieved from https://www.ernestangley.org/read/article/why_i_lay_hands_on_people.

45. Angley, "Why I Lay Hands on People," p. 1.

46. Ray Summers, *Worthy Is the Lamb* (Nashville, TN: Broadman & Holman, 1951), 26.

47. Ibid, 49.

48. Ernest W. Angley, *Raptured: A Novel on the Second Coming of the Lord!* (Akron, OH: Winston Press, 1950).

49. Fee, *NewTestament Exegesis*, 184.

CHAPTER 3

1. Exodus 4:5.

2. Robin Roberts, *Good Morning America,* ABC, WWAY, Wilmington, NC, March 3, 2007.

3. ABC News, WWAY, Wilmington, NC, March 7, 2007.

4. Chris Cuomo, *Good Morning America*, ABC, WWAY, Wilmington, NC, March 29, 2007.

5. Kirk Johnson, "Back from the Dead, Teenager Casts Light on Shadowy Game," *The New York Times,* March 28, 2007, http://web.lexis-nexis.com/universe/document (accessed May 22, 2007).

6. ABC News, WWAY, Wilmington, NC, May 7, 2007.

7. Wade H. Boggs Jr., *Faith Healing and the Christian Faith* (Richmond, VA: John Knox Press, 1956), 30.

8. Quoted in *America Undercover: A Question of Miracles,* HBO Film, Time Warner Cable, Wilmington, NC, April 15, 2001.

9. Ibid.

10. Gary McCarron, "Lost Dogs and Financial Healings: Deconstructing Televangelist Miracles," in *The God Pumpers,* ed. Marshall Fishwick and Ray B. Browne (Bowling Green, OH: Bowling Green State University Popular Press, 1987), 19–31. For a similar definition of "miracle," see Richard Swinburne, *The Concept of Miracle* (New York: Macmillan Publishing Co., 1970), 14, 70.

11. See, for example, Kathryn Kuhlman, *I Believe in Miracles* (Old Tappan, NJ: Fleming H. Revell, 1970), 20.

12. Stephen J. Pullum *"Foul Demons, Come Out!": The Rhetoric of Twentieth-Century American Faith Healing* (Westport, CT: Praeger, 1999), 158.

13. For a similar story, see the conception of John the Baptist to Elisabeth and Zacharias in Luke 1. Verse 18 describes Zacharias as "an old man" and Elisabeth as "well stricken in years."

14. C. S. Lewis, *Miracles* (New York: Macmillan Publishing Co., 1947), 59.

15. Roy E. Cogdill, *Miraculous Divine Healing* (Bowling Green, KY, Oct. 5, 1952), 14.

16. W. E. Vine. *An Expository Dictionary of New Testament Words* (Nashville, TN: Royal Publishers, Inc.), 747, 1240.

17. Gary McCarron, "Lost Dogs and Financial Healing," 30.

18. Ibid., 19.

19. William A. Nolen, *Healing: A Doctor in Search of a Miracle* (New York: Random House, 1974), 76–77.

20. Ibid., 81.

21. Personal observation of the author, who attended a Friday night miracle service at Ernest Angley's Grace Cathedral in Akron, Ohio, Feb. 19, 1988.

22. R. C. Foster, *Gospel Studies, Vol. 2: The Life of Christ: A Chronological Study of the Four Gospels* (Cincinnati, OH: Cincinnati Bible Seminary, 1971), 54–55.

23. In his book *The Healing Anointing* (Tulsa, OK: Faith Library Pub, 1997), 84, faith healer Kenneth E. Hagin asserts that "On many occasions, I've ministered to sick people and I've known that their diseases had departed. Yet the people still had their symptoms for a little while. Sometimes it was ten minutes, an hour, or maybe three days before a person was all right." This experience is not characteristic of healings recorded in the New Testament.

24. Kathryn Kuhlman, *Dry Land, Living Waters: Las Vegas Miracle Service* (videotape, directed by Dick Ross, 1975).

25. Personal observation of the author, who attended a Benny Hinn revival in Nashville, TN, Oct. 23–24, 1997.

26. Personal observation of the author, who attended a Benn Hinn revival in Nashville, TN, Oct. 23–24, 1997; a Gloria Copeland healing school in Nashville, TN, Oct. 17, 1992; and an Ernest Angley miracle service in Akron, OH, Feb. 19, 1988.

27. For other narratives that support the idea that the miracles of Jesus were used to produce faith in his audiences, see John 2:11, 23; John 11:42; and John 20:30.

28. Phil Roberts, "What Is a Miracle?" *The Plano Provoker*, April 17, 1975, 3–4.

29. Waymon D. Miller, *Modern Divine Healing*, (Fort Worth, TX: Miller Publishing Co., 1956), 110–13.

30. Ibid., 110–113.

31. See, for example, Ernest W. Angley, *Faith in God Heals the Sick* (Tampa, FL: no pub., 1952), 98; and Kenneth E. Hagin, *The Healing Anointing* (Tulsa, OK: Faith Library Publications, 1997), 43.

32. Vine, *New Testament Words*, 899.

33. James Strong, "A Concise Dictionary of the Words in The Greek Testament," in *The New Strong's Exhaustive Concordance of the Bible* (New York: Nelson, 1984), 61.

34. Wayne Jackson, "A Study of the Providence of God," *Reason & Revelation* 3 no. 1 (Jan. 1988), 1–2.

35. Ibid.

36. Dee Bowman, "Providence," *Christianity Magazine*, Nov. 1992, 2.

37. See, for example, Matt. 5:45; Matt 6:33; and Rom. 13:1 (compare to Dan. 2:21).

38. Bowman, *Providence*, 2.

39. Jackson, *A Study of the Providence of God*, 2.

40. Ibid., 3.

41. Ibid.

42. Bowman, *Providence*, 2.

43. Tommy Hagewood, "Is God Showing Me Something Through My Circumstances?" *Locust Light* 22, no. 10, May 15, 1990, 2.

44. Jackson, *A Study of the Providence of God*, 3.

45. Allan Turner, "Is It Possible to Interpret Providence?" unpublished manuscript, n.d. 4–5. Manuscript in author's personal files.

46. Miller, *Healing*, 20.

47. There were at least two examples in the New Testament where the Apostle Paul could have performed a miracle to benefit two people, had that been the purpose of miracles. However, he chose not to. In 2 Tim. 4:20, we read that he left Trophimus at Miletus, "sick." In 1 Tim. 5:23, he told Timothy to "use a little wine for thy stomach's sake and thine often infirmities." If miracles were intended as social benefits, why did Paul not heal these two people?

48. Vine, *New Testament Words*, 846.

49. Jonathan David Moorhead, "1 Corinthians 13:8–13 and Ephesians 4:11–16: A Canonical Parallel," unpublished manuscript presented to Dr. Robert Pyne, Dallas Theological seminary, in partial fulfillment of RS1001, Research Seminar, August, 2004, 70–73. Manuscript in author's possession.
50. Ibid., 70–71.
51. Ibid., 73.
52. David E. Pratte, *The God of the Bible: A Study of the Father, Son, and Holy Spirit* (www.lighttomypath.net/sales, 2013), 137.

CHAPTER 4

1. Malachi Martin, *Hostage to the Devil: The Possession and Exorcism of Five Living Americans* (New York: Reader's Digest Press, 1976).
2. *The Exorcist*, directed by William Friedkin (1973; Los Angeles: Warner Brothers).
3. Martin, *Hostage to the Devil*, title page. See also Michael W. Cuneo, *American Exorcism: Expelling Demons in the Land of Plenty* (New York: Doubleday), 15.
4. Carl Vogl, *Begone Satan! A Soul-Stirring Account of Diabolical Possession*, trans. C. Kapsner (Rockford, IL: TAN Books, original work published n.d.).
5. Gerald Daniel Brittle, *The Demonologist: The Extraordinary Career of Ed and Lorraine Warren* (Lincoln, NE: iUniverse, 1980).
6. Felicitas D. Goodman, *The Exorcism of Anneliese Michel* (New York: Doubleday, 1981).
7. M. Scott Peck, *People of the Lie: The Hope for Healing Human Evil* (New York: Simon and Schuster, 1983).
8. Gabriele Amorth, *An Exorcist Tells His Story*, trans. N. V. MacKenzie (San Francisco: Ignatius Press, original work published 1990).
9. Gabriele Amorth, *An Exorcist: More Stories*, trans. N. V. MacKenzie (San Francisco: Ignatius Press, original work published 1992).
10. John Zaffis and Brian McIntyre, *Shadows of the Dark* (Lincoln, NE: iUniverse, 2004).
11. Jose A. Fortea, *Interview with an Exorcist: An Insider's Look at the Devil, Demonic Possession, and the Path to Deliverance* (West Chester, PA: Ascension Press, 2006).
12. David M. Keily, and Christina McKenna, *The Dark Sacrament: True Stories of Modern-Day Demon Possession and Exorcism* (New York: Harper One, 2007).
13. Anne Palagruto, *Deliver Us From Evil: A Guide to Spiritual Warfare and Exorcism*, 3rd ed. (Philadelphia, PA: TPA Publishing, 2008).
14. Stephen J. Conn, *The Devil Called Collect: The Exorcism of Jessica Leek* (New York: iUniverse, 2008).
15. Matt Baglio, *The Rite: The Making of a Modern Exorcist* (New York: Doubleday, 2009).
16. Ernest Angley, *The Deceit of Lucifer* (Akron, OH: Winston Press, 1989), 43.
17. Ibid., 44.

18. Ibid., 45.
19. Ibid., 68.
20. Ibid., 63.
21. Ernest W. Angley, *Faith in God Heals the Sick* (Tampa, FL: no pub., 1952), 132–33.
22. Benny Hinn, personal observation of the author, Nashville, TN, Oct. 23–24, 1997.
23. Anthony Thomas, producer, *America Undercover: A Question of Miracles*, HBO series (April 15, 2001; Wilmington, NC: Time Warner Cable).
24. Cited in Hank Hanegraff, *Christianity in Crisis* (Eugene, OR: Harvest House: 1993), 256–57.
25. Cuneo, *American Exorcism*, 271.
26. Ibid., 209.
27. Ibid., 273.
28. Ibid., 271–72.
29. Ibid., 112.
30. *Deliver Us From Evil*, television broadcast, The Learning Channel (Feb. 11, 2003; Wilmington, NC: Time Warner Cable).
31. Cuneo, *American Exorcism*, 82.
32. Ibid., 88.
33. Quoted in Richard L. Johannesen, Rennard Strickland, and Ralph T. Eubanks, eds., *Language Is Sermonic: Richard Weaver on the Nature of Rhetoric* (Baton Rouge: Louisiana State Univ. Press, 1970), 210.
34. W. E. Vine, *An Expository Dictionary of New Testament Words*, (Nashville, TN: Royal, 1939), 992.
35. Ibid., 298.
36. Clinton D. Hamilton, "From Heaven or From Men," *Guardian of Truth*, Jan. 3, 1991, 5.
37. Darrell Conley, *The Gospel Versus Occultism* (Montgomery, AL: Apologetics Press, 1997), 23.
38. Steve Rudd, *Demons and Demon Possession*, Retrieved from http://www.bible.ca/su-demons.htm, 1–16.
39. Vine, *An Expository Dictionary of New Testament Words*, 283.
40. Ernest Angley, *The Deceit of Lucifer* (Akron, OH: Winston Press, 1989).
41. Wayne Jackson, "Demons: Ancient Superstition or Historical Reality?" *Christian Courier*, Nov. 27, 1998, 2, http://www.christiancourier.com/articles/21-demons-ancient-supersition-or-historical-reality.
42. Ibid.
43. Steve Rudd, *Demons and Demon Possession*, Retrieved from http://www.bible.ca/su-demons.htm, 2.
44. Hamilton, "From Heaven or From Men," 6.
45. Jackson, "Demons: Ancient Superstition or Historical Reality?" 3.
46. Donald Capps, *Jesus the Village Psychiatrist* (Louisville, KY: Westminster John Knox), cited in J. Harold Ellens, "Biblical Miracles and Psychological

Process: Jesus as Psychotherapist," in *Miracles: God Science, and Psychology in the Paranormal, Vol. 1*, ed. J. Harold Ellens (Westport, CT: Praeger, 2008), 3.

47. Ibid.
48. Cited in Steve Rudd, *Demons and Demon Possession*, retrieved from http:// www.bible. ca/su-demons.htm, 3.
49. Ibid., 2.
50. Jackson, "Demons: Ancient Superstition or Historical Reality?"
51. *Deliver Us From Evil*, television broadcast, The Learning Channel (Feb. 11, 2003); Cuneo, *American Exorcism*, 168, 174.
52. Cuneo, *American Exorcism*, 247.
53. Fortea, *Interview with an Exorcist*, 104.
54. *Deliver Us From Evil*, television broadcast, The Learning Channel (Feb. 11, 2003).
55. Fortea, *Interview with an Exorcist*, 105.
56. Cuneo, *American Exorcism*, 274–75.
57. Conley, *The Gospel Versus Occultism*, 44.
58. Conley, *The Gospel Versus Occultism*, 34.
59. Jackson, "Demons: Ancient Superstition or Historical Reality?" 5.
60. Ibid.
61. Hamilton, "From Heaven or From Men," 7.
62. Conley, *The Gospel Versus Occultism*, 34–35.
63. Ibid., 35.
64. Greg Gwinn, *Some Thoughts on Demon Possession*, unpublished manuscript in author's possession, n.d., 3–4.
65. Quoted in Homer Hailey, *A Commentary on the Minor Prophets* (Grand Rapids, MI: Baker, 1972), 319.
66. Ibid., 392.
67. Ibid.
68. Jackson, "Demons: Ancient Superstition or Historical Reality?" 8.
69. Robert C. Carson and James N. Butcher, *Abnormal Psychology and Modern Life*, 9th ed. (New York: Harper Collins, 1992), 208.
70. D. L. Bull, "A Phenomenological Model of Therapeutic Exorcism for Dissociative Identity Disorder," *Journal of Psychology and Theology*, 29: 2 (2001): 131.
71. Cited in Bull, 131.
72. Stefano Ferracuti, Roberto Sacco, Renato Lazzari, "Dissociative Trance Disorder: Clinical and Rorschach Findings in Ten Person Reporting Demon Possession and Treated by Exorcism," *Journal of Personality Assessment* 66: 3 (1996): 525.
73. Ibid.
74. Ibid.
75. Ibid., 536.
76. Colleen A. Ward and Michael H. Beaubrun, "The Psychodynamics of Demon Possession," *Journal for the Scientific Study of Religion* 19: 2 (1980): 205.
77. *Deliver Us From Evil*, television broadcast, The Learning Channel (Feb. 11, 2003).
78. Ibid.

79. Ward and Beaubrun, "The Psychodynamics of Demon Possession," 206.

80. Ibid.

81. Ibid.

82. Colin A. Ross and Shaun Joshi, "Paranormal Experiences in the General Population," *Journal of Nervous and Mental Disease* 180 (1992): 1.

83. *Deliver Us From Evil*, television broadcast, The Learning Channel (Feb. 11, 2003).

84. Cited in Steve Rudd, *Demons and Demon Possession*.

85. *The Exorcism of Emily Rose*, directed by Scott Derrickson (2005; Los Angeles: Screen Gems).

86. *The Last Exorcism*, directed by Daniel Stamm (2010; United States: Lionsgate).

CHAPTER 5

1. "The Players," accessed Oct. 31, 2013, http://www.armynavy2001.com/ANgame/The. See also "From Philadelphia to Fallujah," accessed Oct. 31, 2013, http://www.youtube.com/ watch?v=Jr_KpyPel6.

2. Todd Burpo, *Heaven Is For Real: A Little Boy's Astounding Story of His Trip to Heaven and Back* (Nashville, TN: Thomas Nelson, 2010), 91.

3. "Sports Center," *ESPN*, Time Warner Cable, Wilmington, NC, Jan. 2, 2013.

4. Oral Roberts, "The Media Have Had Their Say. Now the Truth," *Abundant Life*, Sept./Oct. 1987.

5. Ibid., 3.

6. Ibid.

7. Oral Roberts, "Tremendous Revelations From God that Have Changed the Lives of Millions of People," *Abundant Life*, July/Aug. 1987, 11.

8. Marjoe Gortner, *Marjoe*, directed by Howard Smith and Sara Kernochan (1972, Mauser Production, Inc.).

9. Todd V. Lewis, "Charisma and Media Evangelists: An Explication and Model of Communication Influence," *The Southern Communication Journal* 54 (Fall 1988): 103.

10. Ibid.

11. See "'When God Talks Back' to the Evangelical Community," published interview by Terry Gross, *Fresh Air*, NPR, April 9, 2012.

12. Kevin DeYoung, *Just Do Something: A Liberating Approach to Finding God's Will* (Chicago: Moody, 2009), 49.

13. Gary Friesen, *Decision Making and the Will of God: A Biblical Alternative to the Traditional View* (Portland, OR: Multnomah Press, 1980), 118–119.

14. Nate Jackson, interview on National Public Radio, Sept. 27, 2013.

15. I am using the word "minister" here the way that some people use the word "clergy."

16. Friesen, *Decision Making and the Will of God*, 110–11.

17. Friesen, *Decision Making and the Will of God*, 182.

18. See, for example, Todd Burpo, *Heaven Is For Real*, 12.

19. For a more detailed analysis of Peter's sermon, see Stephen J. Pullum, "The Persuasion of the Apostle Peter: Pentecost Revisited," *Tennessee Speech Communication Association Journal* (Fall 1987): 11–19.

20. DeYoung, *Just Do Something*, 68.

21. Faith healer Benny Hinn, for example, tells of many occasions when he either saw or heard Jesus speak to him audibly. Hinn tells about one occasion when he was only eleven years old: "I saw Jesus walk into my bedroom. He was wearing a robe that was whiter than white and a deep red mantle was draped over the robe. I saw His hair. I looked into His eyes. I saw the nail-prints in His hands." See Benny Hinn, *Good Morning, Holy Spirit* (Nashville, TN: Thomas Nelson Publishing, 1997), 22.

22. Friesen, *Decision Making and the Will of God*, 130–31.

23. DeYoung, *Just Do Something*, 52.

24. Ibid., 84.

25. See Tanya Marie Luhrman, personal website, accessed Dec. 3, 2013, http://luhrmann.net/ when-god-talks-back/description/.

26. Tanya Marie Luhrman, *When God Talks Back: Understanding the American Evangelical Relationship With God* (New York: Vintage Books, 2012), xxi.

27. Tanya Marie Luhrman, personal website, accessed Dec. 3, 2013, http://luhrmann.net/ when-god-talks-back/description/.

28. Quoted in Erin Benziger, "Psychological Anthropologist Says Hearing God Speak Audibly Does Not Mean You're 'Crazy,'" Dec. 30, 2012, http://christian-researchnetwork. org/2012/12/30 psychological-anthropologist-says-hearing.

29. Luhrman points out that "The person who hears a voice when alone has a sensory perception without a material cause." Tanya Marie Luhrman, *When God Talks Back*, xxiv.

30. Benziger, "Psychological Anthropologist Says Hearing God Speak Audibly Does Not Mean You're 'Crazy.'"

CHAPTER 6

1. Anthony Thomas, producer, *America Undercover: A Question of Miracles*, HBO series (April 15, 2001; Wilmington, NC: Time Warner Cable).

2. Oral Roberts, "The Media Have Had Their Say. Now the Truth," *Abundant Life*, Sept./Oct. 1987, 10.

3. Richard Roberts: Oral Roberts Ministry, http://oralroberts.com/category/living-proof-video/ accessed Dec. 5, 2013.

4. David Edwin Harrell, *All Things Are Possible: The Healing and Charismatic Revivals in Modern America* (Bloomington, IN: Indiana Univ. Press, 1975).

5. In what has sometimes been referred to as the Great Commission, Christ told his apostles to "Go into all the world and preach the gospel to all creation" (Mark 16:15, NASV). Christ did not mean literally every creature; obviously he did not mean dogs and cats and other animals. Nor did he even mean every person. There are some individuals—the severely developmentally disabled, for

example, who are not held accountable. So "every" does not always mean literally every. Context and common sense dictate how a verse is to be understood.

6. This is not to imply that people other than Christians are not worthy of an individual Christian's help. What I am suggesting in this paragraph is that Paul's instruction to the church at Corinth, for whatever reason, was that their benevolence as a congregation be limited only to Christians in this instance. Those were the only ones whom Paul had in mind in 2 Cor. 9.

7. Kathryn Kuhlman, *Heart to Heart with Kathryn Kuhlman, Volume 1* (North Brunswick, NJ: Bridge-Logos Publishers, 1998), 48.

8. Marshall E. Patton, "Answers For Our Hope," *Searching the Scriptures*, 24 (July 1983): 5.

9. David Lipscomb and J.W. Shepherd, *A Commentary on the New Testament Epistles: Romans*, 2nd ed. (Nashville, TN: Gospel Advocate, 1943), 1: 157.

10. Patton, "Answers For Our Hope," 5.

11. Ibid.

12. Elsewhere in the New Testament, we are told that "*Things* which eye saw not and ear heard not, and which entered not into the heart of man, *Whatsoever things* God prepared for them that love him," he revealed (1 Cor. 2:9—emphasis mine). 1 Pet. 1:10–12 discusses things like salvation and the unfolding of God's plan of salvation before suggesting, "which *things* angels desire to look into" (emphasis mine). It was these "things" that Paul has in mind in Romans 8, things that God has done *for* humans, not things that have happened *by accident* to humans.

13. Patton, "Answers For Our Hope," 6.

14. D. A. Carson, *Exegetical Fallacies*, 2nd ed. (Grand Rapids, MI: Baker Books, 1996), 116.

15. The word "needle" in these three verses comes from the translation of the Greek word *rhaphis. Rhaphis* is akin to the verb *rhapto*, meaning "to sew." Thus, *rhaphis* denotes a sewing instrument, not a wide gate, as some have suggested. See James Strong, *A Concise Dictionary of the Words in The Greek Testament* in *The New Strong's Exhaustive Concordance of the Bible* (New York: Nelson, 1984), 738, 63.

16. R. C. Foster, *Gospel Studies, Volume 2. The Life of Christ: A Chronological Study of the Four Gospels* (Cincinnati, OH: Cincinnati Bible Seminary, 1971), 80.

17. J. W. McGarvey, *A Commentary on Matthew and Mark* (Delight, AR: Gospel Light, 1875), 318.

18. In discussing the resurrection of Christ in his first epistle to the Corinthians, the Apostle Paul wrote, among other things, that if Christ were not resurrected from the dead, then their faith was "vain" and "we [Christians] are of all men most pitiable" (1 Cor. 15:17–19).

19. C. S. Lewis, *The Grand Miracle and Other Selected Essays on Theology and Ethics from God in the Dock* (New York: Ballantine Books, 1970), 55. For Lewis, the "Grand Miracle" is the "Incarnation" of Christ. Lewis writes, "In the Christian story God descends to re-ascend. He comes down . . . But He

goes down to come up again and bring the whole ruined world up with Him." This includes, but is not limited to, the crucifixion and resurrection. See also C. S. Lewis, "The Grand Miracle," in *Miracles* (New York, McMillan: 1947), 111–112.

CHAPTER 7

1. Rom. 8:14.
2. See Hank Hanegraff, *Christianity in Crisis* (Eugene, OR: Harvest House Publishers, 1993), 39, 56.
3. Kenneth E. Hagin, *The Healing Anointing* (Tulsa, OK: Faith Library Publications, 1997), 69.
4. Ibid., 56–58.
5. Ibid., 58–59.
6. Ibid., 124.
7. Ibid., 165.
8. Kathryn Kuhlman, *Heart to Heart with Kathryn Kuhlman, Volume 1, 2* (North Brunswick, NJ: Bridge Logos Publishers, 1998).
9. Ibid., 2.
10. Ibid., 9–17.
11. Ernest Angley, *The Greatness of the Fire of the Holy Spirit* (Akron, OH: Winston Press, 1987), 2.
12. Ibid., 15.
13. Ibid., 1.
14. Ibid., 18–22.
15. Ernest W. Angley, *Faith in God Heals the Sick* (Tampa, FL: no pub, 1952), 139–140.
16. Benny Hinn, *Good Morning, Holy Spirit* (Nashville, TN: Thomas Nelson, 1997), 106.
17. James Strong, *A Concise Dictionary of the Words in The Greek Testament* in *The New Strong's Exhaustive Concordance of the Bible* (New York: Nelson, 1984), 423.
18. For verses that reveal the three personalities of the Godhead, see Gen. 1:1–2, 26; John 1:1–3; Matt. 3:16–17; and Matt. 28:19.
19. For a more exhaustive discussion of the Holy Spirit's attributes, see Steve Rudd's *The Personality & Deity of the Holy Spirit Proven From the Bible!* http://www.bible.ca/trinity/tinity-holy-spirit-personality-deity.htm, 1–6.
20. For other, similar verses, see John 15:26–27 and John 16:13.
21. T.W. Brents, *The Gospel Plan of Salvation*, 16th ed. (Nashville, TN: Gospel Advocate, 1973), 579.
22. Brents, *Gospel Plan of Salvation*, 580.
23. Ibid., 588.
24. John MacArthur, *Strange Fire: The Danger of Offending the Holy Spirit With Counterfeit Worship* (Nashville, TN: Nelson Books, 2013), 190–191; 203.
25. Brents, *Gospel Plan of Salvation*, 580.

26. This is the baptism that Christ spoke of when the mother of James and John wanted Christ to place her two sons in positions of authority and prominence when he came into his kingdom. Christ told her, "Ye know not what ye ask. Are ye able to drink the cup that I am about to drink?" Elsewhere in Luke 12:50, Christ said, "But I have a baptism to be baptized with; and how am I straitened till it be accomplished!" Brents suggests, "The awful sufferings of Jesus may well be called a baptism, for truly he was overwhelmed in them." See Brents, *Gospel Plan of Salvation*, 355.

27. In this context there were two classes of people to whom John was preaching: (1) apostles, who were to receive the baptism of the Holy Spirit, and (2) Pharisees and Sadducees, who were called "offspring of vipers." These were the ones who were to receive the baptism by fire, a type of punishment. John suggested in verse 12 that "he will thoroughly cleanse his threshing-floor; and he will gather his wheat into the garner, but the chaff he will burn up with unquenchable fire." This is the baptism of fire mentioned in verse 11.

28. This is a figurative reference to the Jews who wondered in the wilderness under the guidance of Moses when they came out of Egyptian bondage.

29. See, for example, the conversions of the Jews (Acts 2:38–ff; Acts 4:4); the Samaritans (Acts 8:12–13); Saul of Tarsus (Acts 22:16); Cornelius (Acts 10:47); Lydia (Acts 16:15); the Philippian jailor (Acts 16:33); the Corinthians (Acts 18:8); and the Ephesians (Acts 19:3–5).

30. Peter is not suggesting that this is the only thing that saves a person. However, he is pointing out how important water baptism is.

31. Brents, *The Gospel Plan of Salvation*, 580.

32. See also Rom. 5:5 and James 4:5.

33. In the Old Testament, we are told that both Enoch and Noah "walked with God," which necessarily implies that God also walked with them. One cannot walk with another without the other walking with him or her. Yet, we do not believe that either Enoch or Noah walked with God literally or that God walked with either Enoch or Noah literally. The idea is that they were in fellowship with each other. See. Gen. 5:22, 24 and 6:9.

34. David E. Pratte, *The God of the Bible: A Study of the Father, Son, and Holy Spirit* (www.lighttomypath.net/sales, 2013), 151.

35. Ferrell Jenkins, *The Holy Spirit and the Christian* (Athens, AL: CEI Publishing, n.d.), 3.

36. Ferrell Jenkins, *The Finger of God: A Study of the Holy Spirit* (Temple Terrace, FL: no pub., 1984), 24–25.

37. Ibid., 25.

38. MacArthur, *Strange Fire*, 199.

39. Stanley M. Burgess, Gary B. McGee, and Patrick H. Alexander, eds., *Dictionary of Pentecostal and Charismatic Movements* (Grand Rapids, MI: Regency Reference Library, 1988), 790. Also cited in MacArthur, *Strange Fire*, 200.

40. Jenkins, *The Finger of God*, 24.

41. Kyle Pope, *How Does the Holy Spirit Work in a Christian?* (Bowling Green, KY: Guardian of Truth, 2009), 48–49.

42. Pratte, *God of the Bible*, 150.

43. Ibid., 151–52.

44. I am using the word "scripture" here to refer to the gospel, God's word, or the Bible.

45. MacArthur, *Strange Fire*, 206.

46. Franklin T. Puckett, "How The Spirit Indwells," *Searching the Scriptures*, XXIII, no. 9 (Sept. 1982): 8.

47. Ibid.

48. Kenneth E. Hagin, *Why Tongues* (Tulsa, OK: RHEMA Bible Church, 1975), 19–20.

49. Franklin T. Puckett, "The Gift of the Holy Spirit," *Searching the Scriptures*, XXIII, no. 8 (Aug. 1982): 7.

50. Ibid.

51. Ibid., 8.

52. Ibid., 8–9.

53. Jenkins, *The Finger of God*, 18.

54. Brents offers a third view of what the gift of the Holy Spirit in Acts 2:38 is. He suggests that it was given to those on the day of Pentecost who repented and were baptized as a miraculous measure to help them preach the gospel when they returned to their home countries. See *Gospel Plan of Salvation*, 598.

55. MacArthur, *Strange Fire*, 204–205.

56. Pratte, *God of the Bible*, 122.

CHAPTER 8

1. RockWealth Ministries, accessed Feb. 24, 2014, http://www.rockwealth.org/8fold ministry.html.

2. Todd Coontz, *Inspiration Camp Meeting at Evangel World Center*, BET Network, June 22, 2013. This program also aired on the BET Network, Feb. 22, 2014.

3. Ibid.

4. Ibid.

5. Ibid.

6. If 1,089 people were to actually call in with a pledge of $1,000 each, Coontz stood to bring in $1,089,000.

7. Ibid.

8. Dee Bowman, "The Abundant Life and Prosperity," *Searching the Scriptures*, 24, no. 2 (Feb. 1983): 12.

9. Oral Roberts, and Todd Coontz, *The Miracle of Seed Faith: How To Seed and How To Receive Your Harvest* (Aiken, SC: Legacy Media, 2009), 14.

10. Ibid., 15.

11. Ibid., 11–36, 46.

12. "Leadership Team," Lakewood Church, accessed Feb. 25, 2014, http://www.lakewoodchurch.com. "Joel Osteen," accessed Feb. 25, 2014, http://www.

lakewood church.com. See also Ross Douthat, *Bad Religion: How We Became a Nation of Heretics* (New York: Free Press, 2012), 182–83.

13. Joel Osteen, *Your Best Life Now: Seven Steps to Living at Your Full Potential* (New York: Faith Words, 2004), 5.

14. Ibid, 10.

15. Douthat, *Bad Religion*, 184.

16. Quoted in John Ankerberg, and John Weldon, *The Facts on the Faith Movement: Where It Came From, What It Teaches, Who It Hurts* (Eugene, OR: Harvest House, 1993), 35.

17. Quoted in Ibid., 27–28.

18. *The Ministry of Kenneth Copeland: "Living to Give"* (Fort Worth, TX: Kenneth Copeland Ministries, n.d.), n. pag.

19. Dean Merrill, "The Fastest Growing American Denomination," *Christianity Today,* Jan. 7, 1983, 33. For a fuller discussion of the rhetorical appeals of Kenneth Copeland, see Stephen J. Pullum, *No Kind of "Dumb TV Star": The Rhetoric of Televangelist Kenneth Copeland,* paper presented at the Speech Communication Association Convention, Chicago, IL: Nov. 1–4, 1990.

20. Kenneth Copeland, "I Want You To Prosper," *Believer's Voice of Victory,* Jan. 1985, 6.

21. Kenneth Copeland, "I Want You To Prosper: Prosperity in Review," *Believer's Voice of Victory,* July 1985, 2.

22. Kenneth Copeland, "I Want You to Prosper: The Joy of Giving and Receiving," *Believer's Voice of Victory,* Dec. 1985, 4.

23. Kenneth Copeland, "How To Receive From God," *Believer's Voice of Victory,* Aug. 1985, 3. See also Kenneth Copeland, "The Power to Prosper," *Believer's Voice of Victory,* July 1987, 2–4, for more on Copeland's prosperity doctrine.

24. Copeland, "The Power to Prosper," 4.

25. John MacArthur, *Strange Fire* (Nashville, TN: Nelson, 2013), 52.

26. Ibid, 58.

27. Dee Bowman, "The Abundant Life and Divine Healing," *Searching the Scriptures,* 24, no. 1 (Jan. 1983): 9.

28. Ibid., 10.

29. Herman Hilliard, "The Work of the Spirit: A Health and Wealth Gospel?" *Christianity Magazine,* 7, no. 1 (Oct. 1990): 20.

30. Other verses that warn against striving to be rich are Prov. 23:4; Prov. 28:20; and Luke 12:16–21.

31. W. E. Vine. *An Expository Dictionary of New Testament Words* (Nashville, TN: Royal Publishers, Inc., n.d.), 778.

32. See Phil. 2:5–9 for a fuller description of what Christ did.

33. Kenneth Hagin, "A New Creation," *Classic Sermons: Timeless Messages by Kenneth E. Hagin to Stir Up Your Spirit and Inspire Your Faith in God's Word* (Tulsa, OK: Kenneth Hagin Ministries, 1992), 44.

34. Dee Bowman, "The Abundant Life and Atonement," *Searching the Scriptures,* 23, no.12 (Dec. 1982): 7.

35. William Barclay, *The Letters to The Corinthians* (Philadelphia: The Westminster Press, 1956), 261.
36. Ibid., 261–62.
37. Kenneth Copeland, "How To Prosper From the Inside Out," *Believer's Voice of Victory*, Feb., 1991, 2.
38. James Strong, *A Concise Dictionary of the Words in The Greek Testament* in *The New Strong's Exhaustive Concordance of the Bible* (New York: Nelson, 1984), 33.
39. Vine. *An Expository Dictionary of New Testament Words*, 897.
40. Albert Barnes, *Barnes' Notes on the New Testament*, 1st ed. (Grand Rapids, MI: Kregel Publications, 1962), 1506.
41. Hank Hanegraff, *Christianity in Crisis* (Eugene, OR: Harvest House Publishers, 1993), 250.
42. Hanegraff, *Christianity in Crisis*, 251.
43. Kenneth Hagin, "Godliness Is Profitable," *Classic Sermons: Timeless Messages by Kenneth E. Hagin to Stir Up Your Spirit and Inspire Your Faith in God's Word* (Tulsa, OK: Kenneth Hagin Ministries, 1992), 12.
44. Ibid., 15, 19–20.
45. Bowman, "The Abundant Life and Atonement," 8.
46. Ibid.
47. Kenneth E. Hagin, *How God Taught Me About Prosperity* (Tulsa, OK: Kenneth Hagin Ministries, 1985), 17–19.
48. Barnes, *Barnes' Notes on the New Testament*, 202.
49. Bowman, "The Abundant Life and Atonement," 8.
50. McArthur, *Strange Fire*, 59.
51. Raymond Ortlund Jr., *Proverbs* (Wheaton, IL: Crossway, 2012), 60; as cited in McArthur, *Strange Fire*, 78.
52. Ibid., 79.

CHAPTER 9

1. *Cell 15: The Imprisonment of Ernest Angley* (Akron, OH: Winston Press, 1984), 55.
2. "Faith Healer to Continue Work Despite His Arrest," *Press Courier* (Oxnard, CA), Feb. 8, 1956, p. 13, accessed through NewspaperARCHIVE.com.
3. David Edwin Harrell, *All Things Are Possible: The Healing & Charismatic Revivals in Modern America* (Bloomington, IN: Indiana Univ. Press, 1975), 61. See also Tony Cauchi, "Jack Coe," The Voice of Healing: A Revival Library Website, Dec., 2011, http://www.voiceofhealing.info/05otherministries/coe.html; and "Texas 'Faith Healer' Blamed For Injury to Polio Victim," *Evening Journal* (Lubbock, TX), 32, no. 109, Feb. 8, 1956: 1, accessed through NewspaperARCHIVE.com.
4. Ellana Dockterman, "Faith-Healing Parents Jailed After Second Child's Death," *Time*, Feb. 19, 2014, http: //time.com/8750/faith-healing-parents-jailed-after-second-childs-death/.

Author and Subject Index

Scripture Index

About the Author

Stephen J. Pullum, PhD, is a Professor of Communication Studies and former Associate Dean of the College of Arts and Sciences at the University of North Carolina, Wilmington, where he has taught since 1988. He is author of the book *"Foul Demons, Come Out!" The Rhetoric of Twentieth-Century American Faith Healing*, published by Praeger/ABC-CLIO, and other articles on religious discourse. Pullum holds a doctorate in Communication from Indiana University, Bloomington.